David Rabe

Plays:

The Basic Training of Pavlo Hummel, Sticks and Bones, Streamers, The Orphan

David Rabe 'is a remarkable storyteller' *Chicago Tribune*

The Basic Training of Pavlo Hummel: 'rich in humor, irony and insight' *New York Times*

Sticks and Bones: 'you will see few things . . . of an intensity comparable to this' *New York Times*

Streamers: 'beyond question Mr Rabe's most successful play to date – rich in character nuance, tense in its close-quarter hostilities' *New York Times*

The Orphan: 'the writer has tremendous talent for baring tortured souls through scathing dialogue . . . Rabe makes compelling use of his myth-playing' Irwyn Applebaum

David Rabe was born in Iowa. After returning from Vietnam where he worked as a medical corpsman, he was a feature writer for the *New Haven Register* Sunday Magazine and wrote four major plays about the Vietnam experience – *The Basic Training of Pavlo Hummel* (1971), *Sticks and Bones* (1971), *Streamers* (1976) and *The Orphan* (1971). His other plays include *In the Boom Boom Room* (1974), *Goose and Tom Tom* (1986), *Hurlyburly* (1984), *Those the River Keeps* (1992) and *The Dog Problem* (2000). He has also written two novels and his screenplays include *I'm Dancing as Fast as I Can*, *Casualties of War*, *Streamers*, *The Firm* and most recently *Hurlyburly*.

Four of Rabe's plays have been honoured with Tony nominations and *Sticks and Bones* was awarded Best Play in 1972. In addition he has received the American Academy of Arts and Letters Award, and his work has been celebrated at the Drama Desk Awards, the John Gassner Outer Critics Awards, the New York Drama Critics Circle, and he has won the Elizabeth Hull-Kate Warriner Drama Guild Award three times.

DAVID RABE

Plays: 1

The Basic Traning of Pavlo Hummel

Sticks and Bones

Streamers

The Orphan

introduced by Christopher Bigsby

Methuen Drama

METHUEN CONTEMPORARY DRAMATISTS

1 3 5 7 9 10 8 6 4 2

This collection first published in Great Britain in 2002 by
Methuen Publishing Limited,
215 Vauxhall Bridge Road, London SW1V 1EJ

The Basic Training of Pavlo Hummel first published in 1969
by Samuel French Inc.
Copyright © David Rabe, 1969, 1972, 1973, 2002
Sticks and Bones first published as *Bones* in 1969 and revised
and rewritten as *Sticks and Bones* in 1972 by Samuel French Inc.
Copyright © David Rabe, 1969, 1972, 1973, 2002
Streamers Copyright © David Rabe, 1970, 1975, 1977, 2002
The Orphan first published as *Nor the Bones of Birds* in 1970
and as *The Orphan* in 1971
Copyright © David Rabe, 1970, 1971, 1972, 2002

Introduction copyright © 2002 by Christopher Bigsby

David Rabe has asserted his right under the Copyright, Designs and Patents
Act, 1988, to be identified as the author of this work

Methuen Publishing Limited Reg. No. 3543167

A CIP catalogue record for this book is available from the British Library.

ISBN 0 413 73030 1

Typeset in Baskerville by MATS, Southend-on-Sea, Essex
Printed and bound in Great Britain by
Cox & Wyman Ltd, Reading, Berkshire

Caution

Contents

David Rabe
A Chronology

1963   *Bridges* (workshop production at Villanova University, Pennsylvania)

1968   *The Bones of Birds* (workshop production at Villanova University, Pennsylvania)

1969   *Sticks and Bones* (workshop production at Villanova University, Pennsylvania)

1971   *The Basic Training of Pavlo Hummel* first produced at Joseph Papp's Public Theatre, New York, winner of an Obie Award for off-Broadway in 1971
Sticks and Bones first produced by Joseph Papp at the New York Shakespeare Festival Public Theatre
The Orphan (workshop production at Villanova University, Pennsylvania)

1972   *Sticks and Bones* first produced on Broadway at the John Golden Theatre
In the Boom Boom Room (workshop production at Villanova University, Pennsylvania)

1973   *Sticks and Bones* won the Tony Award for Best Play
In the Boom Boom Room produced by Joseph Papp at the Lincoln Centre, New York
The Orphan produced at Manning Street Actors Theater in Philadelphia, Pennsylvania

1974   *In the Boom Boom Room* produced Off-Broadway by Joseph Papp at the Lincoln   Center New York

1976   *Streamers* produced at the Long Wharf Theatre, New
      Haven, Connecticut
      Streamers produced by Joseph Papp at the Lincoln
      Centre, New York

1984   *Hurlyburly* produced at the Goodman Theatre Chicago,
      off Broadway at the Promenade Theatre and on
      Broadway at the Ethel Barrymore Theatre.

1986   *Goose and Tom Tom* produced in a workshop at the
      Lincoln Centre, New York

1992   *Those the River Keeps* produced at McCarter Theatre in
      Princeton New Jersey

1993   *Those the River Keeps* produced at the American
      Repertory Theater in Cambridge, Massechusetts and
      produced by James Freydberg in New York

1994   *Cosmologies* produced at the Wellfleet Harbour Actors
      Theatre, Massachusetts

1997   *A Question of Mercy* produced at New York Theatre
      Workshop

2000   *The Dog Problem* produced at Long Wharf Theatre
      Company

2001   *The Dog Problem* was produced by the Atlantic Theatre,
      New York

Introduction

For many years, David Rabe was thought of as a Vietnam playwright and, as this collection suggests, not without reason. His was a theatre of trauma, detailing the psychological and physical wounds carried by those who had served in the war or faced the draft and by a society that seemingly sought to maintain an air of normality as it cracked apart. Yet his later plays, *Hurlyburly* and its sequel *Those the River Keeps*, along with *Goose and Tomtom* and *A Question of Mercy*, suggest that if Vietnam was a subject it was also chosen as a symptom of a culture under strain, characterised by attenuated relationships, violence and spiritual entropy. Vietnam may have been a special case, a political commitment that seemed to suck the soul out of a country, but the anxieties, the alienation it seemed to breed, were already part of a culture in which myths of masculinity bred unfocused violence and the sexes met across a seemingly unbridgeable divide.

The war was such that in his film *Apocalypse Now!* Frances Ford Coppola would turn to the dark visions of Joseph Conrad, wedded to the iconography of the western, as though the war were a playing-out of familiar rites deformed by their displacement in time and space. But in truth there was a sense in which American society itself was infiltrated by fiction, predisposed to prefer those images projected on the national psyche by Hollywood, television and national myths of innocence and progress, rather than confront truths that threatened a declared national self-confidence. Rabe followed much the same logic. Against the American dream he would pitch nightmare. His individuals are under stress, sometimes to the point at which character and language begin to collapse, but his society, too, is close to breaking point. In his plays we hear the sharp sounds of it falling apart – if they lack conventional plots then so, too, did an America that had lost its way somewhere on its trip from innocence to innocence, from a new Eden to the utopian happiness it was dedicated to pursue.

F. Scott Fitzgerald once wrote an essay called 'The Crack Up', in which he proposed a parallel between the psychological state of an individual (himself) and a society fracturing along the fault line of unsustainable beliefs. It was his portrait of America in the 1930s. Rabe, too, writes as much about those who can barely sustain the integrity of their identities, threatened from within and without, as he does about a culture which seems to him unaware of the dissolution which menaces it as it casually betrays the values for which it supposedly stands. Although he offers a picture of America as the 1960s turned into the 1970s, there is, however, no doubt that it was Vietnam that first focused such concerns – Vietnam as fact but still more as image and metaphor.

Rabe was born in Dubuque, Iowa, in 1940, attending college first there before entering graduate school at Villanova University in Pennsylvania, where he began to write. One of his plays, *Bridges*, had a workshop production at Villanova University 1963. That career was cut short, when he was drafted in 1965, a draft he briefly considered resisting by registering as a conscientious objector. For all that, he thought of the war as a just one, in so far as he thought about it at all. In truth he knew very little about it. It was a war that America entered incrementally. At first it was a distant commitment, in a divided country of which few had heard, a country whose politics seemed confusing. Colonial administration had given way to corrupt government and civil war but the ideological commitments of the north made it seem to fit neatly into Cold War politics. In America it was presented as a war to sustain freedom and democracy, even if neither was in ready supply in South Vietnam.

Until 1965, the scale of the war was not such as to demand attention. Then B-52s began to carpet bomb and American lives to be lost on a scale that registered, not least with those whose own lives were now at risk. Rabe, though, was not a Vietnam protester and not a writer of protest plays, even if he confessed to having a polemical impulse when he first began to write. During his induction he has said that he knew little more of what lay ahead for him than many of his characters in plays in which the shock of violence registers at all levels.

In 1965 the anti-war movement was only just getting under way. The first teach-in, at the University of Michigan, occurred in April, 1965, though this example was quickly taken up around the country. Nonetheless, even in 1966, when his unit was posted to Vietnam, the country was not yet as deeply divided as it would subsequently become. In Washington, President Johnson spoke confidently of inevitable victory while defending the war as part of a necessary battle against world communism, the particularities of the Vietnam situation tending to be accommodated to a more familiar model, the Manichaean struggle between the forces of light and the forces of darkness. Rabe did not serve in a combat unit though he did approach his superiors about a transfer to one, part way through his tour. However bureaucratic difficulties and a change of mind brought the process to a halt. His equivocal state of mind is evident in his refusal to assume any kind of command (he was invited to become a squad leader and to apply to officer training while in basic, but he turned both down). Instead he worked as clerk, a driver and a guard.

Quite the most significant part of that service, however, was the time he spent in a hospital support unit at Long Binh. There, he saw the broken bodies brought in: 'truckloads of human limbs and piles of green uniforms. The impact was terrific on anyone who was over there'. Slowly, he began to change as he was introduced to the reality of Vietnam, albeit a reality that was difficult to apprehend and which seemed to defy expression.

He set himself to keep a journal but found it impossible to capture the essence of what he saw. Language seemed to fall short of the surreal nature of a war in which trucks were piled with body parts, troops increasingly resorted to drugs and the sexual freedom of Saigon provoked the same reductive feelings towards Vietnamese women that were encouraged towards the Vietcong enemy who, as 'gooks', became so much more easily killed. It was a logic that would lead to rape and

massacre as that same war would lead to heroism and self-
sacrifice.

It seemed, he later said, 'a lunatic journey', on which he
had been sent by those who appeared to have little
understanding of the world into which they had propelled
him, with little more than a series of platitudes enforced by
orders. A gap opened up between what he observed and what
he wrote, even in letters home. There seemed no way
adequate to express the world he found himself inhabiting.

When he returned home after a year the nightmare did not
end, nor his sense of unreality. For all the protests that were
now a feature of life in America, protests that extended into
the political system itself, the country seemed to be continuing
much as ever. It was as though he carried a secret he could
not communicate. Now it was America that seemed strange,
the business of day-to-day living seemingly oblivious of the
heroism and betrayals, the mismatch between words and
actions that characterised a distant war.

The war was, indeed, either ignored or seen as a species of
entertainment on the nightly news. It was also, to be sure,
regarded as an issue. You were for it or against it or simply
tuned it out. Its true nature took second place to the *idea* of the
war, to its defence or rejection. Meanwhile, as its young men
died and as jungles blazed thousands of miles away, America
continued much as before, its citizens making money,
watching soap operas, behaving, in general, as if nothing in
particular was happening or, if it was, best left in the hands of
those who understood such matters. Even protests became a
kind of theatre, a series of exemplary acts – the burning of
draft cards, marches, teach-ins, sit-ins – worthy enough but
remote from the inner truth of what was happening to
America, of what was happening to those who had come too
close to the fire and been burned.

He returned to graduate school at Villanova and then left to
become a journalist. He now rejected the war but was equally
repelled by many of the protestors who seemed, to him, not to
understand its real nature. He tried his hand at a play and a
novel. Then, as a reporter on the *New Haven Register*, he was

asked to write a review of two studies of the My Lai massacre in which American soldiers had killed 504 men, women and children in a Vietnamese hamlet, a slaughter only stopped when a pilot manoeuvered his helicopter between the troops and their victims. The result was a curious piece of prose in which rather than offering a realistic account of the events or an assessment of the books, he offered a blend of the personal and the visionary, trying to generate a prose adequate to such an event, struggling to find a correlative for that sense of unreality that had struck him both in Vietnam and in America. He was still looking for a prose that could express something that seemed to defy expression. And it was, finally, precisely this oblique approach, this sense of inhabiting a dream, that proved a key to the drama he now wrote.

He was not the first to address the situation in Vietnam. It is tempting to hear an echo of it in Robert Lowell's 1964 trilogy, *The Old Glory*, with its references to American imperialism. Arthur Miller, repelled by television images of American troops burning friendly Vietnamese villages in order to deny a safe haven for the Vietcong, had written an Op Ed piece for the *New York Times* suggesting that cooperative Vietnamese should be located by the CIA who would voluntarily set fire to their own houses as a gesture of solidarity. He claimed that his 1965 play *Incident at Vichy* and his 1968 drama *The Price*, neither of which mentioned Vietnam, were, if not inspired by, then directly applicable to, the situation in Southeast Asia in their emphasis on the importance of understanding the past, in their exploration of human cruelties and denials.

More directly, though, in 1966 Peter Brook, in England, staged *US*, a play which culminated in the apparent burning of a butterfly, a gesture designed to shock not least because the death of a butterfly fell so far short of lost human lives. In that same year the Open Theatre presented Megan Terry's *Viet Rock* while in 1968 the German playwright Peter Weiss's *Discourse on Vietnam* offered a history of Vietnam and its conflicts. American theatre groups began to focus on the war, some of them moving out of the theatre and on to the street where protest marches, themselves a form of theatre, often incorporated them. The San Francisco Mime Troupe staged

The Dragon Lady's Revenge and Goldoni's anti-war play *L'Amant Militaire*, the Bread and Puppet Theatre, *A Man Says Goodbye to His Mother*, Luis Valdez's El Teatro Campesino, *Vietnam Campesino* (1970) the Performance Group, *Commune* (1970) and the Living Theatre, *Paradise Now*. Interestingly, virtually none of these works was a realistic play. It was as though that was acknowledged to be a form and a style inadequate to addressing a war which seemingly defied rational analysis.

No playwright, however, was to make Vietnam such a central part of his work as David Rabe and if his plays did not begin to reach the public stage until 1971, they had a pre-history that effectively made him one of the first playwrights to address this, the major moral dilemma of a generation.

An early version of *The Orphan* (then called 'The Bones of Birds'), begun in 1967, was produced at Villanova University in 1968, the year of the Tet Offensive in which Vietcong soldiers not only entered Saigon but also penetrated the US Embassy compound, suddenly and publicly exposing as propaganda American assurances that the war was being won. In 1968, the year of the assassinations of Martin Luther King and Robert Kennedy, he was already sketching out his later plays. America's cities burned in the night while in that year's Democratic Convention in Chicago, following the withdrawal of President Johnson, the war became the primary subject, with the peace candidate, Eugene McCarthy defeated and demonstrators clubbed senseless by Mayor Daley's police in full view of television cameras. Vietnam could no longer be wished away. From this point to the final peace agreement in 1975, the war would be the principle political and moral issue in America with President Nixon bombing both North Vietnam and Cambodia while negotiating an end to an adventure that was now taking an unacceptable number of American lives. Even now, though, the meaning of that war, in terms of its impact on those who had served there and the society that sent them, was by no means clear. That a price had been paid was evident enough and Rabe identified what that price had been.

*

He began to write a series of plays, the composition of each overlapping with the others. By 1971 he had largely completed *The Basic Training of Pavlo Hummel* and *Sticks and Bones*, together with a draft of *The Orphan* and *Streamers*. The American theatre, however, was not desperate for his work. The first of these was rejected by a fair number of America's regional theatres as by those New York companies to whom it was offered.

The first in the sequence of his Vietnam plays is *The Basic Training of Pavlo Hummel*, the original draft of which he finished in 1968, a year before Lieutenant Calley and his company carried out their slaughter in My Lai. It concerns the induction of a young recruit and his brief service in Vietnam.

It was finally staged by Joe Papp's Public Theatre in New York and changed a good deal in rehearsal. In the first draft the play was largely realistic. Though far from offering a documentary approach, it did reflect his desire to get the word out, to offer a report of what he had learned. It was linear in form, in contrast to *The Orphan* on which he continued to work. He has said that, 'I felt *Pavlo*, the first written, had to be a play that was primarily about people. Therefore I wanted it done in the theatrical form in which dramatic characters had the best chance of appearing as simply People'. At Papp's urging, however, he largely abandoned this schema so that realism deferred to a kind of impressionism. The set was to be realistic, offering an ironic reassurance in a play in which action and character are anything but realistic. Pavlo Hummel himself is a Woyzeck-like figure, naive but not innocent. He is there to be inducted into the army, learning to obey but understanding little that he is taught. Ironically, what seems on offer is the promise of order in a world which seems to lack precisely that. This is order, though, in the service of death. Pavlo himself seems to understand little of what is going on but the fate for which he is being prepared is prefigured in the inexorable dismantling of one of his fellow soldiers.

Indeed, in *Pavlo Hummel*, time's arrow reverses its direction and the action begins with his death. We thus know his fate before we understand the logic that leads to it, a logic having less to do with rationality than the working out of a faulty premise. The war for which he is being prepared devours its own.

Pavlo is a fantasist. He is chauvinistic, desperate to belong, without questioning what it is he wishes to join. His induction is our induction as he is drilled in something more than military necessities. The suspicion is that the America beyond the camp gates hardly differs in its essentials from the camp itself. Pavlo's naivety is his society's. In the second act we are pitched into a nightmare world as a Sergeant, blown apart by a mine, pleads to be killed, a soldier is tortured by the Vietcong and Pavlo shoots a Vietnamese farmer while being injured himself. In a cycle of violence the only principle seems to be to 'tear and rip apart, though the lesson seems to be that the violence is self-reflexive: a blow offered is a blow returned. There is no sense in which there is a cause to be defended or advanced by such spasms of brutality.

They are carrying out their training. They act efficiently, ruthlessly, but, particularly in the case of Pavlo Hummel, never understand why they act as they do. The fact that he is killed by an American soldier in a Vietnamese brothel underscores equally the self-defeating nature of the action and its moral contamination, ironies beyond Pavlo's capacity to appreciate and equally, it is implied, American society's capacity to understand.

Rabe himself has said that, 'Even though the plays were part of a political movement, in them I was . . . saying: You can do what you want about the war. But don't lie about it. Don't pretend that it's good, or it becomes uglier than it is. Don't pretend it's heroic. Don't pretend that everybody who goes over there is a monster or a hero. Most of the kids didn't know anything about what was going on'.

The *Basic Training of Pavlo Hummel* opened at New York's Public Theatre in 1971. It was followed that same year by *Sticks and Bones*, an early version of which had been staged at Villanova University in 1969. Where *Pavlo Hummel* had been about going to Vietnam, this play focuses on the return of the Vietnam soldier, who finds himself entering a world once familiar but now rendered strange. The blinded protagonist,

David, re-enters a family anxious only to insulate itself from the truth. Indeed the characters are based on figures derived from a popular radio and television series.

David is haunted by memories of the war and in particular by the figure of a Vietnamese girl, an image of his responsibility to a people he encountered and abandoned. His family, however, resent being distracted from the narcotised world which they take for reality. In the end they seem to harbour a cruelty that matches that to be found in the war; they evidence a denial as profound as that of the society which they represent.

He brings into the family home a truth that must be rejected, even if that means rejecting him, their son, in a parody of that rejection that so many Vietnam veterans suffered on their return. What happened in Vietnam is so at odds with American self-images that it must be denied and suppressed.

There are echoes of Ionesco and Albee behind the banalities the family members exchange, as if language were best detached from the business of communication for fear of what might be communicated. The family speak in a reductive prose; their son, David, at times, in a poetry that expresses his sense of a beauty callously destroyed. In a world of images (the television flickers in a corner, slides are projected on a screen), the real seems less commanding.

Somewhere in the background, perhaps, lies Plato's fable of the cave in which philosophers seated in a cave see only shadows cast on the wall, so much more enticing than the diminished reality that lies beyond. There are echoes, too, perhaps, of Harold Pinter's *The Homecoming* in which a family steadfastly deny the significance of what they see as their son returns, and Rabe was a great admirer of Pinter.

Sticks and Bones was designed to be ironic and humorous but Rabe has confessed that the pressures of the moment made this difficult to achieve. There was simply too much at stake, so much, indeed, that a television recording was suppressed. For the playwright, though, it was not about a specifically American dilemma. Vietnam provided the immediate point of reference. It was not the subject. Indeed he insisted that a

Russian production should acknowledge its relevance to Russia.

What was at stake was a human propensity to violence and denial, a failure to understand suffering as a common currency, to acknowledge the power of language to deform reality as well as a failure of imagination as the lives of others seemed irrelevant and remote. Vietnam has literally blinded David but in another sense it has opened his eyes. He is alive as those who close their ears and eyes to the world are not. They choose oblivion. He chooses to remember.

The third play in what then seemed a trilogy, *The Orphan*, followed in 1974. It blends Greek tragedy with modern myths, that of the Charles Manson killings (Manson and his group killed the pregnant film star Sharon Tate) and the My Lai massacre. Originally inspired by an Off-Broadway production of *Iphigenia at Aulis* and subsequently by the Open Theatre's *The Serpent* and the Living Theatre's *Paradise Now*, all of which fused ancient and contemporary myths, it is not best seen as a Vietnam play. It is rather about those trapped by fate, the victims of betrayal.

As *In the Boom Boom Room*, that followed it, it broadens the canvas, in the latter case staging the deeply flawed relation between the sexes, a violence that hardly needed Vietnam as a source. In some ways it anticipated his later play, *Hurlyburly*, a brutal and coruscating, if brilliantly funny account of those alienated from their own lives, people, in Tom Lehrer's words, 'sliding down the razor blade of life'.

The final part of what had now turned into a quartet was *Streamers*, like his other plays this was first sketched out in the late 60s but opened in 1976, when the war in Vietnam was over.

It won the New York Drama Critics Award, as *Pavlo Hummel* had won an Obie. That original version had, he claimed, been written in three hours and then rewritten over seven or eight years. As in the earlier play, it is set on a military base in the 1960s and concerns, among other things, men preparing to go to Vietnam.

Again, however, this not really the subject. *Streamers* explores the lives of those who bring with them problems and

concerns rooted in their daily life beyond the military.
Vietnam does constitute a threat to them, a threat embodied
in those who have already served there, but violence has
already been part of their lives. They are not simply
abandoned by a society at war with itself as well as with a
distant enemy. They are abandoned by those seemingly closest
to them. Race and sexual preference make them vulnerable,
but vulnerability seems one of the few things they share. They
are the victims of an unfocussed fear. Indeed it is that which
leads an enlisted man to attempt suicide.

A streamer, we learn, is a parachutist whose parachute fails
to open. This could be said of virtually all the characters in the
play. Death is a common fate, of course, but these are people
who can find nothing to halt their fall towards absurdity. They
appear to be drawn together by their circumstances but the
spaces between them are more evident than an enforced
solidarity. Death seems to stalk the cadre room where they are
gathered, unravelling whatever coherence they reach for. The
problem is that they become its agents, suspecting the very
human connections that might be the source of redemption.

In an ostensibly realistic play, the force of the central
metaphor, the distorting power of fears and passions ruthlessly
exposed, serves to echo something of that nightmare quality
found in his earlier work.

With Vietnam disappearing in the rearview mirror, Rabe
subsequently went on to write a series of plays in which
psychosis, fragmenting relationships, betrayals, imploding
language serve to define a culture profoundly at odds with
itself, deeply uncommunal, its values infiltrated and corroded
by the media, no longer in touch with the principles that
brought it into being. In other words, Vietnam, which for a
decade was the burning glass – focusing anxieties, profound
distrust of the other, destructive and anarchic impulses – was
an expression rather than a cause of cultural dislocation.

His is not, though, an hermetic world, defined by its own
self-generated limits. Life may be a terminal condition but it
does not imply the need to compound an ultimate absurdity.
The ironies he stages are less evidence of determinism than of
a failure of will and imagination and in a play called *A Question*

of Mercy, mercy and grace are indeed possibilities, even if ambiguously so. That ambiguity, it seems, is an inescapable fact of existence but the primary evil, in Rabe's world, is indifference. His plays are designed to provoke awareness of precisely that fact.

Christopher Bigsby
Professor of American Studies
University of East Anglia
June 2002

The Basic Training of Pavlo Hummel

(*The Basic Training of Pavlo Hummel* was first produced by Joseph Papp, May 20 1971, at the New York Shakespeare Festival Public Theater, under the direction of Jeff Bleckner, with the following cast (listed in order of appearance):

Pavlo Hummel	William Atherton
Yen	Victoria Racimo
Ardell	Albert Hall
Sergeant Tower	Joe Fields
Captain (All Officers)	Edward Cannan
Corporal	Anthony R. Charnota
Kress	Earl Hindman
Parker	Peter Cameron
Pierce	Robert Lehman
Burns	Stephen Clarke
Hendrix	D. Franklyn Lenthall
Hinkle	Edward Herrmann
Ryan	John Walter Davis
Mickey	Frederick Coffin
Voice of Mrs Sorrentino	Victoria Racimo
Mrs Hummel	Sloane Shelton
Sergeant Brisbey	Lee Wallace
Jones	Garrett Morris
Sergeant Wall	John Benson
Mamasan	Christal Kim
Small Boy	Hoshin Seki
Grennel	Tom Harris
Parham	Bob Delegall
First Vietcong	Hoshin Seki
Second Vietcong	Victoria Racimo

Associate Producer Bernard Gersten
Set by David Mitchell
Costume by Theoni V. Aldredge
Lighting by Martin Aronstein

Act One

The set is a space, a platform slanting upward from the downstage area. The floor is nothing more than slats that seem to run in various directions with a military precision. It has a brownish color. The backdrop is dark, touches of green. Along the back of the set runs a ramp that is elevated about two feet off the floor. Stage left and a little down from the ramp stands the drill sergeant's tower. This element is stark and as realistic as is possible. Further downstage and stage left the floor opens into a pit two feet deep. There is an old furnace partly visible. Downstage and stage right are three army cots with footlockers at their base. Upstage and stage right there is the bar area; an army ammunition crate and an army oil drum set as a table and chair before a fragment of sheet-metal wall that is covered partly with beer can labels. All elements of the set should have some military tone to them, some echo of basic training. To start the play, pop American music is heard for an instant in the dark. Then lights up on the bar area: evening. A drunken G.I. sits slumped on the crate and leaning forward on the drum. **Yen** (*pronounced 'Ing'*), *a Vietnamese girl dressed in purple silk pyjamas, slacks and pull-over top, moves about with a beer, trying to settle* **Pavlo** *down.*

Pavlo (*dressed in fatigues, moving with the music, dealing somehow with the other two in the room as he speaks*)   Did I do it to him? The triple-Hummel. Can you hear your boy? (*A sort of shudder runs through his shoulders: he punches.*) A little shuffle and then a triple boom-boom-boom. Ain't bad, man? Gonna eat up Cleveland. Gonna piss on Chicago. (*Banging with his palms on the sides of the oil drum.*)

Yen   Creezy, creezy

Pavlo   Dinky dow!

Soldier (*disturbed by the banging, looking up, deeply drunk*)   Les . . . go . . . home . . .

Yen   Paablo creezy.

Pavlo   Dinky dow.

Yen   Paablo boocoup love. Sleep me all the time . . .

Pavlo Did I ever tell you? – Thirteen months a my life ago – Joanna was her name. Sorrentino, a little bit a guinea-wop made outa all the pins and sticks all bitches are made a. And now I'm the guy who's been with the Aussies. I HAD TEA WITH 'EM. IT WAS ME THEY CALLED TO – 'Hummel!' 'MEDIC!' (*With a fairly good Australian accent.*) 'The dirty little blighters blew me bloody arm off.' (*And* **Yen** *brings a beer.*) Yeh, girl, in the little bit a time. (*And back to the air.*) We had a cat, you know? So we had a kitty box, which is a place for the cat to shit.

Yen Talk 'shit.' I can talk 'shit.' Numba ten talk.

Pavlo Ohhh, damn that Sorrentino, what she couldn't be taught. And that's what I'd like to do – look her up and explain a few things like, 'Your face, Sorrentino, I don't like your ugly face.' Did I ever tell you about the ole lady? Did I ever speak her name, me mudda?

Yen Mudda you, huh, Paablo? Very nice.

Pavlo To be seen by her now, oh, she would shit her jeans to see me now, up tight with this little odd-lookin' whore, feelin' good, and tall, ready to bed down. Ohhh, Jesus Mahoney. You see what she did, she wrote Joanna a letter. My mother. She called Joanna a dirty little slut and when I found out I cried, I wailed, baby, big tears, I screamed and threw kitty litter; I threw it in the air, I screamed over and over, 'Happy Birthday, Happy Birthday,' and then one day there was Joanna in the subway and she said 'Hello' and told me my favorite jacket I was wearing made me look ugly, didn't fit, made me look fat. (*A grenade thrown by a hand that merely flashed between the curtains, hits with a loud clump in the room, and everyone looks without moving.*) GRENA-A-A-DE!

Pavlo *drops to his knees, seizing the grenade, and has it in his hands in his lap when the explosion comes, loud, shattering, and the lights go black, go red or blue. The girl screams. The bodies are strewn about. The radio plays. And a black soldier,* **Ardell**, *now appears, his uniform strangely unreal with black ribbons and medals; he wears sunglasses, bloused boots.* (**Ardell** *will drift throughtout the play, present only when specifically a*

*part of the action, appearing, disappearing without prominent entrances
and exits.) A body detail is also entering, two men with a stretcher to
remove the dead.*

Ardell (*moving to turn the radio off*)   You want me, Pavlo? You
callin'? Don't I hear you? Yeh, yeh, that the way it happen
sometimes. Everybody hit, everybody hurtin', but the radio
ain't been touched, the dog didn't feel a thing; the engine's
good as new but all the people dead and the chassis a wreck,
man. (*Bowing a little toward* **Pavlo**.) Yeh, yeh, some mean
motherfucker, you don't even see, blow you away. Don't I
hear you callin'? (*Pivoting, moving swiftly down center-stage.*) Get off
it. Bounce on up here.

And **Pavlo** *leaps to his feet, runs to join* **Ardell***.*

Pavlo   Pfc Pavlo Hummel, sir, RA-74-313-226.

Ardell   We gonna get you your shit straight. No need to call
me 'sir.'

Pavlo   Ardell!

Ardell   Now what's your unit? Now shout it
out.

Pavlo   Second of the Sixteenth; First Division. BIG RED
ONE!

Ardell   Company.

Pavlo   Bravo.

Ardell   C.O.?

Pavlo   My Company Commander is Captain M.W.
Henderson. My Battalion Commander is Lieutenant Colonel
Roy J.S. Tully.

Ardell   Platoon?

Pavlo   Third.

Ardell   Squad.

Pavlo   Third.

Ardell Squad and platoon leaders.

Pavlo My platoon leader is First Lieutenant David R. Barnes; my squad leader is Staff Sergeant Peter T. Collins.

Ardell You got family?

Pavlo No.

Ardell You lyin', boy.

Pavlo One mother; one half brother.

Ardell All right.

Pavlo Yes.

Ardell Soldier, what you think a the war?

Pavlo It's being fought.

Ardell Ain't no doubt about that.

Pavlo No.

Ardell You kill anybody?

Pavlo Yes.

Ardell Like it?

Pavlo Yes.

Ardell Have nightmares?

Pavlo Pardon?

Ardell What we talkin' about, boy?

Pavlo No.

Ardell How tall you, you lyin' motherfucker?

Pavlo Five-ten.

Ardell Eyes.

Pavlo Green.

Ardell Hair.

Pavlo Red.

Ardell   Weight.

Pavlo   152.

Ardell   What you get hit with?

Pavlo   Hand grenade. Fragmentation-type.

Ardell   Where about it get you?

Pavlo (*gently touching his stomach and crotch*)   Here. And here. Mostly in the abdominal and groin areas.

Ardell   Who you talkin' to? Don't you talk that shit to me, man. Abdominal and groin areas, that shit. It hit you in the stomach, man, like a ten-ton truck and it hit you in the balls, blew 'em away. Am I lyin'?

Pavlo (*able to grin, glad to grin*)   No, man.

Ardell   Hurt you bad?

Pavlo   Killed me.

Ardell   That right. Made you dead. You dead, man; how you feel about that?

Pavlo   Well . . .

Ardell   DON'T YOU KNOW? I THINK YOU KNOW! I think it piss you off. I think you lyin' you say it don't. Make you wanna scream.

Pavlo   Yes.

Ardell   You had that thing in your hand, didn't you? What was you thinkin' on, you had that thing in your hand?

Pavlo   About throwin' it. About a man I saw when I was eight years old who came through the neighborhood with a softball team called the Demons and he could do anything with a softball underhand that most big leaguers can do with a hardball overhand. He was fantastic.

Ardell   That all?

Pavlo   Yes.

Ardell   You ain't lyin'?

Pavlo   No.

A whistle blows loudly and figures run about behind **Pavlo** *and* **Ardell**, *a large group of men in fatigues without markings other than their name tags and U.S. Army. And on the high Drill Instructor's tower, dimly lit at the moment, is a large Negro* **Sergeant**. *A* **Captain** *observes from the distance. A* **Corporal** *prowls among them, checking buttons, etc.*

Pavlo (*looking about*)   Who're they?

Ardell   Man, don't you jive me. You know who they are. That Fort Gordon, man. They Echo Company, 8th Battalion, Third Training Regiment. They basic training, baby.

Pavlo (*removes Pfc stripes and 1st Division patch*)   Am I . . . really . . . dead . . . ?

Ardell   Damn near, man; real soon. Comin' on. Eight more weeks. Got wings as big as streets. Got large, large wings.

Pavlo   It happened . . . to me . . .

Ardell   Whatever you say, Pavlo.

Pavlo   Sure . . . that grenade come flyin', I caught it, held it.

Pause.

Ardell   New York, huh?

Pavlo   Manhattan. 231 East 45th. I –

Ardell   Now we know who we talkin' about. Somebody say 'Pavlo Hummel,' we know who they mean.

Sgt Tower   GEN'L'MEN! (*As the men standing in ranks below the tower snap to Parade Rest and* **Pavlo**, *startled, runs to find his place among them.*) You all lookin' up here and can you see me? Can you see me well? Can you hear and comprehend my words? Can you see what is written here? Over my right tit-tee, can you read it? Tower. My name. And I am bigger than my name. And can you see what is sewn here upon the muscle of my arm? Can you see it? ANSWER!

Men (*yelling*)   No.

Sgt Tower   No, what? WHAT?

Men   NO, SERGEANT.

Sgt Tower   It is also my name. It is my first name.
SERGEANT. That who I am. I you Field First. And you
gonna see a lot a me. You gonna see so much a me, let me tell
you, you gonna think I you mother, father, sisters, brothers,
aunts, uncles, nephews, nieces, and children – if-you-got-'em –
all rolled into one big black man. Yeh, gen'l'men. And you
gonna become me. You gonna learn to stand tall and be
proud and you gonna run as far and shoot as good. Or else
you gonna be ashamed; I am one old man and you can't
outdo no thirty-eight-year-old man, you ashamed. AM I
GONNA MAKE YOU ASHAMED? WHAT DO YOU
SAY?

Men   Yes, Sergeant!

Sgt Tower. NO! NO, GEN'L'MEN. No, I am not gonna
make you ashamed. SERGEANT, YOU ARE NOT
GONNA MAKE US ASHAMED.

Men   SERGEANT, YOU ARE NOT GONNA MAKE US
ASHAMED.

Sgt Tower   WE ARE GONNA DO EVERYTHING YOU
CAN DO AND DO YOU ONE BETTER.

Men   WE ARE GONNA DO EVERYTHING YOU CAN
DO AND DO YOU ONE BETTER!

Sgt Tower   YOU A BUNCH A LIARS. YOU A BUNCH
A FOOLS! Now listen up; you listen to me. No one does me
one better. And especially no people like you. Don't you know
what you are? TRAINEES! And there ain't nothin' lower on
this earth except for one thing and we all know what that is,
do we not, gen'l'men?

Men   YES, Sergeant . . .

Sgt Tower   And what is that? (*Pause.*) And you told me you knew! Did you lie to me? Oh, no, nooo, I can't believe that; please, please don't lie. Gen'lmen, did you lie?

Men (*they are sorry*) Yes, Sergeant.

Sgt Tower No, no, please. If there something you don't know, you tell me. If I ask you something, you do not know the answer, let me know, civilians. That the answer to my question. The only creatures in this world lower than trainees is civilians, and we hate them all. All. (*Quick pause.*) And now . . . and finally . . . and most important, do you see what is written here? Over my heart; over my left tit-tee, do you see? U.S. ARMY. Which is where I live. Which is where we all live. Can you, gen'l'men, can you tell me you first name now, do you know it? (*Quick pause as he looks about in dismay.*) Don't you know? I think you do, yes, I do, but you just too shy to say it. Like little girls watchin' that thing just get bigger and bigger for the first time, you shy. And what did I tell you to do when you don't know the answer I have asked?

Men What is our first name?

Sgt Tower You! . . . You there! (*Suddenly pointing into the ranks.*) You! Ugly! Yeah, you. That right. You ugly. Ain't you? YOU TAKE ONE BIG STEP FORWARD. (*And it is* **Pavlo** *stepping forward. He does not know what he has done or what is expected from him.*) I think I saw you were not in harmony with the rest of these men. I think I saw that you were looking about at the air like some kinda fool and that malingering, trainee, and that intol'able. So you drop, you hear me? You drop down on you ugly little hands and knees and lift up you butt and knees from off that beautiful Georgia clay and you give me TEN and that's push-ups of which I am speaking. (**Pavlo**, *having obeyed the orders step by step, begins the push-ups.* **Tower** *goes back to the* **Men**.) NOW YOU ARE TRAINEES, ALL YOU PEOPLE, AND YOU LISTEN UP. I ASK YOU WHAT IS YOUR FIRST NAMES, YOU TELL ME 'TRAINEE'!

Men (*yelling*) TRAINEE!

Sgt Tower TRAINEE, SERGEANT!

Men TRAINEE, SERGE –

Sgt Tower   I CAN'T HEAR YOU!

Men   TRAINEE, SERGEANT!

Sgt Tower   AND WHAT IS YOUR LAST NAMES?
YOUR OWN FUCKING NAMES? (*The* **Men** *shout a chorus of
American names.*) AND YOU LIVE IN THE ARMY OF THE
UNITED STATES OF AMERICA.

Men   AND WE LIVE IN THE ARMY OF THE UNITED
STATES OF AMERICA.

Sgt Tower   WITH BALLS BETWEEN YOU LEGS!
YOU HAVE BALLS! NO SLITS! BUT BALLS, AND YOU
– (*Having risen,* **Pavlo** *is getting back into ranks.*)

Men   AND WE HAVE BALLS BETWEEN OUR LEGS!
NO SLITS, BUT BALLS!

Sgt Tower (*suddenly back to* **Pavlo**)   UGLY! Now who told
you to stand? Who you think you are, you standin', nobody
tole you to stand. You drop. You drop, you hear me? (*And*
Pavlo *goes back into the push-up position.*) What your name,
boy?

Pavlo   Yes. Sir.

Sgt Tower   Your name, boy!

Pavlo   Trainee Hummel, sir!

Sgt Tower   Sergeant.

Pavlo   Yes, sir.

Sgt Tower   Sergeant. I AM YOUR SERGEANT!

Pavlo   SERGEANT! YOU ARE A SERGEANT!

Sgt Tower   All right. That nice; all right, only in the future,
you doin' push-ups, I want you countin' and that countin' so
loud it scare me so I think there some kinda terrible, terrible
man comin' to get me, am I understood?

Pavlo   Yes, Sergeant.

Sgt Tower   I can't hear you!

Pavlo Yes, Sergeant! Yes, Sergeant!

Sgt Tower All right! You get up and fall back where you was. Gen'l'men. You are gonna fall out. By platoon. Which is how you gonna be doin' most everything from now on – by platoon and by the numbers – includin' takin' a shit. Somebody say to you, ONE, you down; TWO, you doin' it'; THREE, you wipin' and you ain't finished, you cuttin' it off. I CAN'T HEAR YOU!

Men YES, SERGEANT.

Sgt Tower I say to you SQUAT, and you all hunkered down and got nothin' to say to anybody but HOW MUCH? and WHAT COLOR, SERGEANT?

Men Yes, Sergeant.

Sgt Tower You good people. You a good group. Now I gonna call you to attention and you gonna snap to. That's heels on a line or as near it as the conformation of your body permit; head up, chin in, knees not locked; you relaxed. Am I understood?

Men Yes –

Sgt Tower AM I UNDERSTOOD, GODDAMNIT, OR DO YOU WANT TO ALL DROP FOR TWENTY OR –

Ardell, *off to the side, is drifting nearer.*

Men YES, SERGEANT, YES, SERGEANT!

Ardell Pavlo, my man, you on your way!

Corporal PLATOOOON! PLATOOOON!

Sgt Tower I GONNA DO SOME SINGIN', GEN'L'MEN, I WANT IT COMIN' BACK TO ME LIKE WE IN GRAND CANYON –

Corporal TEN-HUT!

Ardell DO IT, GET IT!

Sgt Tower – AND YOU MY MOTHERFUCKIN' ECHO!

Squad Leaders   RIGHT FACE!

Corporal   FORWARD HARCH!

Sgt Tower (*singing*)   LIFT YOUR HEAD AND LIFT IT HIGH!

Men   LIFT YOUR HEAD AND LIFT IT HIGH –

Sgt Tower   ECHO COMPANY PASSIN' BY!

Men   ECHO COMPANY PASSIN' BY!

Ardell (*and the* **Men** *are going off in groups during this*) MOTHER, MOTHER, WHAT'D I DO?

Men   MOTHER, MOTHER, WHAT'D I DO?

Ardell   THIS ARMY TREATIN' ME WORSE THAN YOU!

Men   THIS ARMY TREATIN' ME WORSE THAN YOU!

Sgt Tower   LORD HAVE MERCY I'M SO BLUE!

Men   LORD HAVE MERCY I'M SO BLUE! IT EIGHT MORE WEEKS TILL WE BE THROUGH! IT EIGHT MORE WEEKS TILL WE BE THROUGH! IT EIGHT MORE WEEKS TILL WE BE THROUGH!

And all the **Men** *have marched off in lines in different directions, giving a sense of large numbers, a larger space and now, out of this movement, comes a spin-off of two men,* **Kress** *and* **Parker***, drilling down the center of the stage, yelling the last lines of the song, marching, stomping, then breaking and running stage left and into the furnace room. There is the hulk of the belly of the furnace, the flickering of the fire.* **Kress** *is large, muscular, with a constant manner of small confusion as if he feels always that something is going on that he nearly, but not quite, understands. Yet there is something seemingly friendly about him.* **Parker** *is smaller: he wears glasses.*

Kress   I can't stand it, Parker, bein' so cold all the time and they're all insane, Parker. Waxin' and buffin' the floor at 5:30 in the morning is insane. And then you can't eat till you go down the monkey bars and you gotta eat in ten minutes and can't talk to nobody, and no place in Georgia is warm. I'm from Jersey. I can jump up in the air, if there's a good wind, I'll land in Fort Dix. Am I right so far? So Sam gets me. What's he do? Fort Dix? Uh-uh. Fort Gordon, Georgia. So I can be warm, right? Down South, man. Daffodils and daisies. Year round. (*Hollering*.) BUT AM I WARM? DO YOU THINK I'M WARM? DO I LOOK LIKE I'M WARM? JESUS H! EVEN IN THE GODDAMN FURNACE ROOM, I'M FREEZIN' TA DEATH!

Parker   So, what the hell is hollerin' like a stupid ape gonna do except to let 'em know where we at?

Kress (*as* **Pavlo** *enters upstage, moving slowly in awe toward the tower, looking*)   Heat up my blood!

Ardell (*to* **Pavlo**)   What you doin' strollin' about like a fool, man, you gonna have people comin' down all over you, don't you know –

Officer (*having just entered*)   What're you doin' walkin' in this company area? Don't you know you run in this company area? Hummel, you drop, you hear me. You drop!

Pavlo *goes into push-up position and starts to do the ten push-ups.*

Ardell (*over him*)   Do 'em right, do 'em right!

Kress   Why can't I be warm? I wanna be warm.

Parker   Okay, man, you're warm.

Kress   No; I'm not; I'm cold, Parker. Where's our goddamn fireman, don't he ever do nothin' but push-ups? Don't he ever do nothin' but trouble!

Parker   Don't knock that ole boy, Kress, I'm tellin' you; Hummel's gonna keep us laughin'!

Kress   Yesterday I was laughin' so hard. I mean, I'm stupid, Parker, but Hummel's *stupid*. I mean, he volunteers to be fireman 'cause he thinks it means you ride in a raincoat on a big red truck and when there's nothin' to do you play cards.

Parker   Yeah! He don't know it means you gotta baby-sit the goddamn furnace all night, every night. And end up lookin' like a stupid chimney sweep!

Kress   Lookin' what?

Parker (*as* **Pierce** *enters at a jog, moving across the stage toward* **Ardell** *and* **Pavlo**)   Like a goddamn chimney sweep!

Pavlo   Where you gon'?

Pierce (*without hesitating*)   Weapons room and furnace room.

Pavlo (*getting to his feet*)   Can I come along?

Pierce (*still running, without looking back*)   I don't give a shit. (*Exits,* **Pavlo** *following, as* **Ardell** *is drifting in the opposite direction.*)

Pavlo   . . . great . . .

Kress   Yeh? Yeh, Parker, that's good. Chimney sweeps!

Parker   Yeh, they were these weird little men always crawlin' around, and they used to do this weird shit ta chimneys.

Pierce *and* **Pavlo** *enter. They have their rifles.* **Pierce** *is a trainee acting as a squad leader. He has a cloth marked with corporal stripes on his left sleeve.*

Pierce   At ease!

Kress   Hey, the Chimney Shit. Hey, what's happenin', Chimney Shit?

Pavlo   How you don', Kress?

Kress   Where's your red hat, man?

Pavlo   What?

Parker   Ain't you got no red fireman's hat?

Pavlo   I'm just with Pierce, that's all. He's my squad leader and I'm with him.

Parker   Mr. Squad Leader.

Pavlo   Isn't that right, Pierce?

Parker   Whose ass you kiss to get that job, anyway, Pierce?

Pierce   At ease, trainees.

Kress   He's R.A., man. Regular Army. Him and Hummel. Lifer morons. Whata they gonna do to us today, anyway, Mr. Actin' Sergeant, Corporal? What's the lesson for the day: first aid or bayonet? I love this fuckin' army.

Pierce   The schedule's posted, Kress!

Kress   You know I don't read, man; hurts my eyes; makes 'em water.

Pavlo   When's the gas chamber, that's what I wanna know?

Kress   For you, Chimney Shit, in about ten seconds when I fart in your face.

Pavlo   I'm all right. I do all right.

Kress   Sure you do, except you got your head up your ass.

Pavlo   Yeh? Well, maybe I'd rather have it up my ass than where you got it. (*Slight pause: it has made no sense to* **Kress** *at all.*)

Kress   What?

Pavlo   You heard me, Kress.

Kress   What'd he say, Parker? (*There is frenzy in this.*) I heard him, but I don't know what he said. WHAT'D YOU SAY TO ME, HUMMEL?

Pavlo   Just never you mind, Kress.

Kress   I DON'T KNOW WHAT YOU SAID TO ME, YOU WEIRD PERSON!

Parker (*patting* **Kress**)   Easy, man, easy; be cool.

Kress   But I don't like weird people, Parker. I don't like them. How come I gotta be around him? I don't wanna be around you, Hummel!

Pavlo Don't you worry about it, I'm just here with Pierce. I just wanna know about the gas chamber.

Kress It's got gas in it! Ain't that right, Parker! It's like this goddamn giant asshole, it farts on you. THHPPBBB ZZZZZZZZZZ! (*Silence.*)

Pavlo When is it, Pierce?

Kress Ohhhhh, Jesus, I'm cold.

Pavlo This ain't cold, Kress.

Kress I know if I'm cold.

Pavlo I been colder than this. This ain't cold. I been a lot colder than –

Kress DON'T TELL ME IT AIN'T COLD OR I'LL KILL YOU! JESUS GOD ALMIGHTY, I HATE THIS MOTHER ARMY STICKIN' ME IN WITH WEIRD PEOPLE! DIE, HUMMEL! Will you please do me that favor! Oh God, let me close my eyes and when I open them, Hummel is dead. Please, please. (*Squeezes his eyes shut, clenches his hands for about two seconds and then looks at* **Pavlo** *who is grinning.*)

Pavlo Boy, I sure do dread that gas chamber.

Kress He hates me, Parker. He truly hates me.

Pavlo No, I don't.

Kress What'd I ever do to him, you suppose.

Parker I don't know, Kress.

Pavlo I don't hate you.

Parker How come he's so worried about that gas chamber, that's what I wonder.

Pavlo Well, see, I had an uncle die in San Quentin. (**Kress** *screams.*) That's the truth, Kress. (**Kress** *screams again.*) I don't care if you believe it. He killed four people in a fight in a bar.

Parker Usin' his bare hands, right?

Pavlo   You know how many people are executed every damn day in San Quentin? One hell of a lot. And every one of 'em just about is somebody's uncle and one of 'em was my uncle Roy. He killed four people in a bar-room brawl usin' broken bottles and table legs and screamin', jus' screamin'. He was mean, man. He was rotten; and my folks been scared the same thing might happen to me; all their lives, they been scared. I got that same look in my eyes like him.

Parker   What kinda look is that?

Kress   That really rotten look, man. He got that really rotten look. Can't you see it?

Pavlo   You ever steal a car, Kress? You know how many cars I stole?

Kress   Shut up, Hummel! You're a goddamn chimney sweep and I don't wanna talk to you because you don't talk American, you talk Hummel! Some goddamn foreign language!

Parker   How many cars you stole?

Pavlo   Twenty-three.

Kress   Twenty-three!

Parker *whistles*.

Pavlo   That's a lotta cars, huh?

Parker   You damn betcha, man. How long'd it take you, for chrissake? Ten years?

Pavlo   Two.

Parker   Workin' off and on, you mean.

Pavlo   Sure. Not every night, or they'd catch you. And not always from the same part of town. Man, sometimes I'd hit lower Manhattan, and then the next night the Bronx or Queens and sometimes I'd even cut right on outa town. One time, in fact, I went all the way to New Haven. Boy, that was some night because they almost caught me. Can you imagine that? Huh? Parker? Huh? Pierce? All the way to New Haven and cops on my tail every inch a the way, roadblocks closin' up behind me, bang, bang, and then some highway patrolman, just as I was wheelin' into New Haven, he come roarin' outa this side road. See, they must a called ahead or somethin' and he come hot on my ass. I kicked it, man, arrrrrrgggggggghhhhhh . . . ! 82 per. Had a Porsche; he didn't know who he was after; that stupid fuzz, 82 per, straight down the gut, people jumpin' outa my way, kids and businessmen and little old ladies, all of 'em, and me kickin' ass, up to 97 now, roarin' baby sirens all around me so I cut into this alley and jump. Oh, Jesus, Christ, just lettin' the car go, I hit, roll, I'm up and runnin' down for this board fence, up and over, sirens all over now, I mean, *all over*, but I'm walkin' calm, I'm cool. Cops are goin' this way and that way. One of 'em asks me if I seen a Porsche go by real fast. Did *I* see –

Kress   *Jesus-goddamn* – the furnace room's smellin' like the gas chamber! (*Rising to leave,* **Parker** *following.*)

Parker   Right, Hummel. That's right. I mean, I liked your story about your really rotten uncle Roy better than the one about all the cars.

Kress   Gotta go get our weapons.

Parker   Defend our fuckin' selves.

Pavlo   I'll see you guys later. (*They are gone. Silence.*) Hey, Pierce, you wanna hear my General Orders; make sure I know 'em, Okay? Like we're on Guard Mount and you're on the O.D. . . . You wanna see if I'm sharp enough to be one a your boys. Okay? (*Snapping to attention.*) Sir! My first general order is to take charge of this post and all government property in view, keeping always on the alert and . . .

Pierce   Gimme your eighth, Hummel.

Pavlo   Eighth? No, no, lemme do 'em, one, two, three. You'll mess me up. You'll mess me up I don't do them one, two, three.

Pierce   That's the way it's gonna be, Hummel. The man

comes up to you on Guard Mount, he's gonna be all over you – right on top a you yellin' down your throat. You understand me? He won't be standin' back polite and pretty lettin' you run your mouth.

Pavlo   Just to practice, Pierce. I just wanna practice.

Pierce   You don't wanna practice shit. You just wanna stand there and have me pat your goddamned head for bein' a good boy. Don't you know we stood here laughin' at you lyin' outa your ass? Don't you have any pride, man?

Pavlo   I got pride. And anyway, they didn't know I was lyin'.

Pierce   Shit.

Pavlo   And anyway, I wasn't lyin', it was storytelling. They was just messin' with me a little, pickin' on me. My mom used to always tell my dad not to be so hard on me, but he knew.

Whistle blows loudly from off.

Pierce   Let's go.

Pavlo   See, he was hard on me, 'cause he loved me. I'm R.A., Pierce.

Pierce   You got an R.A. prefix, man, but you ain't Regular Army.

Pavlo   They was just jumpin' on me a little; pickin' on me.

Again the whistle.

Pierce   That whistle means formation, man.

Pavlo   They're just gonna draw weapons, and I already got mine.

Pierce   That ain't what I said, Jerkoff!

Pavlo   Well, I ain't goin' out there to stand around doin' nothin' when I can stay right here and put the time to good use practicin' D and D. (*Again the whistle. The* **Men** *are gathering, we hear their murmuring.*)

Pierce   You ain't no motherin' exception to that whistle!

Pavlo   You ain't any real corporal anyway, Pierce. So don't get so big with me just because you got that hunk a thing wrapped around you –

Pierce   Don't you mess up my squad, Hummel! Don't you make me look bad, or I'll get you your legs broken.

Pavlo (*as the whistle blows and* **Pierce** *is leaving and gone*)   I bet you never heard a individual initiative.

Whistle again as **Soldiers** *rush in to line up in formation at Parade Rest while* **Sgt Tower** *climbs to stand atop the platform.*

Ardell   They don't know, do they? They don't know who they talkin' to.

Pavlo   No.

Ardell   You gonna be so straight.

Pavlo   So clean. (**Sgt Tower** *notices that someone is missing from formation. He turns, descends, exits.*) Port Harms! (*And he does it with only a slight and quickly corrected error.*)

Ardell   Good, Pavlo. Good. (*Slight pause.*) Order Harms!

Pavlo (*does it. There is some skill in the move*)   Okay . . .

Ardell   RIGHT SHOULDER . . . HARMS!

Pavlo *does this, but his head flinches, the rifle nicking the top of his helmet. His back is toward the group and* **Sgt Tower** *enters, watches for a time.*

Pavlo   Goddamnit. Shit. (*Again the rifle back to order.*)

Ardell   RIGHT SHOULDER . . .

Pavlo   HARMS! (*Again it is not good.*) You mother rifle. You stupid fucking rifle. RIGHT SHOULDER, HARMS. (*He tries.*) Mother! Stupid mother, whatsa-matter with you? I'll kill you! (*And he has it high above his head. He is looking up.*) Rifle, please. Work for me, do it for me. I know what to do, just you do it.

Ardell.   Just go easy. Man . . . just easy. It don't mean that much. What's it matter?

Sgt Tower   What you doin', trainee?

Pavlo (*snapping to attention*)   Yes, sir! Trainee Pavlo Hummel, sir.

Sgt Tower   I didn't ask you you name, boy. I asked you what you doin' in here when you supposed to be out on that formation?

Pavlo   Yes, sir.

Sgt Tower   No, I don't have no bars on my collar, do you see any bars on my collar?

Pavlo (*looking*)   No . . . no . . .

Sgt Tower   But what do you see on my sleeve at about the height a my shoulder less a little, what do you see?

Pavlo   Stripes, Sergeant. Sergeant stripes.

Sgt Tower   So how come you call me sir? I ain't no sir. I don't want to be no sir. I am a sergeant. Now do we know one another?

Pavlo   Yes, Sergeant.

Sgt Tower   That mean you can answer my question in the proper manner, do it not?

Pavlo   I was practicin' D and D, Sergeant, to make me a good soldier.

Sgt Tower   Ohhhhhhhhh! I think you tryin' to jive this ole man, that what you doin'. Or else you awful stupid because all the good soldiers is out there in that formation like they supposed to when they hear that whistle. Now which?

Pavlo   Pardon, Sergeant?

Sgt Tower   Which is it? You jivin' on me or you awful stupid, you take your pick. And lemme tell you why you can't put no jive on that old Sarge. Because long time ago, this ole

Sarge was one brand-new, baby-soft, smart-assed recruit. So I
see you and I say 'What that young recruit doin' in that
furnace room this whole company out there bein' talked at by
the C.O.?' And the answer come to me like a blast a thunder
and this voice sayin' to me in my head, 'This here young
recruit jerkin' off, that what he doin',' and then into my head
come this picture and we ain't in no furnace room, we in that
jungle catchin' hell from this one little yellow man and his
automatic weapon that he chained to up on top of this hill.
'Get on up that hill!' I tell my young recruit. And he tell me,
'Yes, Sergeant,' like he been taught, and then he start thinkin'
to hisself, 'What that ole Sarge talkin' about, 'run on up that
hill'? Ah git my ass blown clean away. I think maybe he got hit
on his head, he don't know what he's talkin' about no more –
maybe I go on over behind that ole rock – practice me a little
D and D.' Ain't that some shit the way them young recruits
wanna carry on? So what I think we do, you and me, long
about 2200 hours we do a little D and D and PT and all them
kinda alphabetical things. Make you a good soldier.

Pavlo   I don't think I can, Sergeant. That's night time,
Sergeant, and I'm a fireman. I got to watch the furnace.

Sgt Tower   That don't make me no never mind. We jus'
work it in between your shifts. You see? Ain't it a wonder how
you let the old Sarge do the worryin' and figurin' and he find
a way? (*Turning, starting to leave.*)

Pavlo   Sergeant, I was wondering how many push-ups you
can do. How many you can do, that's how many I want to be
able to do before I ever leave.

Sgt Tower   Boy, don't you go sayin' no shit like that, you
won't ever get out. You be an ole bearded blind fuckin' man
pushin' up all over Georgia.

Pavlo (*speaking immediately and rapidly, a single rush of breath, again
stops* **Sgt Tower**. *Incredulously* **Sgt Tower** *watches, starts to leave,
watches*)   And I was wondering also, Sergeant Tower, and
wanted to ask you – when I was leaving home, my mother
wanted to come along to the train station, but I lied to her

about the time. She would have wanted to hug me right in front of everybody. She would have waved a handkerchief at the train. It would have been awful. (*And* **Sgt Tower** *now leaves, is gone.* **Pavlo** *calls.*) She would have stood there, waving. Was I wrong?

Corporal   TEN HUT! FORWARD HARCH!

And the **Men** *begin to march in place. And* **Pavlo** *without joining them, also marches.*

Sgt Tower   AIN'T NO USE IN GOIN' HOME.

Men (*beginning to exit*)   AIN'T NO USE IN GOIN' HOME

Sgt Tower (*at the side of the stage*)   JODY GOT YOUR GAL AND GONE.

Men   JODY HUMPIN' ON AND ON.

Sgt Tower   AIN'T NO USE IN GOIN' BACK. (*And* **Pavlo**, *in his own area, is marching away.*)

Men   JODY GOT OUR CADILLAC.

Corporal   AIN'T NO MATTER WHAT WE DO.

All   JODY DOIN' OUR SISTER TOO.

Corporal   Count cadence, delayed cadence, count cadence count!

All   One – two – three – four. One, two, three, four. One, two, three, four. *Hey!*

All *are gone now except* **Pavlo** *who comes spinning out of his marching pattern to come stomping to a halt in the furnace-room area, while* **Ardell** *drifts toward him.*

Ardell   Oh, yeh; army train you, shape you up – teach you all kinds of good stuff. Like Bayonet. It all about what you do you got no more bullets and this man after you. So you put this knife on the end a your rifle, start yellin' and carryin' on. Then there hand to hand. Hand to hand cool. (**Pavlo** *is watching, listening.*) It all about hittin' and kickin'. What you do when you got no gun and no knife. Then there CBR. CBR:

Chemical, Biological, and Radiological Warfare. What you do when some mean motherfucker hit you with some kinda chemical. You (**Ardell** *mimes throwing a grenade at* **Pavlo**.) got green fuckin' killin' smoke all around you. What you gonna do? You gotta git on your protective mask. You ain't got it?

Pavlo (*choking*)   But I'm too beautiful to die. (*Rummaging about in the furnace room until* **Ardell** *throws him a mask.*)

Ardell   But you the only one who believe that, Pavlo. You gotta be hollerin' loud as you know how, 'GAS!' And then, sweet lord almighty, little bit later, you walkin' along, somebody else hit you with some kinda biological jive. But you know your shit. Mask on.

Pavlo (*having put the mask on, is waving his arms*)   GAS! GAS! GAS!

Ardell   You gettin' it, Pavlo. All right. Looking real good. But now you tired and you still waitin' and you come up on somebody bad – this boy mean – he hit you with radiation.

Pavlo *goes into a tense, defensive posture.*

Pavlo   Awww. (*Realizing his helplessness.*)

Ardell   That right. You know what you do? You kinda stand there, that what you do, whimperin' and talkin' to yourself, 'cause he got you. You gotta be some kinda fool, somebody hit you with radiation, man, you put on a mask, start hollerin', 'Gas.' Am I lyin'? Pavlo. What do you say?

Pavlo   Aww, no . . . No, man. – No, no. – No, no. No, no. Oh . . . (*And there has been, toward the end of this, a gathering of a group of* **Soldiers** *in the barracks area.* **Pavlo**, *muttering in denial of the radiation, crosses the stage hurriedly, fleeing the radiation, running into* **Parker**, *who grabs him, spins him.*) I did not.

Kress   The hell you didn't!

Parker   You been found out, Jerkoff. (*Kneeling behind* **Pavlo** *to take a billfold from his pocket.*)

Pavlo   No.

Kress　We got people saw you. Straight, honest guys.

Parker　Get that thing off your face. (*Meaning the mask.*)

Burns　The shit I didn't see you.

Parker　You never saw a billfold before in your life, is that what you're tryin' to say? You didn't even know what it was?

Kress　Is that what you're tryin' to say, Hummel?

Pavlo　No.

Kress　What are you tryin' to say?

Pavlo　I'm goin' to bed. (*Moving toward his bed but stopped by* **Kress**.)

Kress　We already had two guys lose money to some thief around here, Shitbird, and we got people sayin' they saw you with Hinkle's billfold in your pudgy little paws.

Hinkle (*deep Southern drawl*)　Is that right, Hummel? (*As* **Parker** *hands him the billfold he found on* **Pavlo**.)

Pavlo　I was just testin' you, Hinkle, to see how stupid you were leavin' your billfold layin' out like that when somebody's been stealin' right in our own platoon. What kinda army is this anyway? You're supposed to trust people with your life, you can't even trust 'em not to steal your money.

Parker　Listen to him.

Pavlo　That's the truth, Parker. I was just makin' a little test experiment to see how long it'd be before he'd notice it was gone. I don't steal.

Kress　What about all them cars?

Pavlo　What cars?

Parker　The New Haven Caper, Jerkoff. You know.

Pavlo　Ohhh, that was different, you guys. That was altogether different.

Kress　Yeh, they were cars and you couldn't fit them in your pocket.

Pavlo   Those people weren't my friends.

Parker   You don't steal from your friends. That what you're sayin'? Kress, Hummel says he don't steal from his friends.

Kress (*jumping up on* **Pavlo***'s bed, standing, walking about*) Don't that make his prospects pretty damn near unlimited.

Pavlo   Hey! Kress, what're you doin'?

Kress   What?

Pavlo   I said, 'What're you up to?' You're on my bed.

Kress   Who is?

Pavlo   You are. You are.

Kress   Where?

Pavlo   Right here. You're on my bed. That's my bed.

Kress   No, it isn't. It's not anybody's. It's not yours, Hummel.

Pavlo   It is too.

Kress   Did you buy it?

Pavlo   Get off my bed, Kress!

Kress   If you didn't buy it, then how is it yours? Ugly!

Pavlo   It was given to me.

Kress   By who?

Pavlo   You know by who, Kress. The army gave it to me. Get off it.

Kress   Are you going to take it with you when you leave here? If it's yours, you ought to be planning on taking it with you; are you?

Pavlo   I can't do that.

Kress   You're taking people's billfolds; you're taking their money; why can't you take this bed?

Pavlo   Because it was just loaned to me.

Kress   Do you have any kind of papers to prove that? Do you have papers to prove that this is your bed?

Pavlo   There's proof in the orderly room; in the orderly room, or maybe the supply room and you know it. That bed's got a number on it somewhere and that number is like its name and that name is by my name on some papers somewhere in the supply room or the orderly room.

Kress   Go get them.

Pavlo   What do you mean?

Kress   Go get them. Bring them here.

Pavlo   I can't.

Kress   If they're yours, you can.

Pavlo   They're not my papers, it's my bed. Get off my bed, Kress. (**Kress** *now kneels down, taking a more total possession of the bed.*) Goddamnit, Kress. GODDAMNIT! (*Silence:* **Kress** *has not moved, seems in fact about to lie down.*) All right. Okay. You sleep in my bed, I'm gonna sleep in yours.

Everyone stands around watching as **Pavlo** *charges off stage toward where* **Kress**'s *bed is located.*

Kress (*rising up a little, tense, looking off, as all look off in the direction* **Pavlo** *has gone*)   No, Hummel.

Pavlo (*yelling*)   The hell I ain't, Kress.

Kress   No, no, I strongly advise against it. I do strongly so advise. Or something awful might happen. I might get up in the middle of the night to take a leak and stagger back to my old bed. Lord knows what I might think you are . . . laying there. Lord knows what I might do.

Pavlo (*yelling*)   Then get out of my bed.

Kress   You don't understand at all, do you, shitbird! I'm sleeping here. This is where I'm going to sleep. You not going to sleep anywhere. You're going to sit up, or sleep on the floor, whatever. And in the morning, you're going to make this bed. This one. Because if you don't it'll be unmade when Sgt Tower comes to inspect in the morning and as we've already discussed, there's papers somewhere in one room or another and they show whose bed this is.

Pavlo (*rushing back, stomping, raging*)   GODDAMN YOU, KRESS, GET OUT OF MY BED! GET OFF MY BED! GET OUT OF IT!

Whistle blows and everyone scrambles to firing range. There is the popping of many rifles firing as on the back platform at the very rear of the set, three or four of the **Men** *are in firing positions; others stand behind them at Port Arms until* **Sgt Tower** *calls 'CEASE FIRE' and the firing stops. The* **Men** *who have been firing put their rifles on their shoulders to be cleared.* **Sgt Tower** *walks behind them tapping each on the head when he has seen the weapon is clear. The* **Men** *leap to their feet.* **Sgt Tower** *then stops out in front of them, begins to pace up and down.*

Sgt Tower   GEN'L'MEN! IT GETTIN' TOWARD DARK NOW AND WE GOT TO GET HOME. IT A LONG LONG WAYS TO HOME AND OUR MOTHER'S GOT SUPPER READY WAITIN' FOR US. WHAT CAN WE DO? WE GOT TO GET HOME FAST AS WE CAN, WHAT CAN WE DO? DO ANYBODY HAVE AN IDEA? LET ME HEAR YOU SPEAK IF YOU DO . . . I HAVE AN IDEA. ANYBODY KNOW MY IDEA? LET ME HEAR YOU IF YOU DO.

Pavlo   Run . . .

Burns   Run?

Sgt Tower   WHAT?

More Men   RUN?

Sgt Tower   I CAN'T HEAR YOU.

Men   WHAT?

Sgt Tower   RUN!

Men   RUN!

Sgt Tower *and* **Men**   RUN! RUN! RUN! RUN! RUN!

Sgt Tower (*as* **Men** *still yell 'RUN!'*)   PORT HARMS –
WHOOO! DOUBLE TIME! WHOOO!

They have been running in place. Now **Sgt Tower** *leads them off.
They exit, running, reappear, exit again. Reappear, spreading out now,
though* **Pavlo** *is fairly close behind* **Sgt Tower**, *who enters once again
and runs to a point downstage where he turns to* **Pavlo** *entering
staggering, leading.*

Sgt Tower   FALL OUT! (*And* **Pavlo** *collapses, the others
struggle in, fall down.*)

Pierce   FIVE GODDAMN MILES! (*All are in extreme pain.*)

Kress   MOTHER-GODDAMN-BITCH – I NEVER
RAN NO FIVE GODDAMN MILES IN MY LIFE. YOU
GOTTA BE CRAZY TO RUN FIVE GODDAMN
MILES . . .

Parker   I hurt. I hurt all over. I hurt, Kress. Oh, Christ.

Pierce   There are guys spread from here to Range 2. You
can be proud you made it, Parker. The whole company, man
– they're gonna be comin' in for the next ten days.

And **Parker** *yells in pain.*

Kress   Pierce, what's wrong with Parker?

Parker   SHIT, TOO, YOU MOTHER!

Kress   It'll pass, Parker. Don't worry. Just stay easy. (*And a
little separate from the others,* **Pavlo** *is about to begin doing push-ups.
He is very tired. It hurts him to do what he's doing.*) Oh, Hummel,
no. Hummel, please. (**Pavlo** *is doing the push-ups, breathing the
count, wheezing, gasping.*) Hummel, you're crazy. You really are.
He really is, Parker. Look at him. I hate crazy people. I hate
'em. YOU ARE REALLY CRAZY, HUMMEL. STOP IT
OR I'LL KILL YOU. (**Pavlo**, *saying the number of push-ups,
stopping, pivoting into a sit-up position.*) I mean, I wanna know
how much money this platoon lost to that thief we got among
us.

Pierce   Three hundred and twelve dollars.

Kress   What're you gonna do with all that money?

Pavlo   Spend it. Spend it.

Kress   Something gonna be done to you! You hear me, weird face? You know what's wrong with you? You wouldn't know cunt if your nose was in it. You never had a piece of ass in your life.

There is a loud blast on a whistle.

Pavlo   Joanna Sorrentino ga'me so much ass my mother called her a slut.

Kress   YOU FUCKING IDIOT!

Again the whistle.

Pierce   Oh, Christ . . .

Pavlo   Let's go. LET'S GO. LET'S GET IT.

Kress   Shut up.

Pavlo   Let's GO, GO, GO – (*Moving – all start to exit.*)

Kress   SHUT YOUR MOUTH, ASSHOLE!

Pavlo   LET'S GO – GO, GO, GO, GO, GO, GO . . .
(*Yelling, leading, yelling as all run off stage.*)

As the light goes on on the opposite side of the stage, two soldiers – the **Corporal** *and* **Hendrix** *– are seen with pool cues at the pool table. There are no pool balls. The game will be pantomime. They use a cue ball to shoot and work with.*

Hendrix   You break.

Corporal   Naw, man, I shoot break on your say-so, when I whip your ass, you'll come cryin'. You call. (*Flipping a coin as* **Pavlo** *comes running back to get his helmet, left where he was doing the push-ups.*)

Hendrix   Heads.

Corporal   You got it.

Pavlo, *scurrying off with his helmet, meets* **Sgt Tower** *entering from opposite side.*

Sgt Tower   Trainee, go clean the dayroom. Sweep it up.

Pavlo   Pardon, Sergeant? I forgot my helmet . . .

Sgt Tower   Go clean the dayroom, trainee.

Pavlo *runs off as at the pool game* **Hendrix** *shoots break.*

Corporal   My . . . my . . . my . . . Yes, sir. You're gonna be tough all right. That was a pretty damn break all right. (*Moving now to position himself for his shot.*) Except you missed all the holes. Didn't nobody tell you you were supposed to knock the little balls in the little holes?

Pavlo (*entering*)   Sergeant Tower said for me to sweep up the dayroom.

Hendrix   And that's what you do – you don't smile, laugh or talk; you sweep.

Corporal   You know what 'buck a ball' means, trainee?

Pavlo   What?

Corporal   Trainee's rich, Hendrix. Can't go to town, got money up the ass.

Pavlo   Sure I know what 'buck a ball' means.

Corporal   Ohh, you hustlin' trainee motherfucker. New game. Right now. Rack 'em up!

Hendrix *moves as if to re-rack the balls.*

Pavlo   You sayin' I can play?

Corporal   Hendrix, you keep an eye out for anybody who might not agree trainee can relax a bit. You break, man.

Pavlo   I'll break.

Corporal   That's right.

Pavlo   You been to the war, huh? That's a 1st Division

Patch you got there, ain't it? (*Shooting first shot, missing, not too good.*)

Corporal That's right.

Pavlo Where at?

Corporal How many wars we got?

Pavlo I mean exactly where.

Corporal (*lining up his shot*) Di An. Ever hear of it?

Pavlo Sure.

Corporal Not much of a place but real close to Da Nang. (*He shoots, watches, moves for the next shot.*)

Pavlo You up there too?

Corporal Where's that?

Pavlo By Da Nang. (**Corporal** *is startled by* **Pavlo** *knowing this. He shoots and misses.*) I mean, I thought Di An was more down by Saigon. D. Zone. Down there. They call that D. Zone, don't they?

Corporal You're right, man; you know your shit. We got us a map-readin' motherfucker, Hendrix. Yeh, I was by Saigon, Hummel.

Pavlo I thought so.

Corporal Your shot. (*Has moved off to the side and* **Hendrix** *who has a hip flask of whiskey.*)

Pavlo (*moving for his shot*) Big Red One, man, I'd be proud wearin' that. (*And he shoots.*) Shit. (*Having missed.*)

Corporal (*moving again to the table*) Good outfit. Top kinda outfit. Mean bastards, all of 'em. Everyplace we went, man, we used ta tear 'em a new asshole, you can believe me. (*Shooting, making it, he moves on.*) I'm gonna win all your damn money, man. You got your orders yet for where you go when you're finished with basic?

Pavlo No.

Corporal   Maybe if you're lucky, you'll get infantry, huh? Yeh, yeh, I seen some shit, you can believe me. (*And he moves about the table, shooting as he speaks.*) But you go over there, that's what you're goin' for. To mess with them people, because they don't know nothin'. Them slopes; man, they're the stupidest bunch a people anybody ever saw. It don't matter what you do to 'em or what you say, man, they just look at you. They're some kinda goddamn phenomenon, man. Can of bug spray buy you all the ass you can handle in some places. Insect repellent, man. You ready for that? You give 'em can a bug spray, you can lay their fourteen-year-old daughter. Not that any of 'em screw worth a shit. (*He thinks it all interesting.*) You hear a lot of people talkin' Airborne, 173rd, 101st, Marines, but you gotta go some to beat the First Division. I had a squad leader, Sergeant Tinden. He'd been there two goddamn years when I got there so he knew the road, man; he knew his way. So we was comin' into this village once, the whole company and it was supposed to be secure. We was Charlie Company and Alpha'd been through already, left a guard. And we was lead platoon and lead squad and comin' toward us on the path is this old man, he must been a hundred, about three foot tall and he's got this little girl by the hand and she's maybe a half-step behind him. He's wavin' at us, 'Okay, Okay, G.I.' And she's wavin', too, but she ain't sayin' nothin', but there's this funny noise you can hear, a kind of cryin' like. (*He still moves about, shooting, speaking, pausing, judging which shot to take.*) Anyway, I'm next to the Sarge and he tells this ole boy to stop, but they keep comin' like they don't understand, smilin' and wavin', so the Sarge says for 'em to stop in Vietnamese and then I can see that the kid is cryin'; she's got big tears runnin' outa her eyes, and her eyes are gettin' bigger and bigger and I can see she's tuggin' at the old man's hand to run away but he holds her and he hollers at her and I'm thinkin', 'Damn, ain't that a bitch, she's so scared of us.' And Tinden, right then, man, he dropped to his knees and let go two bursts – first the old man, then the kid – cuttin' them both right across the face, man, you could see the bullets walkin'. It was somethin'. (*He sets and takes his last shot. He flops the cue onto the table.*) You owe me, man; thirteen bucks. But I'm superstitious, so we'll make it twelve.

(*As **Pavlo** is paying.*) That's right. My ole daddy – the last day he saw me – he tole me good – 'Don't you ever run on nobody, Boy, or if you do I hope there's somebody there got sense enough to shoot you down. Or if I hear you got away, I'll kill you myself.' There's folks like that runnin' loose, Hummel. My ole man. You dig it. (*But **Pavlo** doesn't and is staring at him.*) What the fuck are you lookin' at?

Pavlo   I don't know why he shot . . . them.

Corporal   Satchel charges, man. The both of them, front and back. They had enough T.N.T. on 'em to blow up this whole damn state and the kid got scared. They was wearing it under their clothes.

Pavlo   And he knew . . .

Corporal   That's right. Been around; so he knew. You ready, Hendrix? (*They are moving to exit.*)

Hendrix   Ain't that some shit, Hummel? Ain't that the way to be?

Parker *can be seen far across the stage. In dimness. Nearby,* **Kress** *is with three or four other* **Soldiers**, *crouching among the beds.*

Parker   Dear Mother. It was the oddest thing last night. I sat near my bunk, half awake, half asleep . . .

Corporal   You keep your ear to the ground, Hummel, you're gonna be all (*Exiting.*) right. We'll see you around.

Pavlo   Just to see and to move; just to move. (*Miming with his broom the firing of a rifle, while **Ardell** stares at him across the table and lunges suddenly backwards, rapidly hauling the table off.*)

Parker (*loudly and flamboyantly*)   Yes, yes, good Mother, I could not sleep, I don't know why. And then for further reasons that I do not know, I happened to look behind me and there . . . was a space ship, yes, a space ship, green and golden, good Mother, come down to the sand of our Georgia home. A space ship. (**Pavlo** *wanders nearer.* **Parker** *glances toward* **Kress** – *who is kneeling with a blanket – and the others.*) And out of it, leaping they came, little green men no larger than pins. 'Good

Lord in Heaven,' said I to myself. 'What do they want?
Sneaking among us, ever in silence, ever in stealth.' Then I
saw Hummel. 'Hummel is coming,' said I. 'I will ask
Hummel,' said I to myself. 'Hummel is coming.

Pavlo *enters.*

Parker   THIEF!

Blanket is thrown over **Pavlo***. He is dragged to the floor. They beat and
kick him, calling him 'thief.' He cries out. Squirms. A second blanket is
thrown upon him, a mattress. It is his own bedding they are using, and as
they beat and kick him, a whistle blows; all but* **Pavlo** *go running out,
grabbing rifles and helmets as they go to form up for bayonet practice.* **Sgt
Tower** *is there.*

Pavlo (*emerging from beneath the blankets – no one is there but*
Ardell)   Didn't I do enough push-ups? How many do you
have to do, Ardell?

Ardell   You got to understand, Pavlo, it fun sometimes to
get a man the way they got you. Come down on him, maybe
pivot kick. Break his fuckin' spine. Do him, man. Do . . .
him . . . good.

Sgt Tower (*standing atop his platform, bayonet in hand*)   You got
to know this bayonet shit, gen'l'men, else you get recycled, you
be back to learn it all again. Eight more beautiful weeks in the
armpit a the nation. Else you don't get recycled, you get killed.
Then you wish for maybe half a second, you been recycled.
Do you know the spirit of the bayonet is to kill? What is the
spirit of the bayonet?

Men   To kill! (*While* **Pavlo** *stirs about,* **Pierce** *enters the
barracks. He is disheveled, a little drunk.*)

Sgt Tower   You sound like pussies. You sound like slits.

Men   TO KILL!

Sgt Tower   You sound like pussies.

Men   TO KILL!

Pavlo, *sensing* **Pierce***, hurriedly opens his footlocker, digs out a book,
which he tries to pretend to read.*

Pierce   Look at you. Ohhh, you know how much beer I
hadda drink to get fucked up on 3.2 beer? Hummel, look at
me. You think it's neat to be squad leader? It's not neat to be
squad leader. (**Pavlo** *pretends to read.*) I hear you got beat up
this afternoon.

Pavlo   I got a blanket party.

Pierce   You're in my squad and other guys in my squad
beat you, man; I feel like I oughta do somethin'. I'm older,
see? Been to college a little; got a wife. And I'm here to tell
you, even with all I seen, sometimes you are unbelievable,
Hummel.

Pavlo   I don't care. I don't care.

Pierce   I mean, I worry about you and the shit you do, man.

Pavlo   You do what you want, Pierce.

Pierce   I mean, that's why people are after you, Hummel.
That's why they fuck with you.

Pavlo   I'm trying to study my code a conduct, Pierce, you
mind? It's just not too damn long to the proficiency test.
Maybe you oughta be studyin' your code a conduct too,
insteada sneakin' off to drink at the PX.

Pierce   I wanna know how you got those rocks down your
rifle. It's a two-mile walk out to the rifle range, and you got
rocks in your barrel when we get there. That's what I'm talkin'
about.

Pavlo   I don't know how that happened.

Pierce   And every fight you get into, you do nothin' but
dance, man. Round in a circle, bobbin' and weavin' and
getting' smacked in the mouth. Man, you oughta at least
try and hit somebody. (*And then suddenly, strangely, he is
laughing.*) JESUS CHRIST, Hummel, what's wrong with
you? We're in the shower, and I tell you to maybe throw a
punch once in a while, step with it, pivot, so you try it right
there on that wet floor and damn near kill yourself smashin'
into a wall.

Pavlo   Fuck you, Pierce.

Pierce   Fuck you, Hummel. (*Silence.*)

Pavlo   You know somethin', Pierce? My name ain't even really Pavlo Hummel. It's Michael Hummel. I had it legally changed. I had my name changed.

Pierce   You're puttin' me on.

Pavlo   No, no, and someday, see, my father's gonna say to me, 'Michael, I'm so sorry I ran out on you,' and I'm gonna say, 'I'm not Michael, Asshole. I'm not Michael anymore.' Pierce? You weren't with those guys who beat up on me, were you?

Pierce   No.

Pavlo *begins making his bunk.*

Ardell   Sometimes I look at you, I don't know what I think I'm seein', but it sooo simple. You black on the inside. In there where you live, you that awful hurtin' black so you can't see yourself no way. Not up or down or in or out.

Sgt Tower (*having descended from the platform moves among the* **Men**)   There ain't no army in the world got a shorter bayonet than this one we got. Maneuverability. It the only virtue. You got to get inside that big long knife that other man got. What is the spirit of the bayonet?

Men   TO KILL!

Sgt Tower   You sound like pussies.

Men   TO KILL!

Sgt Tower   You sound like slits!

Men   TO KILL

Sgt Tower   EN GARDE!

Men   AGGGH!

Sgt Tower   LONG THRUST, PARRY LEFT . . . WHOOOOOO!

And the **Men** *make the move, one of them stumbling, falling down, clumsy, embarrassed.*

Where you think you are? You think you in the movies? This here real life, gen'l'men. You actin' like there ain't never been a war in this world. Don't you know what I'm sayin'? You got to want to put this steel into a man. You got to want to cut him, hurt him, make him die. You got to want to feel the skin and muscle come apart with the push you give. It come to you in the wood. RECOVER AND HOLD!

Men   AGGGH! (*They yell and growl with each thrust. Another falls down, gets up.*)

Sgt Tower   EN GARDE!

Men   AGGGH!

Sgt Tower   Lookin' good, lookin' good. Only you ain't mean. (**Men** *growl.*) How come you ain't mean? (**Men** *growl again.*) HORIZONTAL BUTT STROKE SERIES, WHOOO! (*And they move, making the thrust, recovery, then uppercutting butt stroke, horizontal butt stroke and finally the downward slash. The growling and yelling is louder this time.*) Look at you; look at you. Ohhh, but you men put into my mind one German I saw in the war, I got one bullet left, don't think I want to shoot it, and here come this goddamned big-assed German. 'Agggghhhh,' I yell to him and it a challenge and he accept. 'Agggghhhh,' he say to me and set hisself and I just shoot him. Boom! Ohhh, he got a look on his face like I never saw before in my life. He one baffled motherfucker, Jim. (*Without command, the* **Men** *begin to march.*)

Ardell (*singing*)   ONCE A WEEK I GET TO TOWN . . .

Men   THEY SEE ME COMIN', THEY ALL LAY DOWN.

Ardell   IF I HAD A LOWER I.Q. . . . (*All are marching now, exiting.*)

Men   I COULD BE A SERGEANT TOO.

Sgt Tower   LORD HAVE MERCY, I'M SO BLUE . . .

Men   LORD HAVE MERCY, I'M SO BLUE . . .

Sgt Tower   IT SIX MORE WEEKS TILL I BE THROUGH.

Men   IT SIX MORE WEEKS TILL I BE THROUGH.

Sgt Tower   SOUND OFF!

Men   One – Two –

Burns, **Pierce**, **First Soldier** *enter barracks area, still singing as others are exiting, and these three men set up a crap game on a footlocker.*

Sgt Tower   SOUND AGAIN!

Men   Three – Four.

Sgt Tower   COUNT CADENCE, COUNT.

Men   ONE, TWO, THREE, FOUR. ONE, TWO, THREE, FOUR. ONE, TWO, THREE, FOUR.

And they are all spread about the barracks, reading, sleeping.

Pavlo (*to* **Hinkle** *as the crap game goes on nearby*)   Can you imagine that, Hinkle? Just knowin'. Seein' nothin' but bein' sure enough to gun down two people. They had T.N.T. on 'em; they was stupid slope-heads. That Sergeant Tinden saved everybody's life. I get made anything but infantry, I'm gonna fight it, man. I'm gonna fight it. You wanna go infantry with me, Hinkle? You're infantry and good at it, you're your own man. I'm gonna wear my uniform everywhere when I'm home, Hinkle. My mother's gonna be so excited when she sees me. She's just gonna yell. I get nervous when I think about if she should hug me. You gonna hug your mother when you get home?

Hinkle   My mom's a little bitty skinny woman.

Pavlo   I don't know if I should or shouldn't.

Hinkle   What's your mom like?

Pierce   You tellin' him about your barn house exploits, Hinkle?

Hinkle   Oh, no.

Pierce   Hinkle says he screwed sheep. He tellin' you that, Hummel?

Parker   How about pigs, Hinkle?

Hinkle   Oh, yeh.

Kress   I'm tellin' you, Parker, it was too much; all that writin' and shit, and runnin' around. They ain't got no right to test you. Proficiency test, proficiency test; I don't even know what a proficiency is – goddamn people – crawlin' and writin' – I'm tellin' you they ain't got no right to test you. They get you here, they mess with you – they let you go. Who says they gotta test you?

Pierce (*who has the dice and is laying down money*)   Who's back man? I'm shootin' five.

Kress   I got so nervous in hand-to-hand, I threw a guy against the wall. They flunked me for bein' too rough.

Pierce   Who's back man?

Kress   I'll take three. (*Putting down money.* **Parker** *drops a couple of ones.*) I get recycled, I'll kill myself, I swear it. (*As* **Pierce** *is shaking the dice, saying over and over, 'Karen loves me, Karen loves me.'*) I'll cut off my ear.

Pierce (*throwing the dice*)   Karen says I'm GOOD!

Kress   Goddamn! Shit! How they do it again, Parker?

Parker   Pierce, you're incredible.

Kress   Parker!

Parker   They add up your scores, man; your P.T. plus your rifle, plus the score they got today. Then they divide by three. You lettin' it ride, Pierce? (*Throwing down a five.*)

Pierce   Karen loves me.

Kress   Where they get the 'three'? (*Putting in money.*)

Parker   There's three events, man.

Pierce (*throwing the dice*)   Karen say, 'I know the ROAD!'

Kress   You fuckin asshole.

Parker   Goddamnit, Pierce!

Pierce   Who wants me? Back man's got no heart. Shootin' twenty I come seven or eleven – double or nothin'. Whose twenty says I can't come for all out of the gate? . . .

A **Soldier** *enters on the run.*

Soldier   Tower's right behind me; he's got the scores.

General commotion as they hide the dice and the money and **Sgt Tower** *strides across the stage and enters their area.*

Pierce   TENHUT! (*All come to attention before their bunks.*)

Sgt Tower   AT EASE! (**Men** *to Parade Rest.*) Gen'l'men. It's truth and consequences time. The sad tidings and the (*Handing a paper to* **Pierce** *for him to post it on the board.*) glad tidings. You got two men in this platoon didn't make it. They Burns and Kress. They gonna have to stay here eight more weeks and if they as dumb as it look, maybe eight more after that and eight fuckin' more. The rest a you people, maybe you ain't got no spectacular qualities been endowed upon my mind, but you goin' home when you figured. (*He turns, leaving.*)

Pierce   TENHUT!

Sgt Tower   Carry on.

They are silent. **Kress** *stands. All start talking and yelling at once.*

Pierce   Lemme holler . . . just one . . . time, lemme holler . . .

Hinkle   Mother, mother, make my bed!

Soldier (*at the bulletin board*)   Me! My name! Me!

Pierce   AGGGGGGGGHHHHHHHHHHHIIHHHH-HHAAAA!

Parker   Lemme just pack my bags!

Hendrix (*entering with civilian clothes, shirt, trousers, on a hanger, hat on his head*)   Lookee – lookee –

Hinkle   What're them funny clothes?

Pierce   CIVILIAN CLOTHES! CIVILIAN –

Hinkle   CI-WHO-LIAN?

Pierce   PEOPLE OUTSIDE, MAN! THAT'S WHY THEY AIN'T ALL FUNNY AND GREEN, BECAUSE YOU'RE OUTSIDE WHEN YOU WEAR 'EM. YOU'RE BACK ON THE BLOCK. BACK IN THE WORLD!

Pavlo   DON'T NOBODY HEAR ME CALLIN' 'KRESS!' (*He has said the name a few times during the yelling. He is atop his own bed.*) I think we oughta tell him how sorry we are he didn't make it. I'm gonna. I'm gonna tell him. I'm sorry, Kress, that you're gonna be recycled and you're not goin' home. I think we're all sorry. I bet it's kinda like gettin' your head caught in a blanket, the way you feel. It's a bad feelin', I bet, and I think I understand it even if I am goin' back where there's lights and it's pretty. I feel sorry for you, Kress, I just wanna laugh, I feel so sorry – (*And* **Kress** *pushes him off the bed, leaping after him.* **Pavlo** *staggers backward.*) Sonofabitch, what're you – SONOFABITCH! (*Swinging a wild right hand, they flail and crash about,* **Kress** *grabbing* **Pavlo**'s *wrist, drawing him forward, snapping the arm up into a hammer lock.*)

Kress   Down. (*Then Lifting.*) Don't you hear me? Down, I'm sayin'. Don't you hear me? Thata boy . . . Called crawlin'. . . (*And* **Pavlo** *has been thrown to the floor,* **Kress** *diving on top of him.*) You got the hang of it . . . now . . . Crawlin'. . . Yeh. Now I'm gonna ask you something? Okay?

Pavlo   Okay . . .

Kress   What I'd like to know is who is it in this platoon steals money from his buddies? Who is it don't know how to talk decent to nobody? And don't have one goddamn friend? Who is that person? You tell me, Hummel? The name a that person passed his test today by cheatin'.

Pavlo   I don't . . . know . . .

Kress   Who? (*Working the arm.*)

Pavlo   No – (*And the arm is twisted again.*) Stop him, somebody. Pierce. You're my squad leader, Pierce. Ohhhh . . . Pierce, please . . . Aggghhhh . . . Pierce . . .

Kress   WHO? (*And* **Pavlo** *yells.*)

Pierce   Ease off a little . . .

Kress   I CAN'T HEAR YOU!

Pierce   Kress, I –

Pavlo   HUMMEL!

Kress   WHAT? WHAT?

Pavlo   HUMMEL! HUMMEL!

Kress   WHAT?

Pavlo   HUMMEL! HUMMEL! He did 'em. All of those things. All of 'em. He cheated. He cheated. HUMMEL! HUM –

Pierce   Kress, goddamnit. GODDAMNIT! (*Leaping to lift* **Kress** *away from* **Pavlo** *and throw him sideways.*)

Kress   What? What you want, Corporal? Don't mess with me, man. (*Staring at* **Pierce** *who is now between him and* **Pavlo**. **Kress** *backs away; yet he is raging.*) Don't mess with Kress. Not when he's feelin' bad. He'll kill ya, honest to God. He'll pee in your dead mouth. (*And* **Pavlo** *rushes at* **Kress**, *howling.*)

Pierce   Noooooooooo. (*Seizing* **Pavlo**, *pushing him back.*)

Pavlo   I'm all right. I'm all right. I do all right!

Pierce   Will you listen to me, man? You're goin' home, not Kress. You got him.

Pavlo   Fucking asshole!

Pierce   Will you listen? (*Shoving* **Pavlo**, *scolding him.*) You gotta learn to think, Hummel. You gotta start puttin' two and two together so they fit. You beat him; you had ole Kress beat and then you fixed it so you hadda lose. You went after him so he hadda be able to put you down.

Pavlo I just wanted to let him know what I thought.

Pierce No, no!

Pavlo He had no call to hit me like that. I was just talkin' –

Pierce You dared him, man.

Pavlo You shoulda stopped him, that's the problem. You're the squad leader. That's just this whole damn army messin' with me and it ain't ever gonna end but in shit. How come you're a squad leader? Who the fuck are you? I'm not gonna get a chance at what I want. Not ever. Nothin' but shit. They're gonna mess with me – make a clerk outa me or a medic or truck driver, a goddamn moron – or a medic – a nurse – a fuckin' Wac with no tits – or a clerk, some little goddamn twerp of a guy with glasses and no guts at all. So don't gimme shit about what I done, Pierce, it's what you done and done and didn't – (*And during this whole thing,* **Pierce** *has moved about straightening the bunks and footlockers disturbed by the fight and* **Pavlo**, *in growing desperation, has followed him. Now* **Pierce**, *in disgust, starts to leave.*) That's right; keep on walkin' away from your duties, keep –

Pierce You're happy as a pig in shit, I don't know why I keep thinkin' you ain't.

Pavlo I am not.

Pierce Up to your eyeballs!

Pavlo I'm gonna kill myself, Pierce! (*It bursts out of him.*)

Pierce If you weren't in my squad, I'd spit in your face . . . (*He pivots and goes off after* **Kress** *and the soldiers.*)

Pavlo Fuck you, fuck you. (*Rocking backward, then bowing forward. He is alone and yelling after them as* **Ardell** *enters.*) I hate you goddamn people.

Ardell I know.

Pavlo   Ardell. (*At his footlocker,* **Pavlo** *rummages about.*)

Ardell   I know. I know. All you life like a river and there's no water all around – this emptiness – you gotta fill it. Gotta get water. You dive, man, you dive off a stone wall (**Pavlo** *has a canteen and paper bag in his hands.*) into the Hudson River waitin' down dark under you, for a second, it's all air . . . so free . . . do you know the distance you got to fall? You think you goin' up. Don't nobody fall up, man. Nobody.

Pavlo   What is it? I want to know what it is. The thing that Sergeant saw to make him know to shoot that kid and old man. I want to have it, know it, be it.

Ardell   I know.

Pavlo   When?

Ardell   Soon.

Pavlo   If I could be bone, Ardell; if I could be bone. In my deepest part or center, if I could be bone. (*Taking a container from the bag, he takes pills, washes them down with water, while* **Sgt Tower**, *already on the platform, speaks, and* **Pavlo** *crawls under the covers of his bunk.*)

Sgt Tower   Now I'm gonna tell you gen'l'men how you find you way when you lost. You better listen up. What you do, you find the North Star and the North Star show you true north accurate all year round. You look for the Big Dipper and there are two stars at the end a that place in the stars that look like the bowl on the dipper and they called the pointer. They them two stars at where the water would come out the dipper if it had some water, and out from them on a straight line you gonna see this big damn star and that the North Star and it show you north and once you know that, gen'l'men, you can figure the rest. You ain't lost no more.

Men (*entering to position themselves for next scene*)   YESSSS, SERGEANT!

Sgt Tower   I hope so. I do hope so . . . (**Pierce**, **Parker** *and others set up card game on footlocker.*)

Kress (*passing bunk where* **Pavlo** *is a lump beneath his blanket*)   I wonder what the fuckin' chimney shittin' shit is doin' now? (**Hinkle** *settles curiously on the bunk next to* **Pavlo**.)

Parker   You gonna see me, Pierce?

Pierce   And raise you.

Parker   Ten ta one, he's under there jerking off!

Hinkle (*bending near to* **Pavlo**)   No. no, he's got this paper bag and everything smells funny. Y'all some kind of acrobat, Hummel?

Kress   He's got some chick's bicycle seat in a bag, man.

Hinkle   And the noises he's makin'.

Pierce   Poor pathetic motherfucker.

Kress   He ain't pathetic.

Pierce   He is too.

Parker   Under there pounding his pud.

Kress   You musta not seen many pathetic people, you think he's pathetic.

Pierce   I seen plenty.

Parker   Call.

Pierce   Full Boat. Jacks and threes! (*Laying down his cards.*)

Parker   Jesus Goddamn Christ.

Hinkle   I was wonderin' can ah look in you all's bag, Hummel? (*Reaching under the blankets for the bag.*)

Parker   Jesus Goddamn Christ.

Hinkle   Ohhhh . . . it's . . . you been sniffin' airplane glue . . . (*And he laughs, turns toward the others.*) Hummel's been sniffin' airplane glue.

Kress   ATTAWAY TO GO, HUMMEL.

Hinkle   An' where's all the aspirins . . . ? (*Holding the bottle.*)

Pavlo   Tum-tum, Pavlo.

Hinkle   You all kiddin' me.

Pavlo   No.

Hinkle   Y'all ate 'em?

Pavlo   Yeah!

Hinkle   Hey, y'all . . . (*To* **Pavlo**.) Was it full? (**Pavlo**, *attempting to sit up, flops back down.*)

Pavlo   Tippy top.

Hinkle   Hummel just ate – (*Examining the bottle.*) *a hundred* aspirins. Hummel just ate 'em.

Kress   Attaway to go, Hummel.

Parker   Nighty-night.

Hinkle   Won't it hurt him, Pierce?

Kress   Kill him probably.

Parker   Hopefully.

Kress   Hinkle, ask him did he use chocolate syrup?

Hinkle   He's breathin' kinda funny, Pierce, don't you think?

Kress   Hummel does everything funny.

Pierce (*beginning to deal*)   Five cards, gen'l'men; jacks or better.

Hinkle   Pierce.

Pierce   Hummel, you stop worryin' that boy. Tell him no headache big enough in the world, you're gonna take a hundred aspirins. (*Slight pause.* **Kress** *begins imitating* **Pavlo**'s *odd breathing.*) How come everybody's all the time bustin' up my good luck?

Burns   Shit, man, he took a hundred aspirins, he wouldn't be breathing period.

Ryan   Sounds like a goddamn tire pump.

Burns   Hummel, TEN HUT!

Pierce   Hummel, you just jivin' 'cause you don't know what else to do or did you eat them pills?

Burns   Tryin' to blow himself up like a balloon . . . drift away. Float outa the fort.

Parker *begins to imitate breathing.*

Ryan   He's fakin', man.

Burns   How you know?

Ryan   They'd kill you like a bullet.

Hinkle   Get over here, Pierce!

Kress   How come the army don't throw him out, Parker?

Parker   Army likes weird people, Kress.

Kress   I hate weird people.

Parker   Sure you do.

Kress   Weird chimney-shittin' friendless, gutless cheatin' –

Pierce *is examining* **Pavlo**. *And* **Pavlo** *makes a sound and then begins to cough.*

Pierce   NOOO! NOT IN MY SQUAD, YOU MOTHER, GET UP! (*He is trying to get* **Pavlo** *to his feet, another soldier is helping.*) YOU SILLY SONOFABITCH. We got to walk him. (**Pavlo** *is feebly resisting.*) Hinkle, double-time it over the orderly room.

Hinkle   Right.

Pierce   Tell 'em we got a guy over here took a hundred aspirins, they should get an ambulance.

Hinkle (*turning to head for the door*)   Right.

Kress   Hinkle!

Hinkle (*hesitating.*)   Yeh!

Kress   Pick me up a Coke on your way back.

Pierce   Hold him steady, I think we oughta get him outside, more air.

Ardell (*standing over near the base of the tower.*)   Pavlo. You gonna have ambulances and sirens and all kinds a good shit. Ain't you somethin'? It gonna be a celebration. C'mon over here. (*As if **Ardell**'s voice draws them, they lug **Pavlo** toward the tower, walking him; they lay him down, remove all clothes from him but his underwear and T-shirt.*) Pavlo! Look at you. You got people runnin' around like a bunch a fools. That what you wanted? Yeah, that what you want! They sayin' 'Move him. Lift him. Take his shirt off.' They walkin' you around in the air. They all thinkin' about you, anyway. But what you doin' but cryin'? You always think you signifyin' on everybody else, but all you doin' is showin' your own fool self. You don't know nothin' about showboatin', Pavlo. You hear me? Now you get on up off that floor. You don't get up, man, I blow a motherfuckin' whistle up side a you head. I blow it loud. YOU THINK YOU GOT A MOTHERFUCKIN' WHISTLE IN YOUR BRAIN!

Pierce *and the other man have turned away. Everything **Pavlo** does is performed in the manner of a person alone: as if **Ardell** is a voice in his head. The light perhaps suggests this. **Kress**, all others, are frozen.*

Ardell   I'm tellin' you how to be. That right.

Pavlo *slumps back down.*

Ardell   Ohhh, don't act so bad; you actin', man. What you expect, you go out get you head smokin' on all kinds a shit sniffin' that goddamn glue then fallin' down all over yourself. Man, you lucky you alive, carryin' on like that.

Pavlo *is doubled over.*

Ardell   Ain't doin' you no good you wish you dead, 'cause you ain't, man. Get on up.

Pavlo *takes a deep breath and stands.*

Ardell   You go on in the latrine now, get you a Bromo, you wash off you face . . .

Pavlo *exits, staggering.*

Ardell   Then get you ass right back out here. And you don't need no shave, man, you ain't got no beard no ways. (*Sees* **Pavlo***'s uniform lying on the floor.*) What kinda shit this? Your poor ole sarge see this, he sit down on the ground and he cry, man. Poor ole Sarge, he work himself like he crazy trying ta teach you so you can act like a man. An' what you do? (*Turning suddenly*, yelling after **Pavlo**.) PAVLO! You diddlin' in there, you take this long. And you bring out you other uniform. We gonna shape you up.

Pavlo *enters carrying military dress uniform in clothing bag, which he hangs on the tower.*

Ardell   It daytime, man, you goin' out struttin'. You goin' out standin' tall. You tear it open. Trousers first, man. Dig 'em out.

Pavlo, *having selected the trousers, moves as if to put them on.*

Ardell   NOOOO! Damnit, ain't you got no sense at all?

He has rushed to **Pavlo**, *lifted the trouser bottoms from off the floor.*

You drag 'em all over the floor like that, man, they gonna look like shit. Get up on this footlocker!

Now **Pierce** *and the other soldier move to help* **Pavlo** *dress. All is effortless now.*

That right, that it. Make 'em look like they got no notion at all what it like ta be dirty. Be clean, man. Yeh. Now the shirt.

It is a ritual now. **Pavlo** *must exert no effort whatsoever as he is transformed.*

Lemme look you brass over. Ain't too bad. It do. Lemme just touch 'em up a little. (*He brushes with his handkerchief at the brass.*) You put on you tie. Make you a big knot. Big knot make you look tall. Where you boots?

And finished with the jacket, **Pierce** *and other soldier move to the boots.*

Where you boots? An' you got some shades? Lemme get you some shades. (*Walking backward.*) And tuck that tie square. Give her little loop she come off you throat high and pretty.

As **Ardell** *exits,* **Pavlo** *sits on the footlocker.* **Pierce** *and the other soldier kneel to put the boots onto him.*

HUT . . . HOO . . . HEE . . . HAW . . . (*Singing*) IF I HAD A LOWER IQ.

Men   IF I HAD A LOWER I.Q.

Ardell   I COULD BE A SERGEANT TOO.

Men   I COULD BE A SERGEANT TOO!

Across the back of the stage, two men march.

Ardell   LORD HAVE MERCY. I'M SO BLUE.

The two men do an intricate drill-team step.

Men   IT FOUR MORE WEEKS TILL I BE THROUGH.

The two men spin their rifles and strike the ground smartly with the butts, as **Ardell** *returns, carrying a pair of sunglasses.*

Ardell   You gonna be over, man, I finish with you.

Pavlo *stands up, now fully dressed.*

Ardell   You gonna be the fat rat, man; you eatin' cheese.

He moves about **Pavlo**, *examining him, guiding him toward the tower. As* **Ardell** *talks,* **Pavlo** *climbs the tower and stands on it;* **Ardell** *joins him.*

OVER, BABY! Ardell can make you straight; you startin' ta look good now; you finish up, you gonna be the fattest rat, man; eatin' the finest cheese. Put you in good company, you wear that uniform. You go out walkin' on the street, people know you, they say, 'Who that?' Somebody else say, 'That boy got pride.' Yeh, baby, Pavlo, you gonna be over, man. You gonna be that fat fat rat, eatin'. cheese, down on his knees, yeh, baby, doffin' his red cap, sayin', 'Yes, Massa.' You lookee out there.

Both are atop the tower. **Ardell** *is a little behind* **Pavlo** *and gesturing outward.* **Pavlo** *stands. He has sunglasses on.*

Who you see in that mirror, man? Who you see? That ain't no Pavlo Hummel. Noooo, man. That somebody else. An' he somethin' else.

Pavlo *is looking.*

Ardell   Ohhh, you goin' out on the street, they gonna see you. Ardell tellin' you and Ardell know. You back on the block an' you goin' out struttin'. An' they gonna cry when they see you. You so pretty, baby, you gonna make 'em cry. You tell me you name, you pretty baby!

Pavlo (*snapping to attention*)   PAVLO MOTHERHUMPIN' HUMMEL!

Blackout.

Act Two

Set changes: The debris of the bar wall remains upstage and stage right, though the barrel and crate are gone. Downstage and stage right there is a larger, more detailed version of the bar: metal wall, barrel used as table, two crates used as chairs, a footlocker off to the side, beer cans and bottles scattered about. The drill sergeant's tower remains. Far downstage and just a little left of center, a telephone sits on the floor near another footlocker. Stage left of the tower there is an army cot with a green but nonmilitary bedspread.

The lights come up on the men in formation. **Pavlo** *is still atop the tower, standing, looking out as he was. The men face upstage. Standing at the rear of the set are the* **Captain** *and* **Sgt Tower**. *They face the men. Downstage stands* **Mickey**, **Pavlo**'s *half-brother.* **Mickey** *wears slacks, T-shirt, shoes. He is standing as if looking into a mirror about to comb his hair; however he does not move. The* **Captain**, *stiffly formal, addresses the troops.*

Captain   As we enter now the final weeks of your basic training, I feel a certain obligation as your company commander to speak to you of the final purpose of what has gone on here. Normally this is more difficult to make clear. Pleiku, Vietnam, is the purpose of what we have done here. A few nights ago, mortar and machine-gun fire in a sneak attack in the highlands killed nine Americans and wounded 140 serving at our camp there in Pleiku. In retaliation, a bombing of the North has begun and it will continue until the government of Hanoi, battered and reeling, goes back to the North.

Sgt Tower   Company, fall out.

And the troops scatter. Music starts from **Mickey**'s *radio.* **Pavlo** *descends. Picks up duffel bag and AWOL bag.*

Pavlo   Hey, Mickey, it's me. I'm home! (**Mickey**, *in T-shirt, slacks, shoes, combs hair.*) It's me. I'm home, I'm home.

Mickey   Pavlo. Whata you say, huh? Hey, hey, what happened? You took so long. You took a wrong turn, huh?

Missed your stop and now you come home all dressed up like a conductor. What happened? You were down in that subway so long they put you to work? Huh? Man, you look good though; you look good. Where were you again?

Pavlo   Georgia.

Mickey   Hot as a bitch, right?

Pavlo   No. Cold.

Mickey   In Georgia?

Pavlo   Yeh, it was real cold; we used to hide out in the furnace room every damn chance we ever got.

Mickey   Hey, you want a drink? Damn, that don't make much sense, does it?

Pavlo   What?

Mickey   They send you to Georgia for the winter and it's like a witch's tit. Can you imagine that? A witch's tit? Eeeeeeggggggg. Put ice on your tongue. That ever happened to me, man, I'd turn in my tool. Ain't you gonna ask about the ole lady? How's she doin' and all that, 'cause she's doin' fine. Pickin' and plantin' daisies. Doin' fine. (*And* **Pavlo** *laughs softly, shaking his head, taking the drink* **Mickey** *has made him.*) Whatsa matter? You don't believe yo-yos can be happy? Psychotics have fun, man. You oughta know that.

Pavlo   I just bet she's climbin' some kinda wall. Some kinda wall and she's pregnant again, she thinks, or you are or me or somebody.

Mickey   Noo, man, noo, it's everybody else now. Only non-family.

Pavlo (*laughing loudly*)   THAT'S ME AND YOU! NON-FAMILY MOTHERFUCKERS!

Mickey   All the dogs and women of the world!

Pavlo   Yeh, yeh, all the guys in the barracks used to think I was a little weird so I'd –

Mickey – you *are* a little weird –

Pavlo Yeh, yeh, I'd tell 'em, 'You think I'm weird, you oughta see my brother, Mickey. He don't give a big rat's ass for nothin' or nobody.'

Mickey And did you tell 'em about his brains, too? And his wit and charm. The way his dick hangs to his knees – about his eighteen thou a year? Did you tell 'em all that sweet shit?

Pavlo They said they hoped you died of all you got.

Mickey (*has been dressing throughout: shirt, tie, jacket*) How come the troops were thinkin' you weird? You doin' that weird stuff again. You say 'Georgia' and 'the army.' For all I know you been down town in the movies for the last three months and you bought that goddamn uniform at some junk shop.

Pavlo I am in the army.

Mickey How do I know?

Pavlo I'm tellin' you.

Mickey But you're a fuckin' liar; you're a fuckin' myth maker.

Pavlo I gotta go to Vietnam, Mickey.

Mickey Vietnam don't even exist.

Pavlo I gotta go to it.

Mickey Arizona, man; that's were you're goin'. Wyoming.

Pavlo Look at me! I'm different! I'm different than I was! (*This is with fury.*) I'm not the same anymore. I was an asshole. I'm not an asshole anymore. I'm not an asshole anymore! (*Silence as he stares in anguish.*) I came here to forgive you. I don't need you anymore.

Mickey You're a goddamn cartoon, you know that.

Pavlo (*rapidly. A rush of words*) I'm happier now than I ever was, I got people who respect me. Lots of 'em. There was this guy Kress in my outfit. We didn't hit it off . . . and he called

me out . . . he was gonna kill me, he said. Everybody tried to
stop me because this guy had hurt a lot of people already and
he had this uncle who'd taught him all about fightin' and this
uncle had been executed in San Quentin for killing people.
We went out back of the barracks. It went on and on, hitting
and kicking. It went on and on; all around the barracks. The
crowd right with us. And then . . . all of a sudden this look
came into his eye . . . and he just stopped . . . and reached
down to me and hugged me. He just hugged and hugged me.
And that look was in all their eyes. All the soldiers. I don't
need you anymore, Mickey. I got real brothers now.

Mickey   You know . . . if my father hadn't died, you
wouldn't even exist.

Pavlo   No big thing! We got the same mother; that's shit
enough. I'm gonna shower and shave, Okay? Then we can go
out drinkin'.

Mickey   All those one-night stands. You ever think of that?
Ghostly pricks. I used to hear 'em humpin' the ole whore. I
probably had my ear against the wall the night they got you
goin'.

Pavlo (*after a slight silence*)   You seen Joanna lately?

Mickey   Joanna?

Pavlo   Joanna. My ole girl. I thought maybe she probably
killed herself and it was in the papers. You know, on account
of my absence. But she probably did it in secret.

Mickey   No doubt.

Pavlo   No doubt.

Mickey   Ain't she the one who got married? I think the ole
lady tole me Joanna got married and she was gonna write you
a big letter all about it. Sure she was. Anyway, since we're
speaking of old girls and pregnant people, I've got to go to this
little party tonight. Got a good new sweet young thing and she
thinks I'm better than her daddy. I've had a run a chicks lately
you wouldn't believe, Pavlo. They give away ass like Red

Cross girls dealin' out donuts. I don't understand how I get half a what I get. Oh yeah, old lady comes and goes around here. She's the same old witch.

Pavlo   I'm gonna to see Joanna. I'll call her up. Use the magic fuckin' phone to call her up.

Mickey   I'll give you a call later on.

Pavlo   I'll be out, man. I'll be out on the street.

Mickey   You make yourself at home. (*Exiting.*)

And **Soldiers** *appear far upstage, marching forward as* **Ardell**, *off to the side, counts cadence, and other* **Soldiers** *appear at various points about the stage.*

Ardell   HUT . . . HOO . . . HEE . . .

Sgt Tower (*entering as* **Pavlo**, *glancing at him, exits*)   SAW SOME STOCKIN'S ON THE STREET . . .

Men   WISHED I WAS BETWEEN THOSE FEET.

Sgt Tower   WISHED I WAS BETWEEN THOSE FEET. HONEY, HONEY, DON'T YOU FROWN.

Men   I LOVE YOU DRUNK AND LAYIN' DOWN.

Sgt Tower   STANDIN' TALL AND LOOKIN' GOOD. WE BELONG IN HOLLYWOOD.

He is atop the tower as the **Men** *come to a stomping halt.*

Men   WE BELONG IN HOLLYWOOD.

Sgt Tower   Take five, gen'l'men, but the smoking lamp is not lit.

Pavlo *is there, off to the side, disheveled, carrying a pint whiskey bottle. He undresses, speaking his anger, throwing his uniform down. The* **Men** *are relaxing a little.*

Pavlo   Stupid fuckin' uniform. Miserable hunk a green shit. Don't we go to good bars – why don't you work for me? And there's this really neat girl there sayin' to me how do I like bein' a robot? How do I like bein' one in a hundred million robots all marchin' in a row? Don't anybody understand about uniforms? I ain't no robot. You gotta have braid . . . ribbons and patches all about what you did. I got nothin'. What's so complicated? I look like nothin' 'cause I done nothin'. (*In his T-shirt and underwear, he kneels now with the bottle.*)

Sgt Tower   Gen'l'men, you best listen up real close now even though you restin'. Gonna tell you little bit about what you do you coming through the woods, you find a man wounded in his chest. You gotta seal it off. That wound workin' like a valve, pullin' in air makin' pressure to collapse that man's lung; you get him to breathe out and hold his breath. You apply the metal foil side a the waterproof wrappin of the first-aid dressing, tie it off. Gonna hafta tie it extra; you use your poncho, his poncho, you get strips a cloth. You tear up you own damn shirt, I don't care. You let that boy have his lung. You let him breathe. AM I UNDERSTOOD?

Men   YES, SERGEANT!

Sgt Tower   FALL IN. (*The **Men** leap to attention.*) DISMISSED!

*The troops go, leaving **Pavlo** alone, in his underwear, near or on the bed.*

Pavlo   I wanna get laid . . . bed . . . bottle. (*Pause.*) I wanna get laid! I wanna get laid, phone! You goddamn stuck-up motherin' phone. Need a piece of ass, bed. Lemme walk on over to that phone. Lemme crawl on over to that phone. Lemme get there. Gonna outflank you. Goddamn army ant. Thas right. Thas right. Hello. (*Dialing now he has crawled to the phone.*) This is Pavlo, Joanna, hello. Certainly of course. I'd be glad to screw your thingy with my thingy. BSZZZZZZZ . . .

Woman (*over the phone*)   Hello?

Pavlo   BBBZZZZZZZZZZZZZZZZZ . . .

Woman   Hello?

Pavlo   Little bitty creature . . . hello, hello. . . .

Woman   Who is this?

Pavlo   Hollering . . . hollering . . . poor creature . . . locked inside, can't get out, can't –

Woman   Pavlo?

Pavlo   Do you know me? Yes. Yes, it is me, Pavlo. Pavlo Hummel . . . Joanna . . . And I am calling to ask how can you have lived to this day away from me?

Woman   Pavlo, listen.

Pavlo   Yes. I am. I do.

Woman   This isn't Joanna.

Pavlo   What?

Woman   This is Mrs. Sorrentino, Pavlo. Joanna isn't here.

Pavlo   What?

Woman   I said, 'Joanna isn't here,' Pavlo. This is her mother; may I have her call you?

Pavlo   What?

Woman   I said, 'May I have her call you?' Or did you just call to say hello?

Pavlo   Who is this?

Woman   Pavlo, what's wrong with you?

Pavlo   Who are you? I don't know who this is. You get off the line, goddamnit, you hear me, or I'll report you to the telephone company. I'll report you to Bell Telephone. And G.E., too. And the Coke company and General Motors. (*The* **Woman** *hangs up the phone.*) You'll be hurtin', baby. I report you to all those people. Now you tell me where she is. Where is she?

And behind him a light pops on, a table lamp. His mother, a small, dark-haired woman, plump, fashionably dressed. She has been there all the while sitting in the dark, listening. She begins to speak almost at the same instant that the light goes on.

Mrs Hummel   In Stratford, Connecticut, Pavlo. Pregnant
more than likely. Vomiting in the morning. Yes . . . trying to
. . . get . . . rid of . . . it. . . . Hello, Pavlo . . . I wrote you that
. . . I wrote you. (*Silence.*) Hello . . . Pavlo. I wrote you she was
married. Why are you calling? Why? (*Silence.*) Pavlo? Listen,
are you finished on the phone and could we talk a minute? I
don't want to interrupt . . . I only have a few . . . few things to
say. They won't take long. I've been working since you've
been gone. Did you know? (*As she continues to talk,* **Pavlo** *slowly
hangs up the telephone and places it on the footlocker.*) Doing quite
well. Quite well indeed. In a department store. Yes. One of
the smaller ones. Yes. And we had an awful, awful shock there
the other day and that's what I want to tell you about. There's
a woman, Sally Kelly, and Ken was her son, in the army like
you now and he went overseas last August. Well, I talked to
Sally when I went in at noon and she was in the lunch room
writing a little card to Ken and she let me read it. She knew
that you were in the army so she said she was sure I knew the
way it was consolation to write a little note. Then about 5:45,
I was working on the shoes and I saw two army officers come
up the escalator and talk to one of the other clerks. I never
gave them another thought and at 6 o'clock Sally came
through and went down the escalator and made a remark to
me and laughed a little and went on down. In about fifteen
more minutes, I was waiting on a lady and she said to me,
'Isn't that terrible about the lady's son who works downstairs?'
I said, 'Who?' She said, 'The lady who works at your candy
department just got word her son was killed in Vietnam.'
Well, I was really shook when I heard that and – I said, 'Oh,
you must be mistaken. She just went downstairs from her
supper hour and I talked to her and she was fine.' She said,
'Well, that's what I heard on the main floor.' Well, I went
right to the phone and called the reception desk and they said
it was true. This is what happened, this is what I want to tell
you. The officers had gone to Sally's house but no one was
home so they talked to the neighbors and found out Sally
worked at the store. So they went up to our receptionist and
asked for our manager. He wasn't in so they asked for one of
the men and Tommy Bottle came and they told him they

needed his help because they had to tell one of the employees that her son was killed in Vietnam. Tommy really got shook as you can imagine and he took the officers to Mr. Brenner's office and closed the door. While they were in there, Sally came out of the lunch room and came downstairs. Joyce, the girl who is the receptionist, knew by this time and Sally laughed when she went by and said that she better get to work or something like that. Joyce said later on that she could hardly look at her. Anyway, Tommy called the floorman from first floor to come up and he told him what had happened and then he had to go back down to first floor and tell Sally she was wanted in Mr. Bremner's office. She said, 'Oh, boy, what have I done now?' By the time she got to the fourth floor, the office door was open and she saw the two army men and said, 'Oh, dear God, not Kenny.' (*Pause.*) A mother . . . and her children should be as a tree and her branches. A mother spends . . . but she gets . . . change. You think me a fool . . . don't you? There are many who do. (*Pause.*) He joined to be a mechanic and they transfered him to Infantry and he was killed on December 1st. So you see . . . I know what to expect. I know . . . what you're trying to do.

Pavlo   Who . . . was . . . my father? Where is he?

Mrs Hummel   You know that.

Pavlo   No, I want you to tell me.

Mrs Hummel   I've already told you.

Pavlo   No, where is he now? What did he look like?

Mrs Hummel   I wrote it all in a letter. I put it all in an envelope, I sealed it, mailed it.

Pavlo   I never got it.

Mrs Hummel   I think you did.

Pavlo   No!

Mrs Hummel   No, you had many fathers, many men, movie men, filmdom's great – all of them, those grand old men of yesteryear, they were your father. The Fighting 76th, do you remember, oh, I remember, little Jimmy, what a tough little mite he was, and how he leaped upon that grenade, did you see, my God what a glory, what a glorious thing with his little tin hat.

Pavlo   My real father!

Mrs Hummel   He was like them, the ones I showed you in movies, I pointed them out.

Pavlo   What was his name?

Mrs Hummel   I've told you.

Pavlo   No. What was his name? I don't know what it was.

Mrs Hummel   Is it my fault you've forgotten?

Pavlo   You never told me.

Mrs Hummel   I did. I whispered it in your ear. You were three. I whispered the whole thing in your ear.

Pavlo   Lunatic!

Mrs Hummel   Nooooo!

Pavlo   Insane, hideous person!

Mrs Hummel   I've got to go to bed now. I have to get my rest. (*Her back is turned. She is walking to leave him.*)

Pavlo (*yelling*)   I picked this girl up in this bar tonight and when I took her home and got her to the door and kissed her, her tongue went into my mouth. I thought that meant she was going to let me in to her apartment. 'Don't get hurt,' she said, 'and get in touch when you get back; I'd love to see you.' She knew I was going overseas, did you? And then the door was shut and all I wanted to say was, 'What are you doing sticking your tongue in my mouth and then leaving me, you goddamn stuck-up motherin' bitch?' But I didn't say anything.

Mrs Hummel (*as she leaves*)   Yes . . . well . . . I'll . . . see you in the morning.

Ardell (*who has been watching*)   Oh, man, how come? You wanted to get laid, how come you didn't do like the ole Sarge told you steada gettin' all tore up with them walkin' blues? Take you a little money, the old Sarge say, roll it up long ways, put it in your fly, man, so it stickin' out. Then go on walkin' up and down the street that green stickin' right outa your fly. You get laid. You got that money stickin' outa your fly, you get laid. You get your nut! How come you didn't do that?

Officer (*who has been standing on rear platform at Parade Rest*) And the following will depart conus 12 August 1966 for the Republic of Vietnam on assignment to the 23rd Field Hospital. Thomas. Simpson. Horner. Hinkle. Hummel.

Pavlo   I don't wanna be no medic!

And the bar music starts. **Yen** *and* **Mamasan**, *an older Vietnamese woman, enter from one side of the stage;* **Sgt Brisbey** *calling from the other and then entering, his bed on wheels pushed onstage by two* **Soldiers**. *Meanwhile,* **Ardell** *has hauled off the footlocker on which the phone had set, revealing on the floor a pile of clothes,* **Pavlo**'s *jungle fatigues which he immediately starts getting into.* **Yen** *is at the bar. All this happens nearly simultaneously.* **Mamasan**, *scurrying about, exits.*)

Yen   Hey, G.I. cheap Charlie, you want one more beer?

Jones (*offstage*)   One bomniba, one beer.

Brisbey   Pavlo.

Yen (*as* **Jones** *in a bright colored walking suit enters*)   EEEEEE-aaaaaa? What you talk? One bomniba, one beer. Same – same, huh? I no stand. What you want?

Jones (*pursuing her, both are playing yet both have real anger*)   You gimme boucoup now?

Yen   Boucoup what? I don't know what you want. Crazy G.I., you dinky dow.

Brisbey   PAVLO!

Pavlo (*who is still dressing into jungle fatigues*)   I'm in the can, Brisbey, I'll be there in a minute.

Ardell   He be there, Brisbey.

Jones   You got lips as fat as mine, you know that, ho?

Yen   Tôi không biêt!

Jones   Shit, you don't know.

Yen   Shit. I can say, too. I know. Shit. (*And he is reaching for her.*) No. We fini. Fini. You no talk me no more, you numba fuckin' ten. (*And she bounces away to sit on a crate and look at sheet music.*)

Brisbey   Do you know, Pavlo? I saw the metal point of that mine sticking up from the ground just under my foot – I said, 'That's a mine. I'm stepping on a mine.' And my foot went right on down and I felt the pin sink and heard the first small . . . pop. I jumped . . . like a fool. And up she came right outa the ground. I hit at it with my hand as if to push it away, it came up so slow against my hand . . . Steel . . . bits of dirt . . .

Pavlo   I'm off duty now, Brisbey.

Ardell   Ole Brisbey got himself hit by a Bouncin' Betty. That a kind of land mine; you step on it, she jump up to about right here (*Indicating his waist.*), then she blow you in half. That why he got that name. Little yellow man dug a hole, put it in, hoped he'd come around. He an old man, damn near; got seventeen years in the army; no legs no more, no balls, one arm.

A small Vietnamese **Boy** *comes running by and grabs* **Pavlo***'s hand .*

Boy   HEY, G.I., SHOW YOU NUMBA ONE! (*He guides him into the whorehouse-bar and leaves him there.*)

Pavlo (*to* **Jones** *who is sitting there drinking a beer*)   Hey, what's goin' on?

Jones   What's happenin', man?

Mamasan (*returning*)   Hello, hello! You come my house, I am glad. Do you want a beer? I have. Do you want a girl? I have numba-one girl. Numba one. You want?

Pavlo (*pointing to* **Mamasan**)   You?

Mamasan   No, no, I am Mamasan. But I have many girl. You see, maybe you like. Maybe you want short time, huh? Maybe you want long time. I don't know, you tell me. All numba one.

Jones (*laughs*)   Man, don't you believe that ole lady, you just gotta get on and ride. Like her. (*Indicating* **Yen**.) I been. And I'm restin' to go again; an' I don't think it any kinda numba one; but I been outa the world so *damn* long. I jus' close my eyes an' jive my own self – 'That ain't no dead person,' I say, 'that ain't no dead Ho jus' cause she layin' so still. I saw her walk in here.' I mean, man, they so screwed up over here. They got no nature. You understand me, Bro? They got no nature, these women. You – how long you been over here?

Pavlo   Not long; couple weeks.

Jones   You new then, huh?

Pavlo   Yeh.

Jones   You wanna go? (*Reaching out toward* **Yen** *who is across the room, calling to her.*) Hey, Ho! C'mon over here!

Yen   You talk me?

Jones   Yeh, baby, you, c'mon over here. You wanna go, man?

Pavlo   What about the V.D.? (*Taking a seat.*)

Jones (*big laugh*)   What about it?

Yen (*who, approaching with a beer, has heard*)   I no have. I no sick. No. No sweat, G.I. You want short-time me, no sweat.

Jones   Shit, Ho, you insides rotten. You Vietnamee, ain't you? Vietnamee same-same V.D.

Yen   No! No sick. (*As* **Jones** *grabs her, sets her down on* **Pavlo**'s *lap.*) What you do? No.

Jones   I'm jus' tryin' ta help you get some money, baby. I be you sportsman. Okay. (*Holding her in place.*) You just sit on down an' be nice on the man's lap, pretty soon he ain't gonna be worried 'bout no V.D. if you jus' sorta shift . . . (*Demonstrates.*) every now and then. Okay . . . (*She is still now and he turns his attention to* **Pavlo**.) Now, lemme tell you 'bout it, lemme tell you how it is. It be hot, man. I come from Georgia, and it get hot in Georgia, but it ain't ever been this kinda hot, am I lyin'? An' you gonna be here one year and that three-hundred-sixty-five days, so you gonna sweat. Now do you think I'm lyin'?

Yen *is touching* **Pavlo**, *rubbing under his shirt.*

Pavlo   I ain't never sweat so much.

Jones   So that's what I'm sayin'. You gonna be here and you gonna sweat. And you gonna be here and you gonna get V.D. You worried about sweatin'? Ahhhhh. You grinnin'. So I see I have made my meanin' clear. (**Yen** *has been rubbing* **Pavlo**'s *thigh.*) How you feelin' now? She kinda nice, huh? She kinda soft and nice.

Pavlo   Where you work?

Jones (*laughs*)   Don't you be askin' me where I work. That ain't what you wanna know. I gotta get you straight, my man, gotta get outa here, buy myself some supplies. My ole mom all the time tellin' me, 'Don't you go near that P.X. You get blown away for sure. Them V.C.'s gotta wanna get that P.X.'

Pavlo (*to* **Yen**)   What's your name?

Yen   Name me Yen.

Pavlo   Name me Pavlo. Pavlo.

Yen   Paaa-blo.

Pavlo   How much?

Jones   Lord, she says his name, he loves her.

Yen   You want short-time. I ask Mamasan. (*But* **Mamasan** *has been watching.*)

Mamasan (*approaching*)   Okay. Okay. Yen numba one. I am happy. Five hundred Ps.

Jones   Two hundred.

Mamasan   She very beautiful.

Jones   Two-fifty.

Mamasan   Four hundred, can do. No sweat.

Jones   Mamasan, who you think you jivin'?

Mamasan   Yen boucoup boyfriend! She very love!

Jones   Two-fifty.

Mamasan (*to* **Pavlo**)   Three hundred twenty. You, huh? Three hundred twenty.

Jones   Pavlo, give her three hundred, tell her things is tough at home, she don't know.

Mamasan (*as* **Pavlo** *hands her the money*)   No, no, I talk you three hundred twenty.

Jones   And I talk him three hundred, Mamasan, three hundred!

Mamasan (*softly, whiney, to* **Pavlo**)   G.I. You be nice; you give Mamasan ten Ps more. G.I.? Ten Ps very easy you!

Pavlo (*to* **Jones**)   How much *is* ten Ps, man?

Jones   Eight cents, or about –

Pavlo   Eight cents! Eight cents. Over eight goddamn stupid cents I'm still standin' here!

Jones   Man, no! (*As* **Pavlo** *is giving more money to* **Mamasan**.)

Mamasan (*patting him on the back*)   Okay, okay. You numba one –

Yen (*taking* **Pavlo** *by the hand toward the bed*)   I show you.

Jones (*as he leaves*)   Oh man, deliver me from these green troops; they makin' everybody fat but me.

The whistle blows loudly, and the troops come roaring on and into formation facing the tower.

Sgt Tower   GEN'L'MEN! (*And his voice stops* **Pavlo**, *who comes to attention kneeling on the bed.* **Yen** *has jumped onto the bed. And as* **Sgt Tower** *continues his speech, she unbuttons* **Pavlo**'*s pants, unbuttons his shirt, takes his pants down – all this as* **Sgt Tower** *gives instructions. He is holding up a rifle.*) This an M-16 rifle, this the best you country got. Now we got to make you good enough to have it. You got to have feelin' for it, like it a good woman to you, like it you arm, like it you rib. The command is *right shoulder . . . HARMS!* At the command *HARMS*, raise and carry the rifle diagonally across the body, at the same time grasping it at the balance with the left hand, trigger guard in the hollow of the bone. Then carry the left hand, thumb and fingers extended to the small of the stock, and cut away smartly and everything about you, trainee, is at the position of attention. RIGHT SHOULDER. HARMS!

Men (*performing it*)   One – two – three – four. (**Pavlo** *also yells and performs the drill in pantomime.*)

Sgt Tower   You got to love this rifle, gen'l'men, like it you pecker and you love to make love. You got to care about how it is and what can it do and what can it not do, what do it want and need. ORDER. HARMS!

Men   ONE – TWO – THREE – FOUR.

Sgt Tower   RIGHT SHOULDER. HARMS!

Men   ONE – TWO – THREE – FOUR. (**Pavlo** *with them, yelling also.*)

Corporal   FORWARD MARCH! (**Pavlo** *pulls up his trousers and marches.*)

Sgt Tower   AIN'T NO USE IN GOIN' HOME . . .

Men   AIN'T NO USE IN GOIN' HOME . . .

Pavlo'*s marching is joyous.*

Sgt Tower   JODY GOT YOUR GAL AND GONE . . .

Men   JODY HUMPIN' ON AND ON. (*Something of* **Pavlo**'*s making love to* **Yen** *is in his marching.*)

Sgt Tower   AIN'T NO USE IN GOIN' BACK . . .

Men   JODY GOT OUR CADILLAC.

Corporal   LORD HAVE MERCY, I'M SO BLUE.

Men   IT TWO MORE WEEKS TILL I BE THROUGH.

Corporal   Count cadence, delayed cadence, count cadence – count.

And the **Men**, *performing delayed cadence, exit.* **Pavlo** *counts with them, marching away beside the bed, around the bed, leaping upon the bed as the counting comes to its loud end.* **Brisbey**, *who has been onstage in his bed all this while, calls to* **Pavlo**.

Brisbey   Pavlo!

Pavlo   Just a second, Brisbey!

Brisbey   Pavlo!

Pavlo (*crosses toward* **Brisbey**)   Whatta you want, Brisbey?

Brisbey   Pavlo, can I talk to you a little?

Pavlo   Sure.

Brisbey   You're a medic, right?

Pavlo   Yeh.

Brisbey   But you're not a conscientious objector, are you? So you got a rifle.

Pavlo   Sure.

Pavlo *busies himself with* **Brisbey**'s *pulse and chart, straightening the bed, preparing the shot he must give* **Brisbey**.

Brisbey   I like the feel of 'em. I like to hold 'em.

Pavlo   I'm not gonna get my rifle for you, Brisbey.

Brisbey   Just as a favor.

Pavlo   No.

Brisbey   It's the only pleasure I got anymore.

Pavlo Lemme give you a hypo; you got a visitor; you can see him before you sleep.

Brisbey The egg that slept, that's what I am. You think I look like an egg with a head? (**Pavlo** *is preparing the needle. There is a figure off in the shadows.*) Or else I'm a stump. Some guys, they get hit, they have a stump. I am a stump.

Pavlo What about your visitor; you wanna see him? (*And the figure steps forward.*)

Brisbey Henry?

Sgt Wall It's me, Brisbey, how you doin'? (*He is middle-aged, gray-haired, chunky.*)

Brisbey Henry, Henry, who was the first man round the world, Henry? That's what I want to know. Where's the deepest pit in the ocean? You carryin'? What do you have? .45? You must have a blade. Magellan. Threw out a rope. I ever tell you that story? Gonna go sleepy-bye. Been tryin' to get young Pavlo Hummel to put me away, but he prefers to break needles on me. How's the unit? You tell 'em I'll be back. You tell 'em, soon as I'm well, I'll be back.

Sgt Wall I'm off the line . . . now, Brisbey. No more boonies. I'm in Supply now.

Brisbey Supply? What . . . do you supply? (*Slight pause, as if bewildered. Thinking, yet with bitterness.*) If I promise to tell you the secret of life, Henry, will you slit my throat? You can do it while I'm sleeping.

Pavlo Don't he just go on?

Brisbey Young Hummel here, tell him who you love. Dean Martin. Looks at ole Dino every chance he gets. And 'Combat.' Vic Morrow, man. Keeps thinkin' he's gonna see himself. Dino's cool, huh? Drunk all the time.

Pavlo That's right.

Brisbey You fuckin' asshole. Henry. Listen. You ever think to yourself, 'Oh, if only it wasn't Brisbey. I'd give anything.

My own legs. Or one, anyway. Arms. Balls. Prick.' Ever . . . Henry? (*Silence.*)

Sgt Wall   No.

Brisbey   Good. Don't. Because I have powers I never dreamed of and I'll hear you if you do, Henry, and I'll take them. I'll rip them off you. (*Silence.*)

Sgt Wall   You'll be goin' home soon. I thought we could plan to get together . . .

Brisbey   Right. Start a softball team.

Sgt Wall   Jesus Christ, Brisbey, ain't you ever gonna change? Ain't you ever gonna be serious about no –

Brisbey   I have changed, Motherfucker. You blind or somethin', askin' me if I changed? You get the fuck outa here, hear me? (**Sgt Wall** *is leaving, having left a pint of whiskey.*) You take a tree, you cut off its limbs, whatta you got? You got a stump. A living, feeling, thinking stump.

Pavlo   You're not a tree, Brisbey.

Brisbey   And what terrible cruelty is that? Do you know? There is responsibility. I want you to get me that rifle. To save you from the sin of cruelty, Pavlo. (*As* **Pavlo** *is moving with alcohol, cotton, to prepare the shot.*) You are cruel, Pavlo . . . you and God. The both of you.

Pavlo   Lemme do this, man.

Brisbey (*as* **Pavlo** *gives the shot*)   Do you know . . . if you were to get the rifle, Pavlo, I'd shoot you first. It's how you'll end up anyway. I'd save you time. Get you home quicker. I know you, boy.

Pavlo   Shut up, man. Relax. . . .

Brisbey   You've made me hate you.

Pavlo   I'm sorry. I didn't mean that to happen.

Brisbey   No, no, you're not sorry. You're not. You're glad it's me, you're glad it's not you. God's always glad that way because it's never him, it's always somebody else. Except that once. The only time we was ever gonna get him, he tried to con us into thinkin' we oughta let him go. Make it somebody else again. But we got through all that shit he was talkin' and hung on and got him good – fucked him up good – nailed him up good . . . just once . . . for all the billion times he got us.

Pavlo   Brisbey, sometimes I don't think you know what you're sayin'.

A **Captain** *enters upstage left, carrying clipboard.*

Captain   Grennel.

Grennel (*appearing from the back, far upstage*)   Yes, sir.

Captain   Go get me Hummel. He's down with Brisbey.

Brisbey   I keep thinkin', Pavlo, 'bout this kid got his hand blown off, and he kept crawlin' round lookin' for his fingers. Couldn't go home without 'em, he said, he'd catch hell. No fingers. (**Pavlo** *shakes his head.*) I keep thinkin' about ole Magellan, sailin' round the world. Ever hear of him, Pavlo? So one day he wants to know how far under him to the bottom of the ocean. So he drops over all the rope he's got. Two hundred feet. It hangs down into a sea that must go down and down beyond its end for miles and tons of water. He's up there in the sun. He's got this little piece of rope dangling from his fingers. He thinks because all the rope he's got can't touch bottom, he's over the deepest part of the ocean. He doesn't know the real question. How far beyond all the rope you got is the bottom?

Pavlo   Brisbey, I'm gonna tell you somethin'. I tried to kill myself once. Honest to God. And it's no good. You understand me. I don't know what I was thinkin' about. I mean, you understand it was a long time ago and I'd never been laid yet or done hardly anything, but I have since and it's fantastic. I just about blew this girl's head off, it was fantastic, but if I'd killed myself, it'd never a happened. You see what I'm saying, Brisbey? Somethin' fantastic might be comin' to you.

Grennel (*entering*)   Hummel. Man, the captain wants to see you.

Pavlo   Captain Miller? Captain Miller! (*Leaving.*)

Brisbey   Pavlo!

Grennel   How you doin', Brisbey? (*As he wheels* **Brisbey** *off.*)

Pavlo (*rushing up to the* **Captain**, *standing with his clipboard*)   Sir Pfc Hummel reporting as ordered.

Captain   Good afternoon, Hummel.

Pavlo   Good afternoon, sir.

Captain   Are you smiling, Hummel?

Pavlo   Excuse me, sir.

Captain   Your ten-forty-nine says you're not happy at all; it says you want a transfer out of this unit because you're ashamed to serve with us. I was wondering how could you be ashamed and smiling simultaneously, Hummel.

Pavlo   I don't know, sir.

Captain   That's not a very good answer.

Pavlo   No, sir.

Captain   Don't you think what you're doing here is important? You helped out with poor Brisbey, didn't you?

Pavlo   Yes, sir.

Captain   That's my point, Hummel, there are people alive who would be dead if you hadn't done your job. Those invalids you care for, you feed them when they can't, you help them urinate, defecate, simple personal things they can't do for themselves but would die without. Have you asked any one of them if they think what you are doing is important or not, or if you should be ashamed?

Pavlo   Yes, sir . . . more or less. But I . . . just . . . think I'd be better off in squad duty.

Distant firing and yelling are heard to which neither the **Captain** *nor* **Pavlo** *respond. There is a quality of echo to the sounds and then there is a clattering and* **Parham**, *a young black Pfc, appears at the opposite*

side of the stage in full combat gear except for his helmet which is missing.
He has come a few steps onto the stage and he crouches.

Parham   Damn, baby, why that ole sarge gotta pick on me?

Pavlo   I'm Regular Army, sir; I'm going to extend my tour.

Captain   You like it here, Hummel?

Parham   Damn that ole sarge. I run across that field I get
shot sure as hell. (*He breathes.*) Lemme count to five. Lemme do
it on five.

Captain   How many days left in your tour, Hummel?

Parham   Lemme do it like track and field.

Pavlo   I enlisted because I wanted to be a soldier, sir, and
I'm not a soldier here. Four nights ago on perimeter guard, I
tried to set up fields of fire with the other men in the bunker –
do you know what I mean, sir? Designating who would be
responsible for what sector of terrain in case of an attack? And
they laughed at me; they just sat on the bunker and talked all
night and they didn't stay low and they didn't hide their
cigarettes when they smoked or anything.

Parham   FIVE! (*And he runs, taking no more than two steps before
a loud explosion hits and he goes down and hits, bounces and rolls onto
his back, slamming his fist into the ground in outrage.*) DAMNIT! I
KNEW IT! I KNEW IT! I KNEW IT!

Captain   You want the V.C. to come here?

Pavlo   I want to feel, sir, that I'm with a unit Victor Charlie
considers valuable enough to want to get it. And I hope I
don't have to kill anyone; and I hope I don't get killed.

Parham (*still trying but unable to rise*)   Medic? Medic? Man,
where you at? C'mon out here to me! Crawl on out here to
me.

Pavlo   But maybe you can't understand what I'm saying, sir,
because you're an R.O.T.C. officer and not O.C.S., sir.

Captain   You mean I'm not Regular Army, Hummel.

Pavlo   An R.O.T.C. officer and an O.C.S. officer are not the same thing.

Captain   Is that so, Hummel?

Pavlo   I think so, sir.

Captain   You want to get killed, don't you, Hummel?

Pavlo   No, sir. No.

Captain   And they will kill you, Hummel, if they get the chance. Do you believe that? That you will die if shot, or hit with shrapnel, that your arm can disappear into shreds, or your leg vanish, do you believe that, Hummel – that you can and will, if hit hard enough, gag and vomit and die . . . be buried and rot, do you believe yourself capable of that?

Pavlo   Yes . . . sir. I . . . do . . .

Parham   Nooooooo! (*Quick pause. He looks about.*) Ohhh, shit, somebody don't help me, Charlie gonna come in here, cut me up, man. He gonna do me.

Captain   All right, Hummel.

Parham   Oh, Lord, you get me outa here, I be good, man; I be good, no shit, Lord, I'm tellin' it.

Captain   All right . . . you're transferred. I'll fix it. (**Pavlo** *salutes.* **Captain** *salutes, pivots, exits.*)

Pavlo *moves to change into combat gear in darkening light. He finds the gear in a footlocker in the bar area. He exits.*

Parham   What's happenin'? I don't know what's happenin'! (*And the light goes and he is alone in the jungle, in the center of flickering silver; it is night, there are sounds.*) Hummel, c'mon. It's me, man, Parham; and I ain't jivin', mister. I been shot. I been truly shot. (*And he pauses, breathing, and raises his head to look down at himself.*) Ohhhh, look at me; ohhh, look at my poor stomach. Ohhhh, look at me, look at me. Oh, baby, stop it, stop bleedin', stop it, stop it; you my stomach, I'm talkin' to you, I'm tellin' you what to do, YOU STOP IT! (*His hands are pressing furiously down on his stomach. And he lies in silence for a*

moment: before shuddering and beginning again.) SOMEBODY GET
ME A DUSTOFF! Dustoff control, do you hear me? This
here Pfc Jay Charles Johnson Parham. I am coordinates X-
Ray Tango Foxtrot . . . Lima. . . . Do you hear me? I hurtin',
baby . . . hear me. Don't know what to do for myself . . . can't
remember . . . don't know what it is gone wrong . . .
requesting one med-evac chopper. . . . I am one litter patient,
gunshot wounds, stomach. Area secure, c'mon hear me . . .
this ole nigger . . . he gonna die.

First V.C.   Hello, G.I.

Parham   Oh, no. Oh, no. No.

First V.C. (*very sing-song*)   Okay. Okay.

Second V.C.   You numba one.

Parham   Get away from me! I talkin' to you, Charlie, you
get away from me! You guys get away from me! MEDIC!
ME –

*They say 'Okay, Okay' 'You numba one.' And at a nod from the **V.C.**
with the weapon, his partner has jumped forward into a sitting position at
the head of **Parham**, one leg pinning down each shoulder, the hands
grasping under the chin, cocking the head back, stuffing a rag into the
mouth. There are only the sounds of the struggle as the other **V.C.**
approaches and crouches over **Parham** and holds a knife over him.
Parham stares at it, his feet are moving slowly back and forth.*

First V.C.   Numba one, you can see, G.I.? Airplane me . . .
Vietnam. Have many bomb. Can do boom-boom, you stand!
(*He moves the knife up and down.*) Same-same you, many friends
me, fini. Where airplane now, G.I.? Where very gun? (*And he
places the blade against the **Parham**'s chest and **Parham**, behind his
gag, begins to howl and begins to flail his pinioned arms and beat his heels
furiously upon the ground.*) Okay, Okay . . . ! Ông di dâu??! (*Then
the knife goes in and they rise up to stand over him as he turns onto his
side and pulls himself into a knot as if to protect himself, knees tight to his
chest, arms over his head. They unbuckle his pistol belt and take his flack
vest and his billfold from his pocket and are working at removing his shirt
when they both straighten at a sound. They seize his fallen rifle and run to*

disappear. **Pavlo** *appears, moving low, accompanied by* **Ryan**.)

Ryan   Man, I'm tellin' you let's get outa here.

Pavlo (*pointing*)   No, no. There. (*He has a circular belt hooked over his shoulder. As he moves toward the body.*) Just look. (**Ryan** *is following.*) Hey, man . . . hey . . . (*He rolls* **Parham** *over.*) Ohhhhh . . . look at him.

Ryan   It's Parham.

Pavlo   Man, he's all cut. . . .

Ryan   Pavlo, let's get out outa here . . . ! (*And he starts to move off.*) What the hell's it matter?

Pavlo   I'll carry him.

Ryan (*as* **Pavlo** *hands him his rifle*)   I ain't worried about who has to carry him, for Chrissake, I wanna get outa here. (*On the move.*) I'm gonna hustle over there to the side there.

Pavlo   Nooooooo . . .

Ryan   Give you some cover. (*And* **Ryan** *is gone, leaving* **Pavlo** *with the body.*)

The carrier's procedure, which **Pavlo** *undertakes through the following speeches, is as follows: The belt is placed under the buttocks of the man, one length above and along his back, the other below and across his legs so that two loops are formed – one on either side of the man. The carrier then lies down with his back to the dead man and he fits his arms through the two loops. He then grasps the man's left arm with his own right hand and rolls to his right so that the man rolls with him and is on his back. He then rises to one knee, keeping the body pressed tightly to his own. As* **Pavlo** *begins his task,* **Ardell** *is there, appearing as* **Ryan** *departs.*

Ardell   How many that make?

Pavlo   What's that?

Ardell   Whatta you think, man? Dead bodies!

Pavlo   Who the hell's countin'?

Ardell   Looookeeeee. Gettin' ta *beeeee bad!*

Pavlo This one's nothin'. When they been out here a couple a days, man, that's when it's interesting – you go to pick 'em up they fall apart in your hands, man. They're mud – pink mud – like turnin' over a log; all maggots and ants. You see Ryan over there hidin', in the bushes. I ain't hidin' in no bushes. And Parham's glad about that. They're all glad. Nobody wants to think he's gonna be let lay out here.

Ardell Ain't you somethin'.

Pavlo I'm diggin' it, man. Blowin' people away. Cuttin' 'em down. Got two this afternoon I saw and one I didn't even see – just heard him out there jabberin' away – (*And he makes a sound mimicking a Vietnamese speaking.*) And I walked a good goddamn twenty rounds right over where it sounded like he was: he shut up his fuckin' face. It ain't no big thing.

Ardell Like bringin' down a deer . . . or dog.

Pavlo Man, people's all I ever killed. Ohhh, I feel you thinkin', 'This poor boy don't know what he's doin'; don't know what he got into.' But I do. I got a dead boy in my hands. In a jungle . . . the middle a the night. I got people maybe ten feet away, hidin' – they're gonna maybe cut me down the minute I move. And I'm gonna . . . (*During all this he has struggled to load the body like a pack on his back. Now he is rising, is on his knees.*) . . . take this dead thing back and people are gonna look at me when I do it. They're gonna think I'm crazy and be glad I'm with 'em. I'm diggin' – (*And the* **Vietcong** *comes streaking out from his hiding place.*) Ryan, Ryan, Ryan! (*And the* **Vietcong**, *without stopping, plunges the knife into* **Pavlo**'s *side and flees off.* **Pavlo** *falls, unable, because of the body on his back, to protect himself.*) What happened?

Ardell The blood goin' out a hole in your guts, man, turn you into water.

Pavlo He hit me . . .

Ardell TURN YOU INTO WATER! Blood goin' in the brain make you think – in your heart make you move, in your prick makes you hard, makes you come. YOU LETTIN' IT

DROP ALL OVER THE GROUND!

Pavlo   I won't . . . I'll . . . noooooo . . . (*Trying to free himself of the body.*) Ryan . . .

Ardell   The knowledge comin', baby. I'm talkin' about what your kidney know, not your fuckin' fool's head. I'm talkin' about your skin and what it sayin', thin as paper. We melt; we tear and rip apart. Membrane, baby. Cellophane. Ain't that some shit!

Pavlo   I'll lift my arm. (*And he can't.*)

Ardell   AIN'T THAT SOME SHIT.

Pavlo   Noooooo . . .

Ardell   A bullet like this finger bigger than all your fuckin' life. Ain't this finger some shit!

Pavlo   RYAN.

Ardell   I'm tellin' you.

Pavlo   Nooooo.

Ardell   RYAN!

Pavlo   RYAN! (*As **Ryan** comes running on with a second **Soldier**.*)

Ardell   Get on in here. (*They struggle to free **Pavlo** from the body. He flails, yelling in his panic as **Sgt Tower** comes striding on and mounts the stairs to his tower. **Pavlo**, being dragged off by the soldiers, yells and yells.*)

Pavlo   Ryan, we tear. We rip apart. Ryan, we tear. (*He is gone.*)

Sgt Tower   You gonna see some funny shit, gen'l'men. You gonna see livin', breathin' people disappear. Walkin', talkin' buddies. And you gonna wanna kill and say their name. When you been in so many fights and you come out, you a survivor. It what you are and do. You survive.

*A **Body Detail** removes **Parham**'s body from the stage.*

Ardell   Thin and frail.

Sgt Tower   Gen'l'men, can you hear me?

Ardell   Yes, Sergeant.

Sgt Tower   I saw this rifle one time get blown right outa this boy's hands and him start wailin' and carryin' on right there how he ain't ever goin' back on no line, he'll die for sure, he don't have that one rifle in all the world. You listenin' to me, gen'l'men. I'm gonna tell you now what you do when you lost and it black, black night. The North Star show you true north accurate all year round. You gonna see the Big Dipper and two stars on the end called the pointer and they where the water would be on outa that dipper if it had water in it, and straight out from there is this big damn star, and that the North Star, and once you know north you ain't lost no more! (*And toward the end of this* **Pavlo** *has appeared, rising up from the back of the set, walking slowly as in a dream, looking at* **Sgt Tower**.)

Pavlo   YES, SERGEANT! (*And an explosion hits;* **Pavlo**, *yelling, goes down again.*)

Ardell   What you sayin'? YES, SERGEANT. What you sayin'?

Pavlo   YES, SERGEANT! (*Struggling to rise.*)

Ardell   Ask him what about that grenade come flyin'? How come, if you so cool, if you such a fox, you don't know nothin' to do with no grenade but stand there holdin' it – get your abdominal and groin area blown to shit.

Pavlo   I DON'T KNOW WGAT YOU'RE TALKING ABOUT!

Ardell   You walkin' talkin' scar, what you think you made of?

Pavlo   I got my shit together.

Ardell   HOW MANY TIMES YOU GONNA LET 'EM HIT YOU?

Pavlo   AS MANY TIMES AS THEY WANT.

Ardell   That man up there a fool, Jim.

Pavlo   Shut up.

Ardell   You ever seen any North Star in your life?

Pavlo   I seen a lot of people pointin'. (**Pavlo** *is on the move toward* **Yen** *who is kneeling in the distance*.)

Ardell   They a bunch a fools pointin' at the air. 'Go this way, go that way.'

Pavlo   I want her, man. I need her. (*He touches her*.)

Ardell   Where you now? What you doin'?

Pavlo   I'm with her, man.

Ardell   You . . . in . . . her . . .

Pavlo   . . . soon . . . (*Taking her blouse off her*.)

Ardell   Why you there . . .

Pavlo   I dunno . . . jus' wanna . . .

Ardell   You jus' gonna ride . . .

Pavlo   I jus' wanna . . .

Ardell   There was one boy walkin' . . .

Pavlo   I know, don't talk no shit. (*Seizing her, embracing her*.)

Ardell   Walkin' . . . singin' . . . soft, some song to himself, thinkin' on mosquitoes and Coke and bug spray until these bushes in front of him burst and his fine young legs broke in half like sticks . . .

Pavlo   Leave me alone! (*Rising, trying to get off his own trousers*.)

Ardell   At seven his tonsils been cut out; at twelve there's appendicitis. Now he's twenty and hurtin' and screamin' at his legs, and then the gun come back. It on a fixed traversing arc to tear his yellin' fuckin' head right off.

Pavlo   Good; it's Tanner; it's Weber. It's Smith and not Pavlo. Minneti, not Pavlo. Klaus and you. You motherfucker. But not Pavlo. Not ever.

Ardell   You get a knife wound in the ribs.

Pavlo   It misses my heart. I'm clean.

Ardell   You get shrapnel all up and down your back.

Pavlo   It's like a dozen fifteen bee stings, all up and down my back.

Ardell   And there's people tellin' you you can go home if you wanna. It's your second wound. They're sayin' you can go home when you been hit twice and you don't even check. You wanna go back out, you're thinkin', get you one more gook, get you one more slopehead, make him know the reason why.

Pavlo (*whirling, scooping up a rifle*)   That's right. They're killin' everybody. They're fuckin' killin' everybody! (*The rifle is aimed at* **Ardell**.)

Ardell   Like it's gonna make a difference in the world, man, what you do; and somethin' made bad's gonna be all right with this one more you're gonna kill. Poor ole Ryan gets dinged round about Tay Ninh, so two weeks later in Phu Loi you blow away this goddamn farmer . . .

A **Farmer**, *wearing Vietnamese work clothes and a comical hat, appears in the distance, waving.*

Farmer   Okay, G.I., Okay.

Ardell   And think you're addin' somethin' up.

Pavlo   I blew him to fuckin' smithereens. He's there at twenty yards, wavin'.

Farmer   Okay, G.I., Okay. (*He sways in the distance.*)

Pavlo (*yelling at the* **Farmer**)   DUNG LYE. DUNG LYE. (*This is 'Stop' in Vietnamese.*)

Ardell   You don't know he's got satchel charges.

Pavlo   I do.

Ardell   You don't know what he's got under his clothes.

Pavlo   I do. He's got dynamite all under his clothes. And I shoot him. (*Gunshot, as* **Pavlo** *fires.*) I fuckin' shoot him. He's under me. I'm screamin' down at him. RYAN. RYAN. And he's lookin' up at me. His eyes squinted like he knows by my face what I'm sayin' matters to me so maybe it matters to him. And then, all of a sudden, see, he starts to holler and shout like he's crazy, and he's pointin' at his foot, so I shoot it. (*He fires again.*) I shoot his foot and then he's screamin' and tossin' all over the ground, so I shoot into his head. (*Fires.*) I shot his head. And I get hit again. I'm standin' there over him and I get fuckin' hit again. They keep fuckin' hittin' me. (*Explosion and* **Pavlo** *goes flying forward.*) I don't know where I'm at. In my head . . . it's like I'm twelve . . . a kid again. Ardell, it's going to happen to meeeeeee? (*He is crawling.*)

Ardell   What do you want me to do?

Pavlo   I don't want to get hit anymore.

Ardell   What do you want me to do?

Pavlo   Tell me.

Ardell   He was shot . . . layin' down under you, what did you see?

Pavlo   What?

Ardell   He was squirmin' down under you in that ditch, what did you see?

Pavlo   I saw the grass . . . his head . . .

Ardell   Nooooooooooo.

Pavlo   Help me. I saw the grass, his head.

Ardell   Don't you ever hear?

Pavlo   I want out, Ardell, I want out.

Ardell   When you gonna hear me?

Pavlo   What are you tryin' to tell me? I saw blood . . . bits of brain . . .

Ardell   Nooooooooooo!

Pavlo   The grass, the grass. . . .

Ardell   When you shot into his head, it was like you hit into your own head, fool!

Pavlo   What? NOOOOOOOO.

Ardell   IT WAS YOUR OWN.

Pavlo   NOOOOOOOOO! (*As* **Ardell** *has turned to leave.*) Don't leave me, you sonofabitch. (*And* **Ardell** *has stopped, back turned, far upstage,*) JIVE MOTHERFUCKIN' BULLSHIT! (*And* **Ardell** *is gone.*) And I stood . . . lookin'. . . . down . . . at that black, black Hudson River . . . There was stars in it . . . I was twelve . . . I remember . . . (*He is turning toward* **Yen** *who is kneeling, singing.*) I went out toward them . . . diving . . . down . . . (*He is moving toward* **Yen**, *crawling.*) They'd said there was no current, but I was twisted in all that water, fighting to get up . . . all my air burning out, couldn't get no more. . . . (*Still moving toward* **Yen**.) and I was going down, fighting to get down. I was all confused, you see, fighting to get down, thinking it was up. I hit sand. I pounded. I pounded the bottom. I thought the bottom was the top. Black. No air. (*As the* **Officer** *enters, striding swiftly.*)

Officer   Yes! (*Carries a clipboard on which he writes as* **Pavlo** *runs up to him.* **Yen**, *though she remains kneeling, stops singing.*)

Pavlo   Sir! I've just been released from Ward 17, gunshot wound in my side, and I've been ordered back to my unit, Second of the 16th, 1st Division, and I don't think I should have to go. This is the third time I been hit. I been hit in the ribs and leg and back. I think there should be more trainin' in duckin' and dodgin', sir. I been hit by a knife, shrapnel, and bullets.

Officer   Could you get to the point?

Pavlo   That is the point. I want to know about this regulation sayin' you can go home after your second wounding?

Officer   Pardon, Hummel?

Pavlo   I been told there's this regulation you can go home after your second wound. When you been hit twice, you can go home.

Officer   Hummel, wouldn't you be home if you were eligible to be home?

Pavlo   I don't know, sir; but I wanted to stay the first two times, so I don't know and I was told I had the option the second time to go home or not, but I never checked and if I passed it by, sir, I'd like to go back and pick it up.

Officer   You didn't pass it by; there's no such regulation.

Pavlo   It was a sergeant who told me.

Officer   These orders are valid.

Pavlo   Could you check, sir?

Officer   I'm an expert on regulations, Hummel. These orders are valid. You've earned the Purple Heart. Now, go on back and do your job. (*Raising his hand to salute, pivots, exits as* **Pavlo** *is about to salute.*)

Ardell   NO! NO!

Pavlo   I do my job.

Sgt Wall *enters the bar, calling to* **Yen**. *He wears civilian clothes — slacks and a flowered, short-sleeved shirt.* **Yen** *moves quickly to the bar area where she pets him and then moves to prepare a drink for him.*

Sgt Wall   Come here, Pretty Piggy, we talk boocoup love; okay? Make plans go my home America.

Yen   Sao. (*Vietnamese for 'Liar'*)

Sgt Wall   No lie.

Sgt Tower (*in a kind of brooding, mournful rage atop his tower as* **Pavlo** *stands before him*)   Gen'l'men, lemme tell you what you do, the enemy got you, he all around you. You the prisoner. You listenin', gen'l'men?

Ardell   Yes, Sergeant. (*All despairing sarcasm.*)

Sgt Wall   You got to watch out for the enemy. He gonna try to make you feel alone and you got no friends but him. He gonna make you mean and afraid; then he gonna be nice. We had a case with them North Koreans, this group a American P.O.W.s, one of 'em was wounded so he cried all night. His buddies couldn't sleep. So, one night his buddies picked him up, I'm tellin' you, they carried him out the door into that North Korean winter, they set him down in the snow, they lef' him there, went on back inside. They couldn't hear him screamin' the wind was so loud. They got their sleep. You got to watch out for the enemy.

Pavlo *pivots, turning away from* **Sgt Tower** *and into the bar, where* **Mamasan** *greets him.* **Yen** *is with* **Sgt Wall** *who is taking a big drink.*

Mamasan   Paaablooooo . . . how you-you. I give you beer, okay?

Pavlo (*unmoving, rigid*)   Mamasan, chow ba.

Sgt Wall (*having finished his drink, takes up as if in mid-sentence*) '. . . so who,' he says, 'was the first motherfucker to sail round the world? Not Vasco Da Gama.' I don't know what he's sayin'. 'Who was the first motherfucker to measure the ocean?' (*He is loud and waving his arms.*) I don't know! He wasn't even asking. MAMASAN! MAMASAN! ONE BEER! ONE BEER, ONE SAIGON TEA! (*He reaches now to take* **Yen***'s hand and tug her gently around to his side of the table, drawing her near to sit on his lap.*) Come here; sit down. No sao. Fini sao. Boocoup love, Co Yen. Boocoup love. (*His hand on her breast, as she nibbles his ear.*)

Yen   I think you maybe papasan America. Have many babysan.

Sgt Wall   No . . . no.

Yen   I think you sao.

Sgt Wall   No lie, Yen. No wife America, no have babysan. Take you, okay?

Pavlo   Sarge! (**Sgt Wall** *looks up to* **Pavlo**.) Listen; I don't have too much time, I got to go pretty soon; how long you gonna be talkin' shit to that poor girl? I mean, see, she's the whore I usually hit on, I'm a little anxious, I'd like to interrupt you, you gonna be at her all fuckin' night. I'll bring her back in half an hour.

Sgt Wall   Sorry about that. Sorry –

Pavlo   I didn't ask you was you sorry.

Sgt Wall   This little girl's my girl.

Pavlo   She's a whore, man –

Sgt Wall   We got a deal, see, see; and when I'm here, she stays with me.

Pavlo   You got a deal, huh?

Sgt Wall   You guessed it, Pfc.

Pavlo   Well, maybe you shoulda checked with me, you shoulda conferred with me maybe before you figured that deal was sound.

Sgt Wall   You have been informed.

Pavlo   But you don't understand, Sarge. She's the only whore here who move me.

Sgt Wall   My baby.

Pavlo   You rear-echelon asshole!

Sgt Wall (*beginning to rise*)   What's that?

Pavlo   Where you think you are, the goddamn P.X.? This the garbage dump, man, and you don't tell me nothin' down here let alone who I can hit on, who I can't hit on, you see what I'm sayin' to you, Fuckface.

Yen   Paablo . . . no, no. . . .

Pavlo   You like this ole man?

Yen   Can be nice, Paablo . . . (*Moving to face* **Pavlo** *and explain.*)

Pavlo   Old man. Papasan. Can do fuck-fuck maybe one time one week. Talk, talk. Talk. No can do boom-boom. PAPASAN. NUMBA FUCKIN' TEN!

Yen (*angry at his stupidity*)   Shut up. Paablo, I do him. Fini him. Do you. Okay.

Pavlo   Shut up?

Sgt Wall   You heard her.

Pavlo   Shut up? (*His hand twisting in her hair.*) I don't know who you think this bitch is, Sarge, but I'm gonna fuck her whoever you think she is. I'm gonna take her in behind those curtains and I'm gonna fuck her right side up and then maybe I'm gonna turn her over, get her in her asshole, you understand me? You don't like it you best come in pull me off.

Sgt Wall (*switchblade, popping open in his hand*)   I ain't gonna have to, punk.

Pavlo *kicks him squarely in the groin.* **Wall** *yells, falls.*

Pavlo   The fuck you ain't. Hey . . . were you ready for that? Were you ready for that, ole man? Called crawlin', you gettin (*Dragging along the ground, shoving him.*) the hang of it, you ole man. Get up, get up. (*And* **Wall** *moans as* **Pavlo** *lifts him.*) I want you gone, you mother, you understand. I don't wanna see you no more. You gonna disappear. You are gonna vanish. (*And he flings* **Wall** *away. He staggers, falls, and* **Pavlo** *picks the knife off the floor, goes for a beer, as* **Sgt Tower** *begins to speak.*)

Sgt Tower   This is a grenade, gen'l'men. M-26-A-2 fragmentation, 5.5 ounces, composition B, time fuse, thirteen feet a coiled wire inside it like the inside a my fist a animal and I open it that animal leap out to kill you. Do you know a hunk a paper flyin' fast enough cut you in half like a knife, and when this baby hit, fifteen meters in all directions, ONE THOUSAND HUNKS A WIRE GOIN' FAST ENOUGH! (*And* **Ardell** *enters, joining* **Pavlo**, *who celebrates.*)

Pavlo   Did I do it to him, Ardell? The triple Hummel? Got to be big and bad. A little shuffle. Did I ever tell you? Thirteen months a my life ago.

Yen   Paaaabloooo, boocoup love!

Pavlo   Thirteen months a my life ago. (*And* **Sgt Wall**, *pulling pin on a grenade, is there in the corner, beginning to move.*) What she did my ole lady, she called Joanna a slut and I threw kitty litter, screamin'– cat shit – 'happy birthday!' She called that sweet church-goin' girl a whore. To be seen by her now, up tight with this odd-lookin' whore, feelin' good and tall, ready to bed down. Feelin' – (*And the grenade lands, having been thrown by* **Sgt Wall**, *moving in a semicircle and fleeing.* **Pavlo** *drops to his knees, seizing the grenade, looking up in awe at* **Ardell**. *The grenade is in* **Pavlo**'s *hands in his lap.*) Oh Christ!

And the explosion comes, loud; it is a storm going into darkness and changing lights. Silence. **Body Detail** *enters as* **Ardell**, *looking at* **Pavlo** *lying there, begins to speak. The* **Body Detail** *will wrap* **Pavlo** *in a poncho, put him on a stretcher, carry him to* **Ardell**.

Ardell   He don't die right off. Take him four days, thirty-eight minutes. And he don't say nothin' to nobody in all that time. No words; he just kinda lay up and look and when he die, he bitin' on his lower lip, I don't know why. So they take him, they put him in a blue rubber bag, zip it up tight, and haul him off to the morgue in the back of a quarter ton, where he get stuck naked into the refrigerator 'long with the other boys killed that day and the beer and cheese and tuna and stuff the guys who work at the morgue keep in the refrigerator except when it inspection time. The bag get washed, hung out to dry on a line out back a the morgue. (*Slight pause.*) Then . . . lemme see, well, finally, he got shipped home and his mother cry a lot and his brother get so depressed he gotta go out and lay his chippie he so damn depressed about it all. And Joanna, she read his name in the paper, she let out this little gasp and say to her husband across the table, 'Jesus, Jimmy, I used to go with that boy. Oh, damn that war, why can't we have peace? I think I'll call his mother.' Ain't it some kinda world? (*And he is laughing.*) Sooooooooo . . . that about it. That about all I got to say. Am I right, Pavlo? Did I tell you true? You got anything to say? Oh, man, I know you do, you say it out. (*Slight pause as* **Ardell** *moves to uncover* **Pavlo**.) Man, you don't say it out, I don't wanna know you. Be cool as you wanna be, Pavlo! Beee cool; lemme hear you . . . You tell it to me: what you think of the cause? What you think a gettin' your ass blown clean off a freedom's frontier? What you think a bein' R.A. Regular Army lifer?

Pavlo (*softly, with nearly embarrassed laughter*)   Sheeeeee . . . itttttt . . . Oh, Lord . . . oh . . .

Ardell   Ain't it what happened to you? Lemme hear it.

Pavlo   . . . Shit!

Ardell   And what you think a all the 'folks back home,' sayin' you a victim . . . you a animal . . . you a fool . . .

Pavlo   They shit!

Ardell   Yeh, baby; now I know you. It all shit.

Pavlo   It all shit!

Ardell   You my man again.

Pavlo   It shit.

Ardell   Lemme hear it! My *main* man.

Pavlo   SHIT!

Ardell   Main motherfuckin' man.

Pavlo   OH, SHIT!

Ardell   GO!

Pavlo   SHIT!

Ardell   GET IT! GET IT!

Pavlo (*a howl into silence*)   SHHHHHHHHHHHHHHHIIIIIII-IIITTTTTTTTTTTTTTttttttttttt!

And **Four Men** *enter carrying the aluminum box of a coffin, while two other men go across the back of the stage doing the drill, the marching and twirling rifles that were done at the end of the first act. They go now, however, in the opposite direction, and the coffin is placed beside* **Pavlo**.

Ardell That right. How you feel? You feel all right? You gotta get that stuff outa you, man. You body know that and you body smart; you don't get that outa you, it back up on you, man, poison you.

The **Four Men** *are placing* **Pavlo** *in the coffin.*

Pavlo But . . . I . . . I'm dead!

The **Men** *turn and leave.*

Ardell Real soon; got wings as big as streets; got large, large wings. (*Slight pause.*) You want me to talk shit to you? Man, sure, we siftin' things over. We in a bar, man, back home, we got good soft chairs, beer in our hands, go-go girls all around; one of 'em got her eye on you, 'nother one thinkin' little bit on me. You believe what I'm sayin'. You *home*, Pavlo. (*Pause.*) Now . . . you c'mon and you be with me . . . We gonna do a little singin'. You be with me. Saw some stockin's . . . on the street . . .

Pavlo (*faltering*) Saw some . . . stockin's . . . on . . . the street . . .

Ardell (*slight pause*) . . . wished I was . . . between those . . . feet . . .

Pavlo Wished I was between those feet! (*Slight pause.*)

Ardell *and* **Pavlo** Once a week, I get to town. They see me comin', they jus' lay down . . .

Ardell Sergeant, Sergeant, can't you see . . .

Pavlo Sergeant, Sergeant, can't you see . . .

Ardell All this misery's killin' . . . me . . .

Pavlo All this misery's killin' –

Ardell *lets the coffin slam shut, cutting* **Pavlo** *off.*

Ardell Ain't no matter what you do . . . Jody done it . . . all to you . . .

Slight pause. **Ardell** *is backing away.*

Lift your heads and lift 'em high . . . Pavlo Hummel . . .
passin' by . . .

Ardell *disappears upstage. The coffin stands in real light.*

Sticks and Bones

Sticks and Bones was first performed at the New York Shakespeare Festival Public Theater on 7 November 1971. The cast was as follows:

Ozzie	Tom Aldredge
Harriet	Elizabeth Wilson
David	David Selby
Rick	Cliff DeYoung
Sgt Major	Hector Elias
Father Donald	Charles Siebert
Zung ('The Girl')	Asa Gim

Directed by Jeff Bleckner
Setting by Santo Loquasto
Costumes by Theoni V. Aldredge
Lighting by Ian Calderon
Produced by Joseph Papp

Time
Autumn 1968

Place
The family home

The family home.

Darkness: Silence. Slides appear on either side of stage: black-and-white medium close-up of a young man, mood and clothing of the eighteenth century. He is lean, reasonably handsome, black hair parted in the center. Voices speak offstage. They are slow and relaxed with an improvisational quality.

Child 1 Who's zat?

Male Adult Grandpa Jacob's Father. (*Slide 2: Group photo, same era, eight or ten people, all ages.*)

Child 2 Look at 'em all!

Child 1 How come they're all so serious? (*Slide 3: Small boy, black hair, black knickers.*)

Female Adult There's Grandpa Ozwald as a little boy.

Child 1 Grandpa? (*Slide 4: Different boy, same pose.*)

Female Adult And that's his brother Thomas. He died real young.

Male Adult Scarlet fever. (*As there is a new slide: Young girl, seventeen or eighteen.*) And that's his sister Christina.

Female Adult No, that's Grandma.

Male Adult No.

Female Adult Sure. (*As there is a new slide:* **Ozzie** *and* **Harriet**, *young, 1940s era.*) There's the two of them.

Male Adult Mmmmm, you're right, because that's Grandpa. (*As there is a new slide, two young boys, five and nine years old.*)

Female Adult The taller one's David, right? (*New slide: Photo, close-up of* **David** *from the last moment of the play, a stricken look.*)

Child 1 What's that one?

Male Adult Somebody sick.

Child 1   Boy . . . ! (*New slide:* **Ozzie**, **Harriet** *and* **Father Donald**. **Father Donald**, *wearing a gym suit, his back to the camera, stands holding a basketball in one hand.* **Ozzie** *and* **Harriet** *face him, one on either side.*)

Child 2   Oh, look at that one!

Male Adult   That's a funny one, isn't it.

Female Adult   That's one – I bet somebody took it – they didn't know it was going to be taken.

There is a bright flash and the stage is immediately illuminated. The set is an American home, very modern, a quality of brightness, green walls, green rug. A large number of plants stand about on shelves, in the windows. Perhaps the number of plants increases as the play progresses. There is a sense of space and, oddly, a sense also that this room, these stairs belong in the gloss of an advertisement. Downstage, on wheels, a TV faces upstage, glowing, murmuring. **Ozzie**, **Harriet**, **Father Donald** *are standing as they were in the slide last seen.*

Father Donald   A feel for it is the big thing. A feel for the ball. You know, I mean, bouncing it, dribbling it. You don't even look at it. (*Phone rings.*)

Ozzie   I'll get it.

Father Donald   You can do it, Harriet. Give it a try. (*Bouncing the ball to* **Harriet**.)

Ozzie   – Hello? –

Father Donald (*as she catches it*)   – That a girl –

Harriet   – Oh, Father –

Ozzie (*hanging up*)   Nobody there.

Father Donald   That's what I'm telling you. You gotta help kids. Keeps 'em outa trouble. We help organize sports activities; it does 'em a world a good. You know that. And they need you.

Ozzie   Well, I was a decent basketball player – I could get around but my strong suit was track and field. I was quite a miler. Dash man too. I told you, Father. (*Telephone rings.*) I could throw the discus. (*As he runs for the phone.*)

Father Donald   But this is basketball season. (*Moving for* **Harriet** *and then the door as* **Ozzie** *goes to the phone, says 'Hello' then listens intently.*) You listen to me, Harriet, you get that husband of yours out there to help us. It'll do him good and he's the kind of man we need. Leaders. We need leaders.

Harriet   Oh, Father Donald, bless me.

Father Donald   Of course. (*He blesses her, holding the ball under his left arm.*) Bye, bye.

Harriet (*as* **Father Donald** *goes*)   Goodbye, Father. (*And she turns to look for a moment at* **Ozzie** *on the phone.*) Why aren't you talking? (*Silence: she is looking at him.*) Ozzie, why aren't you talking?

Ozzie (*slowly lowering the phone*)   They're gone. They hung up.

Harriet   You didn't say a word. You said nothing.

Ozzie   I said my name.

Harriet   What did they want?

Ozzie   I said hello.

Harriet   Were they selling something – is that what they wanted?

Ozzie   No, no.

Harriet   Well . . . who was it?

Ozzie   What?

Harriet   What are we talking about?

Ozzie   The Government. It was . . . you know . . .

Harriet   Ozzie! (*In fear.*) No!

Ozzie (*some weariness in him*)   No, he's all right, he's coming home!

Harriet   Why didn't you let me speak? Who was it?

Ozzie   No, no.

Harriet   Was it David.

Ozzie   No, somebody else. Some clerk. I don't know who.

Harriet   You're lying.

Ozzie   No. There was just all this static – it was hard to
hear. But he was coming home as part of it, and they had had
his records and papers but I couldn't talk to him directly even
though he was right there, standing right there.

Harriet   I don't understand.

Ozzie   That's what they said . . . and he was fine and
everything. And he wanted them to say 'Hello' for him. He'd
lost some weight. He would be sent by truck. I could hear
truck engines in the background – revving. They wanted to
know my name. I told them.

Harriet   No more?

Ozzie   They were very professional. Very brusque . . .

Harriet   No more . . . at all . . . ?

And the door opens and **Rick** *comes in. He is young, seventeen; and the
door slams. His hair is long and neat, sideburns. His clothing is
elaborate, very, very up to date. He carries a guitar on his shoulder.*

Rick   Hi, Mom, hi, Dad.

Harriet   Hi, Rick.

Ozzie   Hi, Rick.

Harriet   Ohhh, Ricky, Ricky, your brother's on his way
home. David's coming home!

Ozzie   We just got a call.

Rick   Ohhh, boy!

Harrie   Isn't that wonderful? Isn't it? Your father talked to
him. Oh, I bet you're starving, sit, sit.

Ozzie   I talked to *somebody*, Rick.

Harriet There's fudge and ice cream in the fridge, would you like that?

Rick Oh, yeah, and could I have some soda? (*She is on her way to the kitchen, nodding.*) Wow, that sure is some news. I'm awful hungry.

Ozzie Never had a doubt. A boy like that – if he leaves, he comes back.

Rick How about me? What if I left? (*As he picks up a comic book.*)

Ozzie Absolutely. Absolutely. (*Silence.* **Ricky** *reads the comic.*) I built jeeps . . . tanks, trucks.

Rick What?

Ozzie In the other war, I mean. Number Two. I worked on vehicles. Vehicles were needed and I worked to build them. Sometimes I put on wheels, tightened 'em up. I never . . . served . . . is what I mean. (*Slight pause.*) They got all those people – soldiers, Rick – you see what I mean? They get 'em across the ocean, they don't have any jeeps or tanks or trucks, what are they gonna do, stand around? Wait for a bus on the beachhead? Call a cab?

Rick No public transportation in a war.

Ozzie That's right, that's right. (*As* **Harriet** *enters, carrying fudge and ice cream.*)

Harriet Oh, Ozzie, Ozzie, do you remember – I just remembered that time David locked himself in that old ice box. We didn't know where he was. We looked all over. We couldn't find him. And then there was this ice box in this clearing . . . out in the middle. I'll bet you don't even remember.

Ozzie Of course I remember.

Harriet And he leaped to us. So frightened.

Ozzie He couldn't even speak – he couldn't even speak – just these noises.

Harriet   Or that time he fell from that tree.

Ozzie   My God, he was somethin'! If he wasn't fallin', he was gettin' hit.

Harriet   And then there was that day we went out into the woods. It was just all wind and clouds. We sailed a kite!

Ozzie   I'd nearly forgotten . . . !

Rick   Where was I?

Harriet   You were just a baby, Rick. We had a picnic.

Rick   I'm gonna get some more soda, okay? (**Harriet** *touches him as he passes*.)

Ozzie   What a day that was. I felt great that day.

Harriet   And then Hank came along. Hank Grenweller. He came from out of the woods calling that –

Ozzie   That's right.

Harriet   He was happy.

Ozzie   We were all happy. And then we had that race. Wasn't that the day?

Harriet   I don't remember.

Ozzie   Hank and me! Hank Grenweller. A foot race. And I beat him. I did it; got him.

Harriet   Noooo.

Ozzie   It was only inches, but –

Harriet   You know that's not true. If it was close – that race you ran – and it was – (*There's a nostalgia to this for her, a fondness.*) I remember now – it was because he let it – no other reason. We were all having fun. He didn't want to make you feel badly.

Rick (*calling from the kitchen*)   You people want some more fudge!

Harriet   No, Rick.

Ozzie   I don't know he didn't try. I don't know that. (*Staring at* **Harriet** *as* **Rick** *returns, eating.*)

Harriet   I think I'll be going up to bed; take a little nap.

Rick   Sleepy, Mom?

Harriet   A little. (*She is crossing toward* **Ozzie**.)

Rick   That's a good idea then.

Harriet   Call me.

Rick   Okay.

Harriet   Do you know, the day he left? It was a winter day. November, Ozzie. (*Moving toward the stairs.*)

Ozzie   I know.

Harriet   I prayed; did you know that? Now he's home.

Ozzie   It was a winter day.

Harriet   I know.

Rick   Night, Mom. (*He is toying with his guitar. She doesn't answer, disappears walking down the hall. He looks up, yells.*) Night, Mom!

Harriet (*from off*)   Turn off the T.V. somebody.

Rick *crosses to the T.V. He turns it off and starts to walk away.* **Ozzie** *watches. Silence.*

Ozzie   I knew she was praying. She moves her lips. (**Ricky** *does not look up. He begins, softly, to strum and tune the guitar.*) And something else – yes, sir, boy, oh, boy, I tell you, huh? What a day, huh? (*Slight pause.*) I mean, they got seventeen hundred million men they gotta deal with, how they gonna do that without any trucks and tanks and jeeps? But I'm some kinda jerk because I wasn't out there blastin' away, huh? I was useful. I put my time to use. I been in fights. Fat Kramer. How we used to fight. Black eyes. Bloody noses. That's all we did. (**Ricky** *strums some notes on the guitar.* **Ozzie** *stares at him.*) How come I'm so restless? I . . . seen him do some awful, awful

things, ole Dave. He was a mean . . . foul-tempered little baby.
I'm only glad I was *here* when they sent him off to do his
killing. That's right. (*Silence.*) I feel like I swallowed ants, that's
how restless I am. Outran a bowlin' ball one time. These guys
bet me I couldn't do it and I did, beat it to the pins. Got a
runnin' start, then the – (*A faint, strange rapping sound has stopped
him, spun him around.*) Did you do that?

Rick   Somebody knockin'.

Ozzie   Knockin'?

Rick   The door, Dad.

Ozzie   Oh.

Rick   You want me to get it?

Ozzie   No, no. It's just so late. (*As he moves for the door.*)

Rick   That's all right.

Ozzie   Sure. (*Opens the door just a crack, as if to kind of stick his
head around. But the door is thrust open and a black man, large, dressed
in the uniform of a sgt major, steps in.*)

Sgt Major   Excuse me. Listen to me. I'd like to speak to the
father here. I'd like to know who . . . is the father? Could . . .
you tell me the address?

Ozzie   May I ask who it is who's asking?

Sgt Major   I am. I'm asking. What's the address of this house?

Ozzie   But I mean, who is it that wants to know?

Sgt Major   We called; we spoke. Is this 717 Dunbar?

Ozzie   Yes.

Sgt Major   What's wrong with you?

Ozzie   Don't you worry about me.

Sgt Major   I have your son.

Ozzie   What?

Sgt Major   Your son.

Ozzie   No.

Sgt Major   But he is. I have papers, pictures, prints. I know your blood and his. This is the right address. Please. Excuse me. (*He pivots, reaches out, into the dark.*) I am very busy. I have your father, David. (*Drawing* **David** *in from the dark, a tall thin boy, blond and, in the shadows wearing sunglasses and a uniform of dress greens. In his right hand is a long, white, red-tipped cane. He moves, probing the air, as the* **Sgt Major** *moves him past* **Ozzie** *toward the couch where he will sit the boy down like a parcel.*)

Ozzie   Dave . . . ?

Sgt Major   He's blind.

Ozzie   What?

Sgt Major   Blind.

Ozzie   I don't . . . understand.

Sgt Major   We're very sorry.

Ozzie   Ohhhhh. Yes. Ohhhh. (*Realizing.*) I see . . . sure. I mean, we didn't know. Nobody said it. I mean, sure, Dave, sure; it's all right – don't you worry. Rick's here too, Dave – Rick, your brother, tell him 'Hello.'

Rick   Hi, Dave.

David   You said 'Father.' (*Worried.*)

Ozzie   Well . . . there's two of us, Dave; two.

David   Sergeant, you said 'home.' I don't think so.

Ozzie   Dave, sure.

David   It doesn't feel right.

Ozzie   But it is, Dave – me and Rick – Dad and Rick; and Mom. Harriet! (*Calling up the stairs.*) Harriet!

David   Let me touch their faces . . . I can't see. (*Rising, his fear increasing.*) Let me put my fingers on their faces.

Ozzie   (*hurt, startled*)   What? Do what?

Sgt Major   Will that be all right, if he does that?

Ozzie   Sure . . . Sure . . . Fine.

Sgt Major (*helping* **David** *to* **Ozzie**)   It will take time.

Ozzie   That's normal and to be expected. I'm not surprised. Not at all. We figured on this. Sure, we did. Didn't we, Rick?

Rick (*occupied with his camera, an instamatic*)   I wanna take some pictures. How are you, Dave?

David   What room is this?

Ozzie   Middle room, Dave. TV room TV's in –

Harriet   David . . . ! Oh, David . . . ! (*She is on the stairs.*) David . . . (*And* **Ozzie** *hurries toward the stairs, leaving* **David**, *looking up at her as she falters, stops, stares up and* **Rick** *moving near, snaps a picture of her.*)

Ozzie   Harriet . . . don't be upset . . . they say . . . Harriet, Harriet . . . he can't see . . . ! Harriet . . . they say – he can't . . . see. That man.

Harriet (*as she is standing very still*)   Can't see? What do you mean?

Sgt Major   He's blind.

Harriet   No. Who's says? No, no.

Ozzie   Look at him; he looks so old. But it's nothing, Harriet, I'm sure.

Sgt Major   I hope you people understand

Ozzie   It's probably just how he's tired from his long trip.

Harriet (*moving toward him*)   Oh, you're home now, David. You're home.

Sgt Major (*with a large sheet of paper waving in his hands*)   Who's gonna sign this for me, mister? It's a shipping receipt. I got to have somebody's signature to show you got him. I got to have somebody's name on the paper.

Ozzie   Let me. All right?

Sgt Major   Just here and here, you see? Your name or mark three times.

As they move toward a table and away from **Harriet**, *who is near* **David**.

Ozzie   Fine, listen, would you like some refreshments?

Sgt Major   No.

Ozzie   I mean while I do this. Cake and coffee. Of course you do.

Sgt Major   No.

Ozzie   Sure.

Sgt Major   No. I haven't time. I've got to get going. I've got trucks out there backed up for blocks. Other boys. I got to get on to Chicago and some of them to Denver and Cleveland, Reno, New Orleans, Boston, Trenton, Watts, Atlanta. And when I get back they'll be layin' all over the grass; layin' there in pieces all over the grass, their backs been broken, their brains jellied, their insides turned into garbage. No-legged boys and one-legged boys. I'm due in Harlem; I got to get to the Bronx and Queens, Cincinnati, St. Louis, Reading. I don't have time for coffee. I got deliveries to make all across this country.

David   Nooooooo . . . (*With* **Harriet**, *his hands on her face, a kind of realization.*) Sergeant . . . nooo; there's something wrong; it all feels wrong. Where are you? Are you here? I don't know these people!

Sgt Major   That's natural, soldier; it's natural you feel that way.

David   Nooooo. (*He rises.*)

Harriet (*attempting to guide him back to a chair*)   David! Just sit, be still.

David   Don't you hear me?

Ozzie   Harriet, calm him.

David   The air is wrong; the smells and sounds, the wind.

Harriet   David, please, please. What is it? Be still. Please . . .

David   GODDAMN YOU, SERGEANT, I AM LONELY HERE! I AM LONELY!

Sgt Major   I got to go. (*And he pivots to leave.*)

David   Sergeant! (*Following the sound of the* **Sgt Major**'s *voice.*)

Sgt Major (*whirling, bellowing*)   YOU SHUT UP. YOU PISS-ASS SOLDIER, YOU SHUT THE FUCK UP!

Ozzie (*walking to the* **Sgt Major**, *putting his hand on the man's shoulder*)   Listen, let me walk you to the door. All right? I'd like to take a look at that truck of yours. All right?

Sgt Major   There's more than one.

Ozzie   Fine.

Sgt Major   It's a convoy.

Ozzie   Good.

They exit, and **Rick**, *running close behind them, looks out.*

Rick   Sure are lots a trucks, Mom!

Harriet   Are there? (*As he reenters.*)

Rick   Oh, yeah. (*He slams the door shut.*) Gonna rain some more, too.

Harriet   Is it?

Rick   Yeh. (*Turning, he runs up the stairs.*) See you in the morning. 'Night, Dave.

Harriet   It's so good to have you here again; so good to see you. You look . . . just . . . fine.

As **Ozzie** *steps back into the room behind her; he stands, looking.*

You must be so relieved to be out of there – to be – (*She senses* **Ozzie**'s *presence and whirls on him.*) He bewilders you, doesn't he.

Ozzie   What?

Harriet   Of course he does.

And **Ozzie**, *jauntily, heads for the stairs.*

Where are you going? You thought you knew what was right, all those years, didn't you, teaching him sports and fighting.

Ozzie *stops; he doesn't know. And she is both happy and sad now as she speaks, sad for poor* **Ozzie** *and* **David**, *they are so whimsical, so childlike.*

Harriet   Do you understand what I'm trying to say? A mother knows THINGS . . . a father cannot ever know them. The measles, smallpox, cuts and bruises. Never have you come upon him in the night as he lay awake and staring . . . praying.

Ozzie   I saw him put a knife through the skin of a cat. I saw him cut the belly open.

David   Noooo . . .

Harriet   David, David . . .

David   Ricky! (*There is a kind of accusation in this as if he were saying* **Rick** *killed the cat. He says it loudly and directly into her face.*)

Harriet   He's gone to bed.

David   I want to leave. (*There is furniture around him; he is caged, he pokes with his cane.*)

Harriet   What is it?

David   Help me. (*He crashes.*)

Ozzie   Settle down! Relax.

David   I want to leave! I want to leave! I want to leave. I – (*As he smashes into the stairs, goes down, flails, pounding his cane.*) want to leave.

Ozzie *and* **Harriet**   Dave! David! Davey!

David   . . . to leave! Please. (*He is on the floor, breathing. Long silence in which they look at him until she announces the solution.*)

Harriet Ozzie, get him some medicine. He needs some medicine. Get him some Easy Sleep.

Ozzie Good idea.

Harriet It's in the medicine cabinet; a little blue bottle, little pink pills.

Ozzie I'll be right back. (*Hurrying up the stairway and down the hall.*)

Harriet (*she stands over* **David**) It'll give you the sleep you need, Dave; the sleep you remember. You're our child and you're home. Our good . . . beautiful boy.

And the door to the outside bursts open. There is a small girl in the doorway, an Asian **Girl**. *She wears the Vietnamese Ao Dai, black slacks and white tunic slit up the sides.*

Oh, my goodness. (*As she goes racing over to slam the door shut, leaving the girl outside.*) What an awful . . . wind.

Blackout. Music.

Lights rise slightly. A match flickers as **Harriet** *lights a candle.* **Ozzie** *is asleep sitting up in a chair. As* **Harriet** *moves toward the stairs,* **Ozzie** *startles.*

Harriet Oh! I didn't mean to wake you. I lit a candle so I wouldn't wake you. (**Ozzie** *stares at her.*) I'm sorry.

Ozzie I wasn't sleeping. (*As he turns on a flashlight.*)

Harriet I thought you were. (*At the base of the stairs.*)

Ozzie Couldn't. Tried. Couldn't. Thinking. Thoughts running very fast. Trying to remember the night David . . . was . . . well . . . made. You know. Do you understand me? I don't know why. But the feeling was in me that I had to figure something out and if only I could remember that night, the mood . . . I would be able. You're shaking your head.

Harriet I don't understand. (*She starts climbing the stairs.*)

Ozzie No. Well . . . I don't either. (*He waves his flashlight.*) I'm going to look around outside. I heard a sound before. Like mice in the walls.

Harriet   We don't have any mice.

Ozzie   I know. (*He opens the door. The Vietnamese* **Girl** *is still standing there.*) I'm just going to look around.

Harriet (*as the* **Girl** *steps in*)   Well . . . good night.

As **Ozzie**, *with his flashlight, goes out the front door, the* **Girl** *stands there looking up at* **Harriet**, *moving to rap softly at* **David**'*s door, and then she opens the door.* **David** *lies unmoving on the bed, as* **Harriet** *leans in.*

I heard you call.

David   What?

Harriet   I heard you call.

David   I didn't.

Harriet   Would you like a glass of warm milk?

David   I was sleeping.

Harriet (*after a slight pause*)   How about that milk? Would you like some milk?

David   I didn't call. I was sleeping.

Harriet   I'll bet you're glad you didn't bring her back. Their skins are yellow, aren't they?

David   What?

Harriet   You're troubled; warm milk would help. Do you pray at all anymore? If I were to pray now, would you pray with me?

David   What . . . do you want?

Harriet   They eat the flesh of dogs.

David   I know. I've seen them.

Harriet   Pray with me; pray.

David   What do you want?

Harriet   Just to talk, that's all. Just to know that you're home and safe again. Nothing else; only that we're all together, a family. You must he exhausted. Don't worry; sleep. (*She is backing into the hallway.*) Good night. (*A whisper; she blows out the candle and is gone, moving up stairs that lead to additional second- and third-floor rooms. The **Girl** enters **David**'s room, and **David** bolts up.*)

David   Who's there? (*As she drifts by, he waves the cane at the air.*) Who's there? (*He stands.*) Is someone there? Cho, Co Zung? (*He moves for the door, which he opens, and steps into the hall, leaving her behind him in the room.*) CHO, CO ZUNG? Are you there? (*And he moves off up the hallway. She follows.*) Is someone there . . . ?!

Blackout. Music.

*Lights up: It is a bright afternoon, and **Ozzie**, with a screwdriver in his hand, pokes about at the T.V. set.*

Ozzie   C'mon, c'mon. Ohhh, c'mon, this one more game and ole State's bowl bound. C'mon, what is it. Ohhh, hey . . . ohhhhh. . . .

Harriet (*as she enters, carrying a tray with a pitcher of orange juice, some glasses, a bowl of soup*)   Ozzie, take this up to David, make him eat it.

Ozzie   Harriet, the T.V. is broke.

Harriet   What?

Ozzie   There's a picture but no sound. I don't – (*Grabbing her by the arm, pulling her toward a place before the set.*)

Harriet   Stoppit, you're spilling the soup. (*Pulling free.*)

Ozzie   It's Saturday. I want to watch it. I turned it on, picture came on just like normal. I got the volume up full blast. (*Having set the soup down, she pulls the screwdriver from his hand.*) Hey! I want to fix it!

Harriet   I want to talk about David.

Ozzie   David's all right. (*As he turns, crosses toward the phone; he picks up the phone book.*) I'm gonna call the repairman.

Harriet (*following him. She will take the phone book from him*)
Ozzie, he won't eat. He just lays there. I offer him food, he
won't eat it. No, no. The T.V. repairman won't help, you silly.
He doesn't matter. There's something wrong with David. He's
been home days and days and still he speaks only when spoken
to; there's no light in his eyes, no smile, he's not happy to be
here and not once has he touched me or held me, and I don't
think he's even shaken your hand. Has he shaken your hand?

Ozzie (*flops down in a chair*)   Oh, I don't mind that. Why
should I mind –

Harriet   And now he's talking to himself! What about that?
Do you mind that? He mutters in his sleep.

Ozzie   Ohhhhhh. (*Exasperated, denying her.*)

Harriet   Yes. And it's not a regular kind of talking at all. It's
very strange – very spooky.

Ozzie   Spooky?

Harriet   That's right.

Ozzie   I never heard him.

Harriet   You sleep too deeply. I took a candle and followed.
I was in his room. He lay there, speaking.

Ozzie   He was speaking? Speaking what?

Harriet   I don't know. I couldn't understand.

Ozzie   Was it words?

Harriet   All kind of funny and fast.

Ozzie   Maybe prayer; praying.

Harriet   No. No, it was secret. Oh, Ozzie, I know praying
when I hear it, and it wasn't praying he was doing. We meant
our son to be so different from this – I don't understand –
good and strong. And yet . . . he is. I know he is. But there are
moments when I see him . . . hiding . . . in that bed behind
those awful glasses . . . and I see the chalkiness that's come
into his skin, the –

Ozzie   Those glasses are simply to ease his discomfort. (*Headed for the kitchen, looking for juice to drink.*)

Harriet   I hate them.

Ozzie   They're tinted glass and plastic – Don't be so damn suspicious. (*Moving to the pitcher to pour some juice.*)

Harriet   I'm not, I'm not. It's seeing I'm doing, not suspicion. Suspicion hasn't any reasons. It's you – now accusing me for no reason when I'm only worried. (*As she sees what he's doing.*) No, no, that's for David. (*And she picks up the tray.*)

Ozzie   I want some juice.

Harriet   This is for him. He needs his nourishment.

Ozzie   I want a little juice, Harriet.

Harriet   Shut up. You're selfish. You're so selfish.

Ozzie   I'll walk over there; I'll pour it on the floor. I'll break the glass.

Harriet   A few years ago you might have done that kind of thing. (*Starting to pour the juice.*)

Ozzie (*pacing away*)   I didn't get much sleep last night. You woke me up with all your snorting and snoggling around. I woke up and I looked at you and all I could see was the lovely way you looked when you were young. And there you were, struggling to breathe. You were trying to breathe. (*As she is approaching him to hand him the juice.*) What do you give me when you give me this?

Harriet   Your juice. And I always looked pretty much the way I do now. I never looked much different.

David   Good morning. (*Happy sounding, yet moving with urgency, he appears from off upstairs and descends toward them dressed in a red robe.*)

Ozzie   Oh, David, ohhh, good morning. Hello. How do you feel this fine bright morning; how do you feel?

David   He was a big man, wasn't he?

Ozzie   What?

David   Hank. You were talking about Hank Grenweller. I thought you were.

Ozzie   Oh, yes. Hank. Very big. Big. A good fine friend, ole Hank.

David   You felt when he was with you he filled the room.

Ozzie   It was the way he talked that did that. He boomed. His voice just boomed.

David   He was here once and you wanted me to sit on his lap, isn't that right? It was after dinner. He was in a chair in the corner.

Harriet   That's right.

David   His hand was gone – the bone showed in the skin.

Ozzie   My God, what a memory – did you hear that, Harriet? You were only four or five. He'd just had this terrible awful auto accident. His hand was hurt, not gone.

David   No. It was congenital.

Ozzie   What?

David   That hand. The sickness in it.

Ozzie   Congenital?

David   I'd like some coffee. (*He is seated now.*)

Harriet   Of course. And what else with it?

David   Nothing.

Harriet   Oh, no, no, you've got to eat. To get back your strength. You must. Pancakes? How do pancakes sound? Or wheat cakes? Or there's eggs? And juice? Orange or prune; or waffles. I bet it's eggs you want. Over, David? Over easy? Scrambled?

David   I'm only thirsty.

Harriet   Well, all right then, coffee is what you'll have and I'll just put some eggs on the side; you used to love them so, remember? (*And picking up the tray, she is off toward the kitchen.*)

Pause.

Ozzie   I mean, I hate to harp on a thing, but I just think you're way off base on Hank, Dave. I just think you're dead wrong –

David   He told me.

Ozzie   Who?

David   Hank.

Ozzie   You . . . talked to Hank?

David   In California. The day before they shipped me overseas.

Ozzie   No, no. He went to Georgia when he left here. We have all his letters postmarked Georgia.

David   It was California, I was in the barracks. The C.Q. came to tell me there was someone to see me. It was Hank asking did I remember him. He'd seen my name on a list and wondered if I was Ozzie's boy. He was dying, he said. The sickness was congenital. We had a long, long talk. (*There is great urgency in* **David**.)

Ozzie   But his parents were good fine people, David.

David   Don't you understand? We spoke.

Ozzie   Did he wanna know about me? Did he mention me?

David (*after thinking a moment*)   He asked . . . how you were.

Ozzie   Well, I'm fine. Sure. You told him. Fine. Fine.

Harriet (*entering with a cup of coffee*)   It must be so wonderful for you to be home. It must just be so wonderful. A little strange, maybe . . . just a little, but time will take care of all that. It always does. You get sick and you don't know how you're going to get better and then you do. You just do. You must have terrible, awful, ugly dreams, though.

Slight pause.

Ozzie She said you probably have terrible awful ugly dreams . . . though.

David What?

Harriet Don't you remember when we spoke last night?

David Who?

Harriet You called to me and then you claimed you hadn't.

David I didn't.

Harriet Ohhh, we had a lovely conversation, David. Of course you called. You called, we talked. We talked and laughed and it was very pleasant. Could I see behind your glasses?

David What? Do . . . what? (*Moving away.*)

Harriet See behind your glasses; see your eyes.

Ozzie Me too, Dave; could we?

David My eyes . . . are ugly.

Ozzie We don't mind.

Harriet We're your parents, David.

David I think it better if you don't.

Ozzie And something else I've been meaning to ask you – why did you cry out against us that first night – to that stranger, I mean, that sergeant?

Harriet And you do dream. You do.

Ozzie Sure. You needn't be ashamed.

Harriet We all do it. All of us.

Ozzie We have things that haunt us.

Harriet And it would mean nothing at all – it would be of no consequence at all – if only you didn't speak.

David   I don't understand.

Ozzie   She says she heard you, Dave.

Harriet   I stood outside your door.

David   No.

Ozzie   A terrible experience for her, Dave; you can see that.

Harriet   Whatever it is, David, tell us.

Ozzie   What's wrong?

David   No.

Harriet   We'll work it out.

Ozzie   You can't know how you hurt us.

David   I wasn't asleep.

Ozzie   Not until you have children of your own.

Harriet   What? Not . . . asleep . . . ?

David   No. No. I was awake; lying awake and speaking.

Ozzie   Now wait a minute.

David   Someone was with me – there in the dark – I don't know what's wrong with me – but I feel, I feel –

Harriet   It was me. I was with you. There's nothing wrong with you.

David   No. In my room. I could feel it.

Harriet   I was there. (*And they have him cornered.*)

David   No.

Ozzie   Harriet, wait!

Harriet   What are you saying, 'Wait'? I was there.

Ozzie   Oh, my God. Oh, Christ, of course. Oh, Dave, forgive us.

Harriet   What?

Ozzie   Dave, I understand. It's buddies left behind.

David   What?

Ozzie   Maybe your mother can't, but I can. Men serving together in war, it's a powerful thing – and I don't mean to sound like I think I know it – all of it, I mean – I don't, I couldn't. But I respect you having had it. I almost envy you having had it, Dave. I mean . . . true comradeship.

David   Dad . . .

Ozzie   I had just a taste. Not that those trucks and factory were any battlefield, but there was a taste of it there – in the jokes we told and the way we saw each other first in the morning. We told dirty filthy jokes, Dave, we shot pool, played cards, drank beer late every night, singing all these crazy songs.

David   That's not it, Dad.

Ozzie   But all that's nothing, I'm sure, to what it must be in war. The things you must touch and see. Honor. And then one of you is hurt, wounded, made blind – he has to leave his buddies.

David   No. Not my buddies.

Ozzie   WHAT IS IT THEN?

David   I had fear of all the kinds of dying that there are when I went from here, and then there was this girl . . . with hands and hair like wings. There were candles above the net of gauze under which we lay. Lizards. Cannon could be heard. A girl to weigh no more than dust.

Harriet   A nurse, right . . . David?

Ozzie   No, no, no, Harriet. One of them foreign correspondents, English maybe, or French. (*Silence.*)

Harriet   Oh, how lovely! A Wac or Red Cross girl . . . ?

David   No.

Ozzie   Redhead or blonde, Dave?

David   No.

Ozzie   I mean, all right, what you mean is you whored around a lot. Sure. You whored around. That's what you're saying. You banged some whores . . . Had some intercourse. Sure, I mean, that's my point.

David, *turning away, seems about to rise.*

Ozzie   Now Dave, take it easy. What I mean is, okay, sure, you shacked up with. I mean, hit on. Hit on, Dave. Dicked. Look at me. I mean, you pronged it, right? Right? Sure, attaboy. (*Patting* **David** *on the shoulder.*) Look, Dave, what are you doing?

A rage is building in **David**, *tension forcing him to stand, his cane pressing the floor.*

We can talk this over. We can talk this over.

Heading for the stairs, **David** *crashes into* **Ozzie**.

Don't – goddammit, don't walk away from me. (*He pushes* **David** *backward.*) What the hell do you think you're doing? It's what you did. Who the hell you think you are? You screwed it. A yellow whore. Some yellow ass. You put in your prick and humped your ass. You screwed some yellow fucking whore! (*He has chased,* **David** *backward,* **Harriet** *joining in with him.*)

Harriet   That's right, that's right. You were lonely and young and away from home for the very first time in your life, no white girls anywhere around –

David   She was the color of the earth! They are the color of the earth, and what is white but winter with the earth under it like a suicide!

Harriet's *voice is a high humming in her throat.*

David   Tell me! Tell me! Why didn't you tell me what I was?

And she vomits, her hands at her mouth, her back turning. There is a silence. They stand. **Ozzie** *starts toward her, falters, starts, reaches, stops.*

Ozzie   Why . . . don't . . . you ask her to cook something for you, David, will you? Make her feel better . . . okay?

David   I think . . . some eggs might be good, Mom.

Ozzie (*wanting to help her*)   Hear that, Harriet? David wants some eggs.

Harriet   I'm ALL RIGHT.

Ozzie   Of course you are. We all are. (*Patting her tenderly, he offers his clean white handkerchief.*) Here, here, wipe your mouth; you've got a little something – on the corner; left side. That's it. Whattayou say, David?

Harriet   What's your pleasure, David?

David   Scrambled . . . eggs.

Ozzie   There you go. Your specialty, his pleasure. (*Stepping between* **Harriet** *and* **David**, **Ozzie** *claps his hands;* **Harriet** *darts for the kitchen, and* **Ozzie**, *looking about the room like a man in deep water looking for something to keep him afloat, sees a pack of cigarettes.*) How about a cigarette? I think I'll have one. Filter, see, brand – new idea; I tried 'em, I switched after one puff. (*Running to grab them, show them.*) Just a little after you left, and I just find them a lot smoother, actually; I wondered if you'd notice. Nothing like a good smoke. (*And speaking now, his voice and manner take on a confidence.*) The filter's granulated. It's an off-product of corn husks. I light up – I feel like I'm on a ship at sea. Isn't that one hell of a good-tasting cigarette? Isn't that one beautiful goddamn cigarette?

Harriet *enters with two bowls. One has a grapefruit cut in half; the second has eggs and a spoon sticking out.*

Harriet   Here's a little grapefruit to tide you over till I get the eggs. (*And now she stirs the eggs, in preparation of scrambling them.*) Won't be long, I promise – but I was just wondering wouldn't it be nice if we could all go to church tonight. All together and we could make a little visit in thanksgiving of your coming home.

David *is putting his cigarette out in his grapefruit. They see.*

Harriet   I wouldn't ask that it be long – just –

David *is rising now, dropping the grapefruit on the chair.*

Harriet   I mean, we could go to whatever saint you wanted, it wouldn't . . . matter . . .

He has turned his back, is walking toward the stairs.

Just in . . . just out . . .

He is climbing the stairs.

Ozzie   Tired . . . Dave?

They watch him plodding unfalteringly for his door.

Where are you going . . . bathroom?

David *enters his room, shutting the door.* **Harriet** *whirls and heads for the phone;* **Ozzie** *turns to watch her, startled.*

Ozzie   Harriet, what's up?

Harriet   I'm calling Father Donald.

Ozzie   Father Donald?

Harriet   We need help, I'm calling for help.

Ozzie   Now wait a minute. No; oh, no, we –

Harriet   Do you still refuse to see it? He was involved with one of them. You know what the Bible says about those people. You heard him. You heard what he said.

Ozzie   Just not Father Donald; please, please. That's all I ask – just –

Harriet *is obstinate, shushing him with her finger to her lips, as she turns her back, waiting for someone to answer.*

Ozzie   Why must everything be turned into a matter of personal vengeance?

And the door pops open and **Rick** *comes bounding in, guitar upon his back.*

Rick   Hi, Mom, hi, Dad. (*Happy.*)

Harriet (*waiting, telephone in hand*)   Hi, Rick! (*Overjoyed.*)

Rick   Hi, Mom. (*Happy.*)

Ozzie   Hi, Rick. (*Feeling fine.*)

Rick   Hi, Dad.

Ozzie   How you doin', Rick? (*He is happy to see good ole regular* **Rick**.)

Rick   Fine, Dad. You?

Ozzie   Fine.

Rick   Good.

Harriet   I'll get you some fudge in just a minute, Rick!

Rick   Okay. How's Dave doin', Dad? (*He is fiddling with his camera.*)

Ozzie   Dave's doin' fine, Rick.

Rick   Boy, I'm glad to hear that. I'm really glad to hear that, because, boy, I'll sure be glad when everything's back to the regular way. Dave's too serious, Dad; don't you think so? That's what I think. Whattayou think, Dad? (*He snaps a picture of* **Ozzie**, *who is posing, smiling, while* **Harriet** *waves angrily at them.*)

Harriet   SHHHHHHHH! EVERYBODY! (*And then, more pleasantly, she returns to the phone.*) Yes, yes. Oh, Father, I didn't recognize your voice. No, I don't know who. Well, yes, it's about my son, Father, David. Yes. Well, I don't know if you know it or not, but he just got back from the war and he's troubled. Deeply. Yes.

As she listens silently for a moment, **Rick**, *crouching, snaps a picture of her. She tries to wave him away.*

Deeply.

He moves to another position, another angle, and snaps another picture, then flops in a chair with a comic book.

Deeply, yes. Oh. So do you think you might be able to stop over sometime soon to talk to him or not? Father, any time that would be convenient for you. Yes. Oh, that would he wonderful. Yes. Oh, thank you. And may God reward YOU, Father. (*Hanging up the phone, she stands a moment, dreaming as* **Ozzie** *is pacing, talking to her.*)

Ozzie   I say to myself, 'What does it mean that he is my son? How the hell is it that . . . he . . . is my son?' I mean, they say something of you joined to something of me and became . . . him . . . but what kinda goddamn explanation is that? One mystery replacing another? Mystery doesn't explain mystery!

Rick   Mom, hey, c'mon, how about that fudge? (*Scarcely having looked up from his comic.*)

Harriet   Ricky, oh, I'm sorry. I forgot.

Ozzie   And they've got . . . diseases . .

Harriet   What . . . ? (*Having been stopped by his voice.*)

Ozzie   Dirty, filthy diseases. They got 'em. Those girls. Infection. From the blood of their parents it goes right into in the fluids of their bodies. Malaria, T.B. An actual rot alive in them . . . gonorrhea, syphilis. There are some who have the plague. He touched them. It's disgusting.

Rick   Mom, I'm starving, honest to God; and I'm thirsty, too.

Harriet (*as she scurries off, clapping, for the kitchen*)   Yes, of course. Oh, oh.

Rick   And bring a piece for Dad, too; Dad looks hungry.

Ozzie   No.

Rick   Sure, a big sweet chocolate piece a fudge.

Ozzie   No. Please. I don't feel well.

Rick   It'll do you good.

Harriet (*entering with fudge and milk in each hand*)   Ricky, here, come here.

Rick (*hurrying toward her*)   What?

Harriet (*as she hands him fudge and milk*)   Look good? (*And she moves toward* **Ozzie**.)

Ozzie   Or maybe we're just – I mean, maybe – MAYBE it's just that he's growing away from us, like he's supposed to – like we did ourselves, from our own parents, only we thought it would happen in some other way, some –

Harriet (*putting the fudge and milk into* **Ozzie**'s *hands*)   What are you talking about, 'going away' – he's right upstairs.

Ozzie   I don't want that.

Harriet   You said you did.

Ozzie   He said he did.

Rick (*having gobbled the fudge and milk*)   You want me to drive you, Mom?

Harriet   Would you, Ricky, please?

Rick (*running*)   I'll go around and get the car.

Harriet (*scolding, as* **Ozzie** *has put the fudge and milk down on a coffee table*)   It's all cut and poured. Ozzie, it'll just be a waste.

Ozzie   I don't care – I don't want it.

Harriet   You're so childish. Honest to God, you're like a two-year-old sometimes. (*As she marches off toward the door, where she takes a light jacket from a hook, starts to slip it on.*)

Ozzie   Don't you know I could throw you down onto this floor and make another child live inside you now!

Harriet   I doubt that, Ozzie.

Ozzie   You want me to do it?

Harriet (*going out the door*)   Oh, Ozzie, Ozzie, don't we have enough trouble? (*The door slams shut.*)

Ozzie   They think they know me and they know nothing. They don't know how I feel. How I'd like to beat Ricky with my fists till his face is ugly! How I'd like to banish David to the streets. How I'd like to cut her tongue from her mouth! They know nothing . . . ! I was myself (*And turning to the audience now, it's clear that the audience are his friends, his buddies.*) I lived in a time beyond anything they can ever know – a time beyond and separate, and I was nobody's goddamn father and nobody's goddamn husband! I was myself! And I could run. I got a scrapbook of victories; a bag of medals and ribbons. Nobody was faster. In the town in which I lived my name was spoken in the factories and in the fields all around because I was the best there was. I'd beaten the finest anybody had to offer. Summers . . . I would sit out on this old wood porch on the front of our house and my strength was in me, quiet and mine. Around the corner would come some old Model-T Ford and scampering up the walk this bone-stiff, buck-toothed old farmer raw as winter and cawing at me like a crow: they had one for me. Out at the edge of town. A runner from another county. My shoes are in a brown paper bag at my feet and I snatch it up and set out into the dusk, easy as breathing. There'd be an old white fence where we start and we run for the sun. For a hundred yards or a thousand yards or a thousand thousand. It doesn't matter. Whatever they want. I run the race they think their specialty and I beat them. They sweat and struggle, I simply glide on one step beyond . . . no matter what their effort, and the sun bleeds before me . . . We cross rivers and deserts; we clamber over mountains. I run the races the farmers arrange and I win the bets they make; and then, a few days after, the race money comes to me anonymously in the mail; but it's not for the money that I run. In the fields and factories, they speak my name when they sit down to their lunches. If there's a (*as* **David**, *stepping into the hallway from his room, has listened to the latter part of this*) prize to be run for, it's me they send for. It's to be the-one-sent-for that I run.

David (*now at the top of the stairs*)   And . . . then . . . you left.

Ozzie   What? (*Whirling back.*)

David   I said . . . 'And . . . then you left.' That town.

Ozzie   Left?

David   Yes. Went away; traveled. Left it all behind.

Ozzie   No. What do you mean?

David   I mean, you're no longer there; you're here now.

Ozzie   But I didn't really LEAVE it. I mean, not LEAVE. Not really.

David   Of course you did. Where are you?

Ozzie   That's not the point, Dave. Where I am isn't the point at all.

David   But it is. It's everything; all that other is gone. Where are you going?

Ozzie   Groceries. Gotta go get groceries. You want anything at the grocery store? (*Looks at his watch.*) It's late. I gotta get busy.

David (*as* **Ozzie** *exits*)   That's all right, Dad. I'll see you later.
(*As the lights are fading to black.*)

Blackout. Music.

Lights up, the living room aglow in the midst of the surrounding night. **Rick** *enters, toying with his guitar, plinking a note or two, as* **Harriet** *emerges from the kitchen carrying a tray with drinks, glasses, a pot of coffee, and cups, and a bowl of chips on it as* **Ozzie** *appears upstairs, coming the hall, carrying an 8-mm movie projector already loaded with film.*

Harriet   Tune her up now, Rick.

Ozzie   What's the movie about, anyway?

Harriet   It's probably scenery, don't you think? – trees and fields and those little ponds. Everything over there's so green and lovely. Enough chips, Ricky? (*All during this, they scurry about with their many preparations.*)

Rick   We gonna have pretzels, too? 'Cause if there's both pretzels and chips then there's enough chips.

Ozzie   David shoot it, or somebody else . . . ? Anybody know? I tried to peek – put a couple feet up to the light . . . (*He is at the projector.*)

Harriet   What did you see?

Ozzie   Nothing. Couldn't see a thing.

Harriet   Well, I'll just bet there's one of those lovely little ponds in it somewhere.

Ozzie   Harriet, do you know when David was talking about that trouble in Hank's hand being congenital, what did you think? You think it's possible? I don't myself. I mean, we knew Hank well. I think it's just something David got mixed up about and nobody corrected him. What do you think? Is that what you think? Whatsamatter? Oh.

Stopping, startled as he sees she is waving at him. Looking up the stairs which are behind him, he sees **David** *is there, preparing to descend.* **David** *wears his robe and a bright-colored tie.*

Harriet   Hello!

Ozzie   Oh. Hey, oh, let me give you a hand. Yes. Yes. You look good. Good to see you. (*And he is on the move to* **David** *to help him down the stairs.*) Yes, sir. I think, all things considered, I think we can figure we're over the hump now and it's all downhill and good from here on in. I mean, we've talked things over, Dave, what do you say? – The air's been cleared, that's what I mean – the wounds acknowledged, the healing begun. It's the ones that aren't acknowledged – the ones that aren't talked over they're the ones that do the deep damage. That's always what happens.

Harriet (*moving to* **David**)   I've baked a cake, David. Happy, happy being home.

David, *on his own, finds his way to a chair and sits.*

Ozzie   And we've got pop and ice and chips, and Rick is going to sing some songs.

Harriet   Maybe we can all sing along if we want.

Rick   Anything special you'd like to hear, Dave?

Ozzie   YOU just sing what you know, Rick; sing what you care for, and you'll do it best. (*As he and* **Harriet** *settle down upon the couch to listen, all smiles.*)

Rick   How about 'Baby, When I Find You'?

Harriet   Ohhh, that's such a good one.

Rick   Dave, you just listen to me go! I'm gonna build! (*And there is an excited lead into the song.*) I'm gonna build, build, build. (*And he sings.*)

> Baby, when I find you,
> never, gonna stand behind you,
> gonna, gonna lead you
> softly at the start,
> gently by the heart,
> Sweet . . . Love . . . !
>
> Slipping softly to the sea
> you and me both mine
> wondrous as a green
> growing forest vine . . .
>
> Baby, when I find you,
> never, gonna stand behind you,
> gonna, gonna lead you
> softly at the start,
> gently by the heart,
> Sweet . . . Love . . . !
> Baby, when I find you.

Ozzie (*as both he and* **Harriet** *clap and laugh*)   Ohhh, great, Rick, great, you burn me up with envy, honest to God.

Harriet   It was just so wonderful. Oh, thank you so much.

Rick   I just love to do it so much, you know?

Ozzie   Has he got something goin' for him, Dave? Huh? Hey! You don't even have a drink. Take this one; take mine! (*Now they hurry back and forth from* **David** *to the table.*)

Harriet   And here's some cake.

Ozzie   How 'bout some pretzels, Dave?

Rick   Tell me what you'd like to hear.

David   I'd like to sing. (*This stops them. They stare at* **David** *for a beat of silence.*)

Rick   What?

Ozzie   What's that?

David   I have something I'd like to sing.

Rick   Dave, you don't sing.

David (*reaching at the air*)   I'd like to use the guitar, if I could.

Harriet   What are you saying?

Ozzie   C'mon, you couldn't carry a tune in a bucket and you know it. Rick's the singer, Rick and your mom.

Not really listening, thinking that his father has gotten everything back to normal, **Rick** *strums and strums the guitar, drifting nearer to* **David**.

C'mon now, Rick, let's go! That can't be all we're gonna hear.

David   You're so selfish, Rick; your hair is black; it glistens. You smile. You sing. People think you are the songs you sing. They never see you. Give me the guitar. (*And he clamps his hand closed on the guitar, stopping the music.*)

Rick   Mom, what's wrong with Dave?

David   Give it to me.

Rick   Listen, you eat your cake and drink your drink and if you still wanna, I'll let you.

David *stands, straining to the take the guitar.*

David   Now!

Harriet   Ozzie, make David behave.

Ozzie   Don't you play too roughly . . .

David   Ricky . . .

Rick I don't think he's playing, Dad.

*As **David**, following **Rick**, bumps into a chair.*

Ozzie You watch out what you're doing . . .

David *drops his glass on the floor, grabs the guitar.*

Rick You got cake all over your fingers, you'll get it all sticky, the strings all sticky – (*Struggling desperately to keep his guitar.*) Just tell me what you want to hear, I'll do it for you!

Harriet What is it? What's wrong?

David GIVE ME! GIVE ME!

Ozzie David . . . !

David *wrenches the guitar from **Rick**'s hands, sends **Rick** sprawling and loops the strap of the guitar over his shoulder, smiling, smiling.*

Harriet Ohhhh, no, no, you're ruining everything. What's wrong with you?

Ozzie I thought we were gonna have a nice party –

David We are!

Ozzie No, no, I mean a NICE party – one where everybody's happy!

David I'm happy. I'm singing. Don't you see them? Don't you see them?

Ozzie Pardon, Dave?

Harriet What . . . are you saying?

David (*changing, turning*) I have home movies. I thought you knew.

Harriet Well . . . we do.

Ozzie Movies?

David Yes, I took them.

Rick I thought you wanted to sing.

Ozzie   I mean, they're what's planned, Dave. That's what's up. The projector's all wound and ready. I don't know what you had to get so worked up for.

Harriet   Somebody set up the screen.

Ozzie   Sure, sure. No need for all that yelling.

David   I'll narrate.

Ozzie   Fine, sure. What's it about, anyway?

Harriet   Are you in it?

Ozzie   Ricky, plug it in. C'mon, c'mon.

David   It's a kind of story.

Rick   What about my guitar?

David   No.

Ozzie   We oughta have some popcorn, though.

Harriet   Oh, yes, what a dumb movie house, no popcorn, huh, Rick!

Rick   Pretty dumb, Dad. (*As he switches off the lights.*)

Ozzie   Let her rip, Dave.

David *turns on the projector;* **Ozzie** *is hurrying back to a seat.*

Ozzie   Ready when you are, C.B.

Harriet   SHHHHHHH!

Ozzie   Let her rip, C.B. I want a new contract, C.B.

The projector runs, flickering, the screen blank except for a greenish glare, and an intense flickering.

Harriet   Ohhh, what's the matter? It didn't come out, there's nothing there.

David   Of course there is.

Harriet   Noooo . . . It's all funny.

David   Look.

Ozzie It's underexposed, Dave.

David No. Look. (*Moving nearer.*)

Harriet What?

David They hang in the trees. They hang by their wrists half-severed by the wire.

Ozzie Pardon me, Dave?

Harriet I'm going to put on the lights.

David NOOOOOO! LOOK! (*He uses his cane to point to the flickering screen with great specificity as if the events are there.*) They hang in the greenish haze afflicted by insects; a woman and a man, middle-aged, they don't shout or cry. He's too small. Look: He seems all bone, shame in his eyes that his wife has come even here with him, skinny also as a broom and her hair straight and black, hanging to mask her eyes.

Zung *drifts into the room.*

Ozzie I don't know what you're doing, David; there's nothing up there – I mean, it just didn't –

David LOOK! (*And he points.*) They are all bone and pain, uncontoured and ugly but for the peculiar melon swelling in her middle which is her pregnancy – which they do not see – Look! These soldiers who have found her, as they do not see that she is not dead but only dying until saliva and blood bubble at her lips. Look . . . ! And yet she dies. Though a doctor is called in to remove the bullet-shot baby she would have preferred to keep since she was dying and it was dead.

And **Zung**, *silently, drifting, picks up a soda and drinks, watching the movie.*

In fact, as it turned out they would have all been better off left to hang as they had been strung on the wire – he with the back of his head blown off and she – the rifle jammed exactly and deeply up into her and a bullet fired directly into the child living there. For they ended each buried in a separate place; the husband by chance alone was returned to their village, while the wife was dumped into an alien nearby plot of dirt, while the child, too small a piece of meat, was burned. (*He strums the guitar.*) Thrown into fire as the shattered legs and arms cut off of men are burned. There is an oven. It is not a ceremony. It's the disposal of garbage . . . !

Harriet *gets to her feet, marches to the projector, pulls the plug.*

Harriet It's so awful the things those yellow people do to one another. Yellow people hanging yellow people. Isn't that right? Ozzie, I told you – animals – Christ burn them. David, don't let it hurt you. All the things you saw. People aren't themselves in war. I mean like that sticking that gun into that poor woman and then shooting that poor little baby, that's not human. That's inhuman. It's inhuman, barbaric and uncivilized and inhuman. It's inhuman. It's inhuman and barbaric and uncivilized.

David I'm thirsty.

Harriet For what? Tell me. Water? Or would you like some milk? How about some milk?

David (*shaking his head*) No.

Harriet Or would you like some orange juice? All golden and little bits of ice.

David Coffee.

Harriet Coffee. Cream only, right? No sugar. (*As she moves to prepare the coffee for him.*)

Ozzie Just all those words and that film with no picture and these poor people hanging somewhere so you can bring them home like this house is a meat house – what do you think you're doing?

Harriet Oh, Ozzie, no, it's not that – no – he's just young, a young boy and he's been through terrible terrible things and now he's home, with his family he loves, just trying to speak to those he loves – just –

David Yes! (*Leaping as if he has suddenly understood something, his* *hand waving the cane so it almost hits* **Ozzie**.) That's right; yes. What I mean is, yes, of course, that's what I am.

And the cane waves, knocking knickknacks, hitting a lamp, as **Harriet** *scurries about, trying to catch and correct these items before they break as* **David** *advances on* **Ozzie**, *who backs up.*

A young . . . blind man in a room . . . in a house in the dark, raising nothing in a gesture of no meaning toward two voices who are not speaking of a certain . . . incredible . . . CON-NECTION!

Rick   Listen, everybody, I hate to rush off like this, but I gotta. Night.

All stare, and **Rick** *leaps up, running for the stairs.*

Harriet   Good night, Rick. Good night.

Ozzie   Good night.

David (*strumming the guitar*)   Because I talk of certain things . . . don't think I did them. Murderers don't even know that murder happens.

Harriet   What are you saying? No, no. (*As she brings* **David** *the coffee.*) We're a family, that's all – we've had a little trouble – David, you've got to stop – please – no more yelling. Just be happy and home like all the others – why can't you?

David (*singing*)   You mean take some old man to a ditch of water, shove his head under, and talk of cars and money till his feeble pawing stops and then head on home to go in and out of doors and drive cars and sing sometimes. (*He stops singing.*) I left her where people are thin and small all their lives. (*The beginning of realization.*) Or did you think it was a place . . . like this? Sinks and kitchens all the world over? Is that what you believe? Water from faucets, light from wires? Trucks, telephones, TV. Ricky sings and sings, but if I were to cut his throat, he would no longer and you would miss him – you would miss his singing. We're hoboes! (*And it is the first time in his life he has ever thought these things.*) We make . . . signs . . . in the dark. You know yours. I understand my own. We share

. . . (*And he takes the coffee from her, or picks it up if she has set it down.*)
. . . coffee! (*He takes a sip and starts for the stairs.*) I'm going up to
bed . . . now. I'm very, very . . . tired.

Ozzie   Well . . . you have a good sleep, son . . .

David   Yes, I think I'll sleep in.

(**Zung** *follows him up the stairs into his room.*)

Ozzie   You do as you please . . .

David   Good night.

Harriet   Good night.

Ozzie   Good night.

Harriet   Good night. (*Slight pause.*) You get a good rest.
(*Silence.*) Try . . . (*Silence; they stand.*) I'm . . . hungry . . . Ozzie
. . . Are you hungry?

Ozzie   Hungry . . . ?

Harriet   Yes.

Ozzie   No. Oh, no.

Harriet   How do you feel? You look a little peaked. Do you
feel all right?

Ozzie   I'm fine; I'm fine.

Harriet   You look funny.

Ozzie   Really. No. How about yourself?

Harriet   I'm never sick; you know that. Just a little sleepy.

Ozzie   Well, that's no wonder. It's been a long day.

Harriet   Yes, it has.

Ozzie   No wonder.

Harriet   Good night. (*She is climbing the stairs toward bed.*)

Ozzie   Good night.

Harriet   Don't stay up too late now.

Ozzie   Do you know when he was waving that cane and he pointed it at me? I couldn't breathe. I felt for an instant that I might never breathe.

Harriet   Mmmmmmmm. Ohhh, I'm so sleepy. So, sooooo sleepy. Aren't you sleepy?

Ozzie (*to make her answer*)   Harriet! I couldn't breathe.

Harriet   WHAT DO YOU WANT? TEACHING HIM SPORTS AND FIGHTING. (*This primal rage should be the first shattering of her motherly, self-sacrificing stance.*) WHAT . . . OZZIE . . . DO YOU WANT?

Ozzie   Well . . . I was wondering . . . Do we have any aspirin down here . . . or are they all upstairs?

Harriet   I thought you said you felt well.

Ozzie   Well, I do. It's just a tiny headache. Hardly worth mentioning.

Harriet   There's aspirin in the desk.

Ozzie (*crossing*)   Big drawer?

Harriet   Second drawer, right-hand side.

Ozzie   Get me a glass of water, would you, please?

Harriet   Of course. (*Getting a nearby glass left over from the party.*)

Ozzie   Thank you. It's not much of a headache, actually. Actually, it's just a tiny headache. (*He pops the pills into his mouth and drinks to wash them down; he swallows.*)

Harriet   Aspirin makes your stomach bleed. Did you know that? Nobody knows why. It's part of how it works. It just does it; makes you bleed. This extremely tiny series, of hemorrhages in those delicate inner tissues. It's like those thin membranes begin, in a very minor way to sweat blood and you bleed; inside yourself you bleed. (*She crosses away.*)

Ozzie   That's not true. None of that. You made all that up . . . Where are you going?

With a raincoat on, **Harriet** *is moving out the door.*

I mean, are you going out? Where . . . are you off to?

Harriet *is gone out the door.*

Goddammit, there's something going on around here; don't you want to know what it is? (*Yelling at the shut door.*) I want to know what it is. (*Turning, marching to the phone, dialing.*) I want to know what's going on around here. I want to – I got to. Police. That's right, goddammit – I want one of you people to get on out to 717 Dunbar and do some checking, some checking at 717 – What? Ohhh – (*Hissing.*) Christ . . . ! just a second, I gotta be – (*And he pulls a handkerchief from his pocket and covers the mouthpiece.*) I mean, they got a kid living there who just got back from the war and something's going on and I want to know what it – No, I don't wanna give my name! It's them, not me – they're the ones who are acting strange! They're acting very goddamn strange, the whole lot of them. It doesn't matter who I am! It only – (*As it seems they've hung up on him.*) Hey! HEY! HEY!

Rick (*popping in at the top of the hallway*)　Hey, Dad! How you doin'?

Ozzie　Oh, Rick! Hi!

Rick　Hi! How you doin'? (*He is heading down the stairs and toward the door.*)

Ozzie　Fine. Just fine.

Rick　Good.

Ozzie　How you doin', Rick?

Rick　Well, I'll see you later.

Ozzie (*running with the guitar* **David** *left*)　I WANT YOU TO TEACH ME GUITAR!

Rick　What? (*Faltering.*)

Ozzie　I want you to teach me . . . guitar . . . ! To play it.

Rick　Sure. Okay.

Ozzie   I want to learn to play it. They've always been a kind of mystery to me, pianos . . . guitars.

Rick   Mystery?

Ozzie (*trying, awkwardly, desperately*)   I mean, what do you think? Do you ever have to think what your fingers should he doing? What I mean is do you ever have to say – I don't know what – 'This finger goes there and this other one does' – I mean, 'It's on THIS ridge, now I chord all the strings and then switch it all.' See? And do you have to tell yourself, 'Now switch it all – first finger this ridge – second finger, down – third – somewhere.' I mean, does that kind of thing ever happen? I mean, HOW DO YOU PLAY IT? I keep having this notion of wanting some . . . thing . . . some material thing, and I've built it. And then there's this feeling I'm of value, that I'm on my way – I mean, moving – and I'm going to come to something eventually, some kind of achievement. All this feelings of a child . . . in me . . . they shoot through me and then they're gone and they're not anything . . . anymore. But it's a . . . wall that I want . . . I think. I see myself doing it sometimes. All brick and stone. Coils of steel. And then I finish . . . and the success of it is monumental and people come from far. To see . . . To look. They applaud. Ricky . . . teach me.

Rick   Ahhh . . . what, Dad?

Ozzie   Guitar, guitar.

Rick   Oh; sure. Great. First you start with the basic 'C' chord. You put the first finger on the second string . . .

Ozzie   But that's what I'm talking about. You don't do that. I know you don't.

Rick (*thinking he has misunderstood*)   Oh.

Ozzie   You just pick it up and play it. I don't have time for all that you're saying. That's what I've been telling you.

Rick   Well, maybe some other day then. (*On his way for the door; all this dialogue, rapid, overlapping.*)

Ozzie   What?

Rick   Maybe Mom'll wanna learn, too.

Ozzie   No, no.

Rick   Just me and you then.

Ozzie   Right. Me and you.

Rick   I'll see you later.

Ozzie   What? Where are you going?

Rick   Maybe tomorrow we can do it.

Ozzie   NO.

Rick   Well, maybe the next day then. (*And he is – gone out the door.*)

Ozzie   NO, NOW! NOW! (*And the door slams shut.*) I grew too old too quick. (*He turns to the audience.*) It was just a town I thought and no one remained to test me. I didn't even know it was leaving I was doing. I thought I'd go away and come back. Not leave. (*And he looks up at* **David**'*s room.*) YOU SONOFABITCH. (*And he is running up to* **David**'*s room.*) NOT LEAVE! (*And he bursts into* **David**'*s room.*) Restless, Dave; restless. Got a lot on my mind. Some of us can't just lay around, you know. You said I left that town like I was wrong, but I was right. A man proved himself by leaving, by going out into the world; he tested himself. So I went and then I ended up in the goddamn Depression, what about that? I stood in goddamn lines of people begging bread and soup. You're not the only one who's had troubles. All of us, by God, David, think about that a little. Just give somebody beside yourself some goddamn thought for a change. (*Stepping out the door, slamming it. He turns to the audience; they are his friends.*) I'm expecting I'll step into the best part of my life and I walk right into the Depression. I lived in goddamn dirty fields with thousands of other men. Baffled. Wondering what hit us. We made tents of our coats. Traveled on freight trains. Again and again . . . the whole of the length of this country, soot in my fingers, riding the rails. A bum, a hobo, but young. And then one day . . . there's a brakeman – this brakeman, who sees me hunched down in that railroad cattle car and he orders me off. He stands distant, ordering that I jump . . . ! I don't understand, and then he stops speaking . . . and . . . when he speaks again, there's pain is in his eyes and voice – 'You're a runner,' he says, 'Christ, I didn't know you were a runner.' Somehow he knows me. And he moves to embrace me, and with both hands he takes me and lifts me high above his head – holds me there, trembling, then flings me far out and I fall, I roll. All in the air, then slam down breathless, raw from the cinders . . . bruised and dizzy at the outskirts of this town. And I'm here, I'm gone from that other town. I'm here. (*Perhaps he has descended the stairs, and he looks around the house now.*) Here. (*He settles down on the couch.*) I make friends. We have good times even though things are rough. We point young girls out in the street. I start thinking about them; I start having dreams of horses and breasts and crotches. And then one day the feeling is in me that I must see a train go by and I'll get on it or I won't, something will happen, but halfway down to where I was thrown off, I see how the grass growing in among the ties is tall, the rails rusted. Grass grows in abundance. Trains no longer come that way; they all go some other way . . . and far behind me, I turn to see Harriet, young and lovely, weaving among the weeds. I feel the wonder of her body moving toward me. She's the thing I'll enter to find my future, I think. Yes. It's her. 'Yes,' I yell. 'Sonofabitch! Bring her here! C'mon! Bring her on! It's my life! I can do it!' Swollen with pride, screaming and yelling, I stand there: 'I'm ready. I'm ready . . . I'm ready.' (*Arms spread, he yells, falling back onto the couch.*)

Blackout. Music.

Lights slowly up. **Ozzie** *sleeps on the couch as* **Rick** *comes in from the kitchen with a plate of several sandwiches and a bottle of Pepsi. He settles in an armchair near the sleeping* **Ozzie**. **Zung**, *is in* **David**'s *room.* **David** *lies in his bed.* **Harriet**, *in a blue robe, comes along the upstairs hallway.*

Harriet   Have you seen my crossword puzzle book?

Rick   In the bathroom, Mom.

Harriet   Bathroom . . . ? Did I leave it there? (*Turning, heading back up the stairs.*)

Rick   Guess so, Mom.

David *sits abruptly up in his bed as if at a sudden, frightening sound.*

David   What? What? Who's there? There's someone there?

Rick *looks up;* **David** *is standing, poking the air with his cane.*

David   Who's there?

Rick   Whatsamatter?

David   What? (*He opens the door to his room.*)

Rick   It's just me and Dad, and Dad's sleeping.

David   Sleeping? Is he?

Rick   On the davenport. You want me to wake him?

David   Nooo . . . noooo. (*Moving swiftly, to descend to the living room.*)

Rick   Hey, could I get some pictures, Dave? Would you mind?

David   Of course not. No.

Rick (*dashing off up the stairs while* **David** *gropes to find the couch*) Let me just go get some film and some flashes, okay?

David (*standing behind the couch on which* **Ozzie** *sleeps, looking after* **Rick**)   Sure.

Ozzie   Pardon? Par . . . don?

David (*whispering into the ear of his father*)   I think you should know I've begun to hate you. I don't think you can tell me any more. I must tell you. Does that disturb you? (**Ozzie** *stirs.*) If I had been an orphan with no one to count on me, I would have stayed there. (**Ozzie** *stirs more.*) Restless, are you? You think us good, and yet we steal all you have.

Ozzie   Good . . . ole . . . Hank.

David   No, no.

Ozzie   . . . nooo . . . nooooooo. . . .

David   Her name was Zung. Zung. She would tell me you would not like her – she would touch her fingers to her eyes and nose, and she knew how I must feel sometimes just like you.

Ozzie   Ohhh, noooo . . . sleeping . . .

David   You must hear me. It is only fraud that keeps us sane. I swear it.

Ozzie   David, sleeping . . . ! Oh, oh . . .

David   It's not innocence I have lost! What is it I have lost?

Ozzie   Oh . . . . oh . . .

Rick *has appeared high in the hallway, where he hesitates.*

David   Don't you know? Do you see her in your sleep? I think I do sometimes.

Rick *(hurrying down)*   I meant to get some good shots at the party, but I never got a chance the way things turned out. You can stay right there.

David *(moving toward the chair on which rests **Rick***'s guitar)*   I'll sit, all right?

Rick *rushes to save the guitar.*

Rick   Sure. How you feelin', anyway, Dave? I mean, honest ta God, I'm hopin' you get better. Everybody is. I mean *(Takes a picture.)* . . . you're not gonna go talkin' anymore crazy like about that guitar and all that, are you? You know what I mean. Not to Mom and Dad, anyway. It scares 'em and then I get scared and I don't like it, okay? *(He moves on, taking more pictures.)*

David   Sure. That guitar business wasn't serious, anyway, Rick. None of that. It was all just a little joke I felt like playing, a kind of little game. I was only trying to show you how I hate you.

Rick   Huh? (*Stunned, he stares.*)

David   To see you die is why I live, Rick.

Rick   Oh.

Harriet (*appearing from off upstairs, the crossword puzzle book is in her hands*)   Goodness gracious, Ricky, it was just where you said it would be, though I'm sure I don't know how it got there because I didn't put it there. Hello, David.

David   Hello.

Ozzie   OHHHHHHHHHHHHHHHH! (*Screaming, he comes awake, falling off the couch.*) Oh, boy, what a dream! Oh . . . (*Trying to get to his feet, but collapsing.*) Ohhhhhhh! God, leg's asleep. Jesus! (*And he flops about, sits there, rubbing his leg.*) Ohhhh, everybody. Scared hell out of me, that dream. I hollered. Did you hear me? And my leg's asleep, too.

He hits the leg, stomps the floor. **Harriet** *sits on the couch, working her crossword puzzle book.* **Rick**, *slumped into a chair, reads a comic.* **David**, *though, leans forward in his chair. He wants to know the effect of his whispering on his father.*

Did anybody hear me holler?

Harriet   Not me.

Rick   What did you dream about, Dad?

Ozzie   I don't remember, but it was awful. (*Stamping his foot.*) Ohhhh, wake up, wake up. Hank was in it, though. And Dave. They stood over me, whispering – I could feel how they hated me.

Rick   That really happened; he really did that, Dad.

Ozzie   Who did?

Rick   What you said.

Ozzie   No. No. I was sleeping. It scared me awful in my sleep. I'm still scared, honest to God, it was so awful.

David   It's that sleeping in funny positions, Dad. It's that sleeping in some place that's not a bed.

Ozzie   Pardon?

David   Makes you dream funny. What did Hank look like?

Harriet   Ozzie, how do you spell 'Apollo'?

Ozzie   What?

Rick   Jesus, Dad, Schroeder got three home runs, you hear about that? Two in the second of the first and one in the third of the second. Goddamn, if he don't make MVP in the National, I'll eat my socks. You hear about that, Dad?

Ozzie   Yes, I did. Yes.

Rick   He's somethin'.

Ozzie   A pro.

Harriet   Ozzie, can you think of a four-letter word that starts with 'G' and ends with 'B'?

Rick   Glub.

Harriet   Glub?

Ozzie (*almost simultaneously*)   Glub?

Rick   It's a cartoon word. Cartoon people say it when they're drowning. G-L-U-B.

Ozzie (*on his feet now*)   Ricky. Ricky, I was wondering . . . when I was sleeping, were my eyes open? Was I seeing?

Rick   I didn't notice, Dad.

Harriet   'Glub' doesn't work, Rick.

Rick   Try GRUB. That's what sourdoughs call their food. It's G-R –

Ozzie   WAIT A MINUTE!

Rick   G-R –

Ozzie   ALL OF YOU WAIT A MINUTE! LISTEN!
Listen. I mean, I look for explanations. I look inside myself. For an explanation. I mean, I look inside MY self. As I would

look into water or the sky . . . the ocean. They're silver.
Answers . . . silver and elusive . . . like fish. But if you can
catch them in the sea . . . book them as they flash by, snatch
them up, drag them down like birds from the sky . . . against
all their struggle . . . when you re adrift and starving they . . .
can help you live. (*He falters; he stands among them, straining to go
further, searching for some sign of comprehension in their faces.*)

Rick   MOM . . . Dad's hungry . . . I think. He wants some
fish, I –

Ozzie   SHUT UP!

Rick (*hurt deeply*)   Dad?

Ozzie   PIECE OF SHIT! SHUT UP! SHUT UP!

Harriet   Ozzie . . .

Ozzie (*roaring down at **David***)   I don't want to hear about
her. I'm not interested in her. You did what you did and I was
no part of it. You understand me? I don't want to hear any
more about her! Look at him. Sitting there. Listening. I'm
tired of hearing you, Dave. You understand that? I'm tired of
hearing you and your crybaby voice and your crybaby stories.
And your crybaby slobbering and your – (*And his voice is
possessed with astonished loathing.*) LOOK . . . AT . . . HIM! YOU
MAKE ME WANT TO VOMIT! HARRIET! YOU(*And he
whirls on **Harriet**.*) YOU! Your internal organs – your internal
female organs – they've got some kind of poison in them.
They're backing up some kind of rot into the world. I think
you ought to have them cut out of you. I MEAN, I JUST
CAN'T STOP THINKING ABOUT IT. I JUST CAN'T
STOP THINKING ABOUT IT. LITTLE BITTY CHINKY
KIDS YOU WANTED TO HAVE! LITTLE BITTY
CHINKY YELLOW KIDS! DIDN'T YOU! FOR OUR
GRANDCHILDREN! (*And he slaps **David** with one hand.*)
LITTLE BITTY YELLOW PUFFY – (*He breaks, groping for the
word.*) . . . creatures . . . ! FOR OUR GRANDCHILDREN!
(*Slaps **David** again, again.*) THAT'S ALL YOU CARED!

David, *a howl in throat, has stood up. And, as he does,* **Ozzie**,
overcome by his own outburst, collapses onto the couch.

Harriet   Ohhh, Ozzie, God forgive you the cruelty of your words. All children are God's children.

David *is standing rigidly as the downstairs front door blows open, and in fierce and sudden light above him, the girl,* **Zung**, *is aflame of light stepping steps forward to the edge of his room and he is looking up at her.*

David   I didn't know you were here. I didn't know. I'll buy you clothing. I've lived with them all my life. I'll make them not hate you. I'll buy you books. (*And she is moving toward him now, coming down the stairs.*) They will see you. The seasons will amaze you. Texas is enormous. Ohio is sometimes green. There will be time. We will learn to speak. And it will be as it was in that moment when we looked in the dark and our eyes were tongues that could speak and the hurting . . . all of it . . . stopped, and there was total understanding in you of me and in me of you . . . and . . . (*They are face to face now, and he is reaching toward her in a tentative way, but he does not touch her.*) . . . such delight in your eyes that I felt it. Yet . . . I . . . discarded you. (*And she turns, moving away and toward the door*) I discarded you. Forgive me. (*He moves after her.*) You moved to leave as if you were struggling not to move, not leave. 'She's the thing most possibly of value in my life,' I said. 'She is garbage and filth and I must get her back if I wish to live. Sickness, I must cherish her.' Zung, there were old voices inside me I had trusted all my life as if they were my own. I didn't know I shouldn't hear them. So reasonable and calm they seemed a source of wisdom. 'She's all of everything impossible made possible, cast her down,' they said. And I did as they told; I did it, and now I know that I am not awake but asleep, and in my sleep . . . there is nothing . . . (*He is there before her, between her and the door, his back to the door. And he takes her in his arms.*) . . . nothing . . . ! What do you want from me to make you stay? I'll do it. I'd do what you want!

Rick   Lookee here, Dad. Cheer up! Cheer up! (*Setting up to take a picture as he crouches at the couch before his father, camera in hand.*) Lookee here, Dad. Cheer up! Cheer up!

David   Noooooooooooo . . . ! STAAAAAAY!

David *slams the door shut, keeping* **Zung** *inside and enfolding her again in his arms, as* **Rick** *takes the picture and there is a huge flash. A slide of* **Ozzie** *appears on the screen, a close-up, of his pained and puzzled face as the lights go black and only the slide of* **Ozzie** *is visible in the dark.*

Voice of Rick   That's a good one. Thata boy.

Voice of Ozzie   No.

Voice of Rick   Sure, Dad. Sure.

The slide blinks out. Music.

Streamers

For Wyle Walker and Mike Nichols

Master Ssu, Master Yü, Master Li and Master Lai

All at once Master Yü fell ill, and Master Ssu went to ask how he was. 'Amazing!' exclaimed Master Yü. 'Look, the Creator is making me all crookedly! My back sticks up like a hunchback's so that my vital organs are on top of me. My chin is hidden down around my navel, my shoulders are up above my head, and my pigtail points at the sky. It must be due to some dislocation of the forces of the yin and the yang . . .'

'Do you resent it?' asked Master Ssu.

'Why, no,' replied Master Yü. 'What is there to resent . . .?'

Then suddenly Master Lai also fell ill. Gasping for breath, he lay at the point of death. His wife and children gathered round in a circle and wept. Master Li, who had come to find out how he was, said to them, 'Shoooooo! Get back! Don't disturb the process of change.'

And he leaned against the doorway and chatted with Master Lai. 'How marvelous the Creator is!' he exclaimed. 'What is he going to make out of you next? Where is he going to send you? Will he make you into a rat's liver? Will he make you into a bug's arm?'

'A child obeys his father and mother and goes wherever he is told, east or west, south or north,' said Master Lai. 'And the yin and the yang – how much more are they to a man than father or mother! Now that they have brought me to the verge of death, how perverse it would be of me to refuse to obey them . . . So now I think of heaven and earth as a great furnace and the Creator as a skilled smith. What place could he send me that would not be all right? I will go off peacefully to sleep, and then with a start I will wake up.'

– Chuang-Tzu

They so mean around here, they steal your sweat.
– Sonny Liston

Streamers was first performed at the Long Wharf Theater in January 1976. The cast was as follows:

Martin	Michael-Raymond O'Keefe
Richie	Peter Evans
Carlyle	Joe Fields
Billy	John Heard
Roger	Herbert Jefferson, Jr
Cokes	Dolph Sweet
Rooney	Kenneth McMillan
M.P. Lieutenant	Stephen Mendillo
PFC Hinson (M.P.)	Ron Siebert
PFC Clark (M.P.)	Michael Kell

Directed by Mike Nichols
Set by Tony Walton
Costumes by Bill Walker
Lighting by Ronald Wallace

Act One

*The set is a large cadre room thrusting angularly toward the audience.
The floor is wooden and brown. Brightly waxed in places, it is worn and
dull in other sections. The back wall is brown and angled. There are two
lights at the center of the ceiling. They hang covered by green metal shades.
Against the back wall and to the stage-right side are three wall lockers,
side by side. Stage center in the back wall is the door, the only entrance to
the room. It opens onto a hallway that runs off to the latrines, showers,
other cadre rooms, and larger barracks rooms. There are three bunks.*
Billy's *bunk is parallel to* **Roger**'s *bunk. They are upstage and on
either side of the room, and face downstage.* **Richie**'s *bunk is downstage
and at a right angle to* **Billy**'s *bunk. At the foot of each bunk is a green
wooden footlocker. There is a floor outlet near* **Roger**'s *bunk. He uses it
for his radio. A reading lamp is clamped onto the metal piping at the head
of* **Richie**'s *bunk. A wooden chair stands beside the wall lockers. Two
mops hang in the stage-left corner near a trash can.*

It is dusk as the lights rise on the room. **Richie** *is seated and bowed
forward warily on his bunk. He wears his long-sleeved khaki summer
dress uniform. Upstage behind him is* **Martin**, *a thin, dark young man,
pacing, worried. A white towel stained red with blood is wrapped around
his wrist. He paces several steps and falters, stops. He stands there.*

Richie   Honest to God, Martin, I don't know what to say
anymore. I don't know what to tell you.

Martin (*beginning to pace again*)   I mean it. I just can't stand it.
Look at me.

Richie   I know.

Martin   I hate it.

Richie   We've got to make up a story. They'll ask you a
hundred questions.

Martin   Do you know how I hate it?

Richie   Everybody does. Don't you think I hate it, too?

Martin   I enlisted, though. I enlisted and I hate it.

Richie   I enlisted, too.

Martin   I vomit every morning. I get the dry heaves. In the middle of every night. (*He flops down on the corner of* **Billy**'s *bed and sits there, slumped forward, shaking his head.*)

Richie   You can stop that. You can.

Martin   No.

Richie   You're just scared. It's just fear.

Martin   They're all so mean; they're all so awful. I've got two years to go. Just thinking about it is going to make me sick. I thought it would be different from the way it is.

Richie   But you could have died, for God's sake. (*Turning, now he is facing* **Martin**.)

Martin   I just wanted out.

Richie   I might not have found you, though. I might not have come up here.

Martin   I don't care. I'd be out.

The door opens and a black man in filthy fatigues – they are grease-stained and dark with sweat – stands there. He is **Carlyle***, looking about.* **Richie***, seeing him, rises and moves toward him.*

Richie   No. Roger isn't here right now.

Carlyle   Who isn't?

Richie   He isn't here.

Carlyle   They tole me a black boy livin' in here. I don't see him. (*He looks suspiciously about the room.*)

Richie   That's what I'm saying. He isn't here. He'll be back later. You can come back later. His name is Roger.

Martin   I slit my wrist. (*Thrusting out the bloody, towel-wrapped wrist toward* **Carlyle**.)

Richie   Martin! Jesus!

Martin   I did.

Richie   He's kidding. He's kidding.

Carlyle   What was his name? Martin? (*He is confused, and the confusion has made him angry. He moves toward* **Martin**.) You Martin?

Martin   Yes.

As **Billy**, *a white in his mid-twenties, blond and trim, appears in the door, whistling, carrying a slice of pie on a paper napkin. Sensing something, he falters, looks at* **Carlyle**, *then* **Richie**.

Billy   Hey, what's goin' on?

Carlyle (*turning, leaving*)   Nothin', man. Not a thing.

Billy *looks questioningly at* **Richie**. *Then, after placing the piece of pie on the chair beside the door, he crosses to his footlocker.*

Richie   He came in looking for Roger, but he didn't even know his name.

Billy (*sitting on his footlocker, he starts taking off his shoes*)   How come you weren't at dinner, Rich? I brought you a piece of pie. Hey, Martin.

Martin *thrusts out his towel-wrapped wrist.*

Martin   I cut my wrist, Billy.

Richie   Oh, for God's sake, Martin! (*He whirls away.*)

Billy   Huh?

Martin   I did.

Richie   You are disgusting, Martin.

Martin   No. It's the truth. I did. I am not disgusting.

Richie   Well, maybe it isn't disgusting, but it certainly is disappointing.

Billy   What are you guys talking about? (*Sitting there, he really doesn't know what is going on.*)

Martin   I cut my wrists, I slashed them, and Richie is pretending I didn't.

Richie   I am not. And you only cut one wrist and you didn't slash it.

Martin   I can't stand the army anymore, Billy. (*He is moving now to petition* **Billy**, *and* **Richie** *steps between them.*)

Richie   Billy, listen to me. This is between Martin and me.

Martin   It's between me and the army, Richie.

Richie (*taking* **Martin** *by the shoulders as* **Billy** *is now trying to get near* **Martin**)   Let's just go outside and talk, Martin. You don't know what you're saying.

Billy   Can I see? I mean, did he really do it?

Richie   No!

Martin   I did.

Billy   That's awful. Jesus. Maybe you should go to the infirmary.

Richie   I washed it with peroxide. It's not deep. Just let us be. Please. He just needs to straighten out his thinking a little, that's all.

Billy   Well, maybe I could help him?

Martin   Maybe he could.

Richie (*suddenly pushing at* **Martin**. **Richie** *is angry and exasperated. He wants* **Martin** *out of the room*)   Get out of here, Martin. Billy, you do some push-ups or something.

Having been pushed toward the door, **Martin** *wanders out.*

Billy   No.

Richie   I know what Martin needs. (*Whirls and rushes into the hall after* **Martin**, *leaving* **Billy** *scrambling to get his shoes on.*)

Billy   You're no doctor, are you? I just want to make sure he doesn't have to go to the infirmary, then I'll leave you alone.

(*One shoe on, he grabs up the second and runs out the door into the hall after them.*) Martin! Martin, wait up!

Silence. The door has been left open. Fifteen or twenty seconds pass. Then someone is heard coming down the hall. He is singing 'Get a Job' and trying to do the voices and harmonies of a vocal group. **Roger**, *a tall, well-built black in long-sleeved khakis, comes in the door. He has a laundry bag over his shoulder, a pair of clean civilian trousers and a shirt on a hanger in his other hand. After dropping the bag on his bed, he goes to his wall locker, where he carefully hangs up the civilian clothes. Returning to the bed, he picks up the laundry and then, as if struck, he throws the bag down on the bed, tears off his tie, and sits down angrily on the bed. For a moment, with his head in his hands, he sits there. Then, resolutely, he rises, takes up the position of attention, and simply topples forward, his hands leaping out to break his fall at the last instant and putting him into the push-up position. Counting in a hissing, whispering voice, he does ten push-ups before giving up and flopping onto his belly. He simply doesn't have the will to do any more. Lying there, he counts rapidly on.*

Roger   Fourteen, fifteen, Twenty. Twenty-five.

Billy *shuffling dejectedly back in, sees* **Roger** *lying there.* **Roger** *springs to his feet, heads toward his footlocker, out of which he takes an ashtray and a pack of cigarettes.*

Roger   You come in this area, you come in here marchin', boy: standin' tall.

Billy *having gone to his wall locker, is tossing a* Playboy *magazine onto his bunk. He will also remove a towel, a Dopp kit, and a can of foot powder.*

Billy   I was marchin'.

Roger   You call that marchin'?

Billy   I was as tall as I am; I was marchin' – what do you want?

Roger   Outa here, man; outa this goddamn typin'-terrors outfit and into some kinda real army. Or else out and free.

Billy   So go; who's stoppin' you; get out. Go on.

Roger   Ain't you a bitch.

Billy   You and me more regular army than the goddamn sergeants around this place, you know that?

Roger   I was you, Billy boy, I wouldn't be talkin' so sacrilegious so loud, or they be doin' you like they did the ole sarge.

Billy   He'll get off.

Roger   Sheee-it, he'll get off.

Sitting down on the side of his bed and facing **Billy**, **Roger** *lights up a cigarette.* **Billy** *has arranged the towel, Dopp kit and foot powder on his own bed.*

Don't you think L.B.J. want to have some sergeants in that Vietnam, man? In Disneyland, baby? Lord have mercy on the ole sarge. He goin' over there to be Mickey Mouse.

Billy   Do him a lot of good. Make a man outa him.

Roger   That's right, that's right. He said the same damn thing about himself and you, too, I do believe. You know what's the ole boy's MOS? His Military Occupation Specialty? Demolitions, baby. Expert is his name.

Billy (*taking off his shoes and beginning to work on a sore toe, he hardly looks up*)   You're kiddin' me.

Roger   Do I jive?

Billy   You mean that poor ole bastard who cannot light his own cigar for shakin' is supposed to go over there blowin' up bridges and shit. Do they wanna win this war or not, man?

Roger   Ole sarge was over in Europe in the big one, Billy. Did all kinds a bad things.

Billy (*swinging his feet up onto the bed, he sits, cutting the cuticles on his toes, powdering his feet*)   Was he drinkin' since he got the word?

Roger   Was he breathin', Billy? Was he breathin'?

Billy   Well, at least he ain't cuttin' his fuckin' wrists.

Silence. **Roger** *looks at* **Billy**, *who keeps on working.*

Man, that's the real damn army over there, ain't it? That ain't shinin' your belt buckle and standin' tall. And we might end up in it, man.

Silence. **Roger**, *rising, begins to sort his laundry.*

Roger . . . you ever ask yourself if you'd rather fight in a war where it was freezin' cold or one where there was awful snakes? You ever ask that question?

Roger   Can't say I ever did.

Billy   We used to ask it all the time. All the time. I mean, us kids sittin' out on the back porch tellin' ghost stories at night. 'Cause it was Korea time and the newspapers were fulla pictures of soldiers in snow with white frozen beards; they got these rags tied around their feet. And snakes. We hated snakes. Hated 'em. I mean, it's bad enough to be in the jungle duckin' bullets, but then you crawl right into a goddamn snake. That's awful. That's awful.

Roger   It don't sound none too good.

Billy   I got my draft notice, goddamn Vietnam didn't even exist. I mean, it existed, but not as in a war we might be in. I started crawlin' around the floor a this house where I was stayin' 'cause I'd dropped outa school, and I was goin' 'Bang, bang,' pretendin'. Jesus.

Roger   (*continuing with his laundry, he tries to joke*)   My first goddamn formation in basic, Billy, this NCO's up there jammin' away about how some a us are goin' to be dyin' in the war. I'm sayin', 'What war? What that crazy man talkin' about?'

Billy   Us, too. I couldn't believe it. I couldn't believe it. And now we got three people goin' from here.

Roger   Five.

They look at each other, and then turn away, each returning to his task.

Billy   It don't seem possible. I mean, people shootin' at you. Shootin' at you to kill you. (*Slight pause.*) It's somethin'.

Roger   What did you decide you preferred?

Billy   Huh?

Roger   Did you decide you would prefer the snakes or would you prefer the snow? 'Cause it look like it is going to be the snakes.

Billy   I think I had pretty much made my mind up on the snow.

Roger   Well, you just let 'em know that, Billy. Maybe they get one goin' special just for you up in Alaska. You can go to the Klondike. Fightin' some snowmen.

Richie bounds into the room and shuts the door as if to keep out something dreadful. He looks at **Roger** *and* **Billy** *and crosses to his wall locker, pulling off his tie as he moves. Tossing the tie into the locker, he begins unbuttoning the cuffs of his shirt.*

Richie   Hi, hi, hi, everybody. Billy, hello.

Billy   Hey.

Roger   What's happenin', Rich?

Moving to the chair beside the door, **Richie** *picks up the pie* **Billy** *left there. He will place the pie atop the locker, and then, sitting, he will remove his shoes and socks.*

Richie   I simply did this rather wonderful thing for a friend of mine, helped him see himself in a clearer, more hopeful light – a little room in his life for hope. And I feel very good. Didn't Billy tell you?

Roger   About what?

Richie   About Martin.

Roger   No.

Billy (*looking up and speaking pointedly*)   No.

Richie looks at **Billy** *and then at* **Roger**. *Richie is truly confused.*

Richie   No? No?

Billy   What do I wanna gossip about Martin for?

Richie (*really can't figure out what is going on with* **Billy***; shoes and socks in hand, he heads for his wall locker*)   Who was planning to gossip? I mean, it did happen. We could talk about it. I mean, I wasn't hearing his goddamn confession. Oh, my sister told me Catholics were boring.

Billy   Good thing I ain't one anymore.

Richie (*taking off his shirt, moves toward* **Roger**)   It really wasn't anything, Roger, except Martin made this rather desperate, pathetic gesture for attention that seems to have brought to the surface Billy's more humane and protective side. (*Reaching out, he tousles* **Billy***'s hair.*)

Billy   Man, I am gonna have to obliterate you.

Richie (*tossing his shirt into his locker*)   I don't know what you're so embarrassed about.

Billy   I just think Martin's got enough trouble without me yappin' to everybody.

Richie *has moved nearer* **Billy**, *his manner playful and teasing.*

Richie   'Obliterate'? 'Obliterate,' did you say? Oh, Billy, you better say 'shit,' 'ain't,' and 'motherfucker' real quick now, or we'll all know just how far beyond the fourth grade you went.

Roger (*having moved to his locker, into which he is placing his folded clothes*)   You hear about the ole sarge, Richard?

Billy (*grinning*)   You ain't . . . shit . . . motherfucker.

Roger (*laughing*)   All right.

Richie (*moving center and beginning to remove his trousers*)   Billy, no, no. Wit is my domain. You're in charge of sweat and running around the block.

Roger   You hear about the ole sarge?

Richie   What about the ole sarge? Oh, who cares? Let's go to a movie. Billy, wanna? Let's go. C'mon. (*Trousers off, he hurries to his locker.*)

Billy   Sure. What's playin'?

Richie   I don't know. Can't remember. Something good, though.

With a Playboy *magazine he has taken from his locker,* **Roger** *is settling down on his bunk, his back toward both* **Billy** *and* **Richie**.

Billy   You wanna go, Rog?

Richie (*in mock irritation*)   Don't ask Roger! How are we going to kiss and hug and stuff if he's there?

Billy   That ain't funny, man. (*He is stretched out on his bunk, and* **Richie** *comes bounding over to flop down and lie beside him.*)

Richie   And what time will you pick me up?

Billy (*pushes at* **Richie**, *knocking him off the bed and onto the floor*) Well, you just fall down and wait, all right?

Richie   Can I help it if I love you? (*Leaping to his feet, he will head to his locker, remove his shorts, put on a robe.*)

Roger   You gonna take a shower, Richard?

Richie   Cleanliness is nakedness, Roger.

Roger   Is that right? I didn't know that. Not too many people know that. You may be the only person in the world who know that.

Richie   And godliness is in there somewhere, of course. (*Putting a towel around his neck, he is gathering toiletries to carry to the shower.*)

Roger   You got your own way a lookin' at things, man. You cute.

Richie   That's right.

Roger   You g'wan, have a good time in that shower.

Richie   Oh, I will.

Billy (*without looking up from his feet, which he is powdering*)   And don't drop your soap.

Richie   I will if I want to. (*Already out the door, he slams it shut with a flourish.*)

Billy   Can you imagine bein' in combat with Richie – people blastin' away at you – he'd probably want to hold your hand.

Roger   Ain't he somethin'?

Billy   Who's zat?

Roger   He's all right.

Billy (*rising, heading toward his wall locker, where he will put the powder and Dopp kit*)   Sure he is, except he's livin' under water.

Looking at **Billy**, **Roger** *senses something unnerving; it makes* **Roger** *rise, and return his magazine to his footlocker.*

Roger   I think we oughta do this area, man. I think we oughta do our area. Mop and buff this floor.

Billy   You really don't think he means that shit he talks, do you?

Roger   Huh? Awwww, man . . . Billy, no.

Billy   I'd put money on it, Roger, and I ain't got much money.

Billy *is trying to face* **Roger** *with this, but* **Roger**, *seated on his bed, has turned away. He is unbuttoning his shirt.*

Roger   Man, no, no. I'm tellin' you, lad, you listen to the ole Rog. You seen that picture a that little dolly he's got in his locker? He ain't swish, man, believe me – he's cool.

Billy   It's just that ever since we been in this room, he's been different somehow. Somethin'.

Roger   No, he ain't.

Billy *turns to his bed, where he carefully starts folding the towel. Then he looks at* **Roger**.

Billy   You ever talk to any a these guys – queers, I mean? You ever sit down, just rap with one of 'em?

Roger   Hell, no; what I wanna do that for? Shit, no.

Billy (*crossing to the trash can in the corner, where he will shake the towel empty*)   I mean, some of 'em are okay guys, just way up this bad alley, and you say to 'em, 'I'm straight, be cool,' they go their own way. But then there's these other ones, these bitches, man, and they're so crazy they think anybody can be had. Because they been had themselves. So you tell 'em you're straight and they just nod and smile. You ain't real to 'em. They can't see nothin' but themselves and these goddamn games they're always playin'. (*Having returned to his bunk, he is putting on his shoes.*) I mean, you can be decent about anything, Roger, you see what I'm sayin'? We're all just people, man, and some of us are hardly that. That's all I'm sayin'. (*There is a slight pause as he sits there thinking. Then he gets to his feet.*) I'll go get some buckets and stuff so we can clean up, okay? This area's a mess. This area ain't standin' tall.

Roger   That's good talk, lad; this area a midget you put it next to an area standin' tall.

Billy   Got to be good fuckin' troopers.

Roger   That's right, that's right. I know the meanin' of the words.

Billy   I mean, I just think we all got to be honest with each other – you understand me?

Roger   No, I don't understand you; one stupid fuckin' nigger like me – how's that gonna be?

Billy   That's right; mock me, man. That's what I need. I'll go get the wax.

Out **Billy** *goes, talking to himself and leaving the door open. For a moment* **Roger** *sits, thinking, and then he looks at* **Richie**'s *locker and gets to his feet and walks to the locker which he opens and looks at the pinup hanging on the inside of the door. He takes a step backward, looking.*

Roger   Sheee-it.

Through the open door comes **Carlyle**. **Roger** *doesn't see him. And*

Carlyle *stands there looking at* **Roger** *and the picture in the locker.*

Carlyle   Boy . . . whose locker you lookin' into?

Roger (*startled, but recovers*)   Hey, baby, what's happenin'?

Carlyle   That ain't your locker, is what I'm askin', nigger. I mean, you ain't got no white goddamn woman hangin' on your wall.

Roger   Oh, no – no, no.

Carlyle   You don't wanna be lyin' to me, 'cause I got to turn you in you lyin' and you do got the body a some white goddamn woman hangin' there for you to peek at nobody around but you – you can be thinkin' about that sweet wet pussy an' maybe it hot an' maybe it cool.

Roger   I could be thinkin' all that, except I know the penalty for lyin'.

Carlyle   Thank God for that. (*Extending his hand, palm up.*)

Roger   That's right. This here the locker of a faggot. (*And he slaps* **Carlyle**'s *hand, palm to palm.*)

Carlyle   Course it is; I see that; any damn body know that.

Roger *crosses toward his bunk and* **Carlyle** *swaggers about, pulling a pint of whiskey from his hip pocket.*

Carlyle   You want a shot? Have you a little taste, my man.

Roger   Naw.

Carlyle   C'mon. C'Mon. I think you a Tom you don't drink outa my bottle.

He thrusts the bottle toward **Roger** *and wipes a sweat- and grease-stained sleeve across his mouth.*

Roger (*taking the bottle*)   Shit.

Carlyle   That right. How do I know? I just got in. New boy in town. Somewhere over there; I dunno. They dump me in amongst a whole bunch a pale, boring motherfuckers. (*He is exploring the room. Finding* **Billy**'s *Playboy, he edges onto* **Billy**'s *bed*

and leafs nervously through the pages.) I just come in from P
Company, man, and I been all over this place, don't see too
damn many of us. This outfit look like it a little short on soul. I
been walkin' all around, I tell you, and the number is small.
Like one hand you can tabulate the lot of 'em. We got few
brothers I been able to see, is what I'm sayin'. You and me
and two cats down in the small bay. That's all I found.

As **Roger** *is about to hand the bottle back,* **Carlyle**, *almost angrily,
waves him off.*

No, no, you take another; take you a real taste.

Roger   It ain't so bad here. We do all right.

Carlyle (*moves, shutting the door, suspiciously, he approaches* **Roger**)
How about the white guys? They give you any sweat? What's
the situation? No jive. I like to know what is goin' on within
the situation before that situation get a chance to be closin' in
on me.

Roger (*putting the bottle on the footlocker, he sits down*)   Man, I'm
tellin' you, it ain't bad. They're just pale, most of 'em, you
know. They can't help it; how they gonna help it? Some of
'em got little bit a soul, couple real good boys around this way.
Get 'em little bit of Coppertone, they be straight, man.

Carlyle   How about the NCOs? We got any brother NCO
watchin' out for us or they all white, like I goddamn well
KNOW all the officers are? Fuckin' officers always white,
man; fuckin' snow cones and bars everywhere you look. (*He
cannot stay still. He moves to his right, his left; he sits, he stands.*)

Roger   First sergeant's a black man.

Carlyle   All right; good news. Hey, hey, you wanna go over
the club with me, or maybe downtown? I got wheels. Let's be
free. (*Now he rushes at* **Roger**.) Let's be free.

Roger   Naw . . .

Carlyle   Ohhh, baby . . .

He is pulling wildly at **Roger** *to get him to the door.*

Roger   Some other time. I gotta get the area straight. Me and the guy sleeps in here too are gonna shape the place up a little. (*He has pulled free, and* **Carlyle** *cannot understand. It hurts him, depresses him.*)

Carlyle   You got a sweet deal here an' you wanna keep it, that right? (*He paces about the room, opens a footlocker, looks inside.*) How you rate you get a room like this for yourself – you and a couple guys?

Roger   Spec 4. The three of us in here Spec 4.

Carlyle   You get a room then, huh? (*And suddenly, without warning or transition, he is angry.*) Oh, man, I hate this goddamn army. I hate this bastard army. I mean, I just got outa basic – off leave you know? Back on the block for two weeks – and now here. They don't pull any a that petty shit, now, do they – that goddamn petty basic training bullshit? They do and I'm gonna be bustin' some head – my hand is gonna be upside all kinds a heads, 'cause I ain't gonna be able to endure it, man, not that kinda crap – understand? (*And again, he is rushing at* **Roger**.) Hey, hey, oh, c'mon, let's get my wheels and make it, man, do me the favor.

Roger   How'm I gonna? I got my obligations. (*And* **Carlyle** *spins away in anger.*)

Carlyle   Jesus, baby, can't you remember the outside? How long it been since you been on leave? It is so sweet out there, nigger; you got it all forgot. I had such a sweet, sweet time. They doin' dances, baby, make you wanna cry. I hate this damn army. (*The anger overwhelms him.*) All these mother-actin' jacks givin' you jive about what you gotta do and what you can't do. I had a bad scene in basic – up the hill and down the hill; it ain't somethin' I enjoyed even a little. So they do me wrong here, Jim, they gonna be sorry. Some-damn-body! And this whole Vietnam THING – I do not dig it. (*He falls on his knees before* **Roger**. *It is a gesture that begins as a joke, a mockery. And then a real fear pulses through him to nearly fill the pose he has taken.*) Lord, Lord, don't let 'em touch me. Christ, what will I do, they DO?! Whoooooooooooooo! And they pullin' guys outa here, too, ain't they? Pullin' 'em like weeds, man; throwin' 'em into the fire. It's shit, man.

Roger   They got this ole sarge sleeps down the hall – just today they got him.

Carlyle   Which ole sarge?

Roger   He sleeps just down the hall. Little guy.

Carlyle   Wino, right?

Roger   Booze hound.

Carlyle   Yeh; I seen him. They got him, huh?

Roger   He's goin'; gotta be packin' his bags. And three other guys two days ago. And two guys last week.

Carlyle (*leaping up from* **Billy***'s bed*)   Ohhh, them bastards. And everybody just takes it. It ain't our war, brother. I'm tellin' you. That's what gets me, nigger. It ain't our war no how because it ain't our country, and that's what burns my ass – that and everybody just sittin' and takin' it. They gonna be bustin' balls, man – kickin' and stompin'. Everybody here maybe one week from shippin' out to get blown clean away and, man, whata they doin'? They doin' what they told. That what they doin'. Like you? Shit! You gonna straighten up your goddamn area! Well, that ain't for me; I'm gettin' hat, and makin' it out where it's sweet and the people's livin'. I can't cut this jive here, man. I'm tellin' you. I can't cut it.

He has moved toward **Roger**, *and behind him now* **Richie** *enters, hair wet, traces of shaving cream on his face. Toweling his hair, he falters, seeing* **Carlyle**. *Then he crosses to his locker.* **Carlyle** *grins at* **Roger**, *looks at* **Richie**, *steps toward him and gives a little bow.*

My name is Carlyle; what is yours?

Richie   Richie.

Carlyle (*turns toward* **Roger** *to share his joke*)   Hello. Where is Martin? That cute little Martin.

Richie *has just taken off his robe as* **Carlyle** *turns back.*

Carlyle   You cute, too, Richie.

Richie   Martin doesn't live here. (*Hurriedly putting on underpants to cover his nakedness.*)

Carlyle (*watching* **Richie**, *he slowly turns toward* **Roger**)   You ain't gonna make it with me, man?

Roger   Naw . . . like I tole you. I'll catch you later.

Carlyle   That's sad, man; make me cry in my heart.

Roger   You g'wan get your head smokin'. Stop on back.

Carlyle   Okay, okay. Got to be one man one more time. (*On the move for the door, his hand extended palm up behind him, demanding the appropriate response.*) Baby! Gimme! Gimme! (*Lunging,* **Roger** *slaps the hand.*)

Roger   G'wan home! G'wan home.

Carlyle   You gonna hear from me. (*And he is gone out the door and down the hallway.*)

Roger   I can . . . and do . . . believe . . . that.

Richie, *putting on his T-shirt, watches* **Roger**, *who stubs out his cigarette, then crosses to the trash can to empty the ashtray.*

Richie   Who was that?

Roger   Man's new, Rich. Dunno his name more than that 'Carlyle' he said. He's new – just outa basic.

Richie (*powdering his thighs and under his arms*)   Oh, my God . . .

As **Billy** *enters, pushing a mop bucket with a wringer attached and carrying a container of wax.*

Roger   Me and Billy's gonna straighten up the area. You wanna help?

Richie   Sure, sure; help, help.

Billy (*talking to* **Roger**, *but turning to look at* **Richie**, *who is still putting powder under his arms*)   I hadda steal the wax from Third Platoon.

Roger   Good man.

Billy (*moving to* **Richie**, *joking, yet really irritated in some strange way*)   What? Whata you doin', singin'? Look at that, Rog. He's got enough jazz there for an entire beauty parlor. (*Grabbing the can from* **Richie**'s *hand.*) What is this? Baby powder! BABY POWDER!

Richie   I get rashes.

Billy   Okay, okay, you get rashes, so what? They got powder for rashes that isn't baby powder.

Richie   It doesn't work as good; I've tried it. Have you tried it?

Grabbing **Billy**'s *waist,* **Richie** *pulls him close.* **Billy** *knocks* **Richie**'s *hands away.*

Billy   Man, I wish you could get yourself straight. I'll mop, too, Roger – okay? Then I'll put down the wax and you can spread it? (*He has walked away from* **Richie**.)

Richie   What about buffing?

Roger   In the morning. (*He is already busy mopping up near the door.*)

Richie   What do you want me to do?

Billy (*grabbing up a mop, he heads downstage to work*)   Get inside your locker and shut the door and don't holler for help. Nobody'll know you're there; you'll stay there.

Richie   But I'm so pretty.

Billy   NOW! (*Pointing to* **Roger**. *He wants to get this clear.*) Tell that man you mean what you're sayin', Richie.

Richie   Mean what?

Billy   That you really think you're pretty.

Richie   Of course I do; I am. Don't you think I am? Don't you think I am, Roger?

Roger   I tole you – you fulla shit and you cute, man. Carlyle just tole you you cute, too.

Richie   Don't you think it's true, Billy?

Billy   It's like I tole you, Rog.

Richie   What did you tell him?

Billy   That you go down; that you go up and down like a yo-yo and you go blowin' all the trees like the wind.

Richie *is stunned. He looks at* **Roger**, *and then he turns and stares into his own locker. The others keep mopping.* **Richie** *takes out a towel, and putting it around his neck, he walks to where* **Billy** *is working. He stands there, hurt, looking at* **Billy**.

Richie   What the hell made you tell him I been down, Billy?

Billy (*still mopping*)   It's in your eyes; I seen it.

Richie   What?

Billy   You.

Richie   What is it, Billy, you think you're trying to say? You and all your wit and intelligence – your HUMANITY.

Billy   I said it, Rich; I said what I was tryin' to say.

Richie   DID you?

Billy   I think I did.

Richie   DO you?

Billy   Loud and clear, baby. (*Still mopping.*)

Roger   They got to put me in with the weirdos. Why is that, huh? How come the army HATE me, do this shit to me – KNOW what to do to me. (*Whimsical, and then suddenly loud, angered, violent.*) Now you guys put socks in your mouths, right now – get shut up – or I am gonna beat you to death with each other. Roger got work to do. To be doin' it!

Richie (*turning to his bed, he kneels upon it*)   Roger, I think you're so innocent sometimes. Honestly, it's not such a terrible thing. Is it, Billy?

Billy   How would I know? (*He slams his mop into the bucket.*) Oh, go fuck yourself.

Richie   Well, I can give it a try, if that's what you want. Can I think of you as I do?

Billy (*throwing down his mop*)   GODDAMMIT! That's it! IT!

He exits, rushing into the hall and slamming the door behind him.
Roger *looks at* **Richie***. Neither quite knows what is going on.*
Suddenly the door bursts open and **Billy** *storms straight over to* **Richie***,*
who still kneels on the bed.

Now I am gonna level with you. Are you gonna listen? You gonna hear what I say, Rich, and not what you think I'm sayin'?

Richie *turns away as if to rise, his manner flippant, disdainful.*

Billy   No! Don't get cute; don't turn away cute. I wanna say somethin' straight out to you and I want you to hear it!

Richie   I'm all ears, goddammit! For what, however, I do not know, except some boring evasion.

Billy   At least wait the hell till you hear me!

Richie (*in irritation*)   Okay, okay! What?

Billy   Now this is level, Rich; this is straight talk. (*He is quiet, intense. This is difficult for him. He seeks the exactly appropriate words of explanation.*) No B.S. No tricks. What you do on the side, that's your business and I don't care about it. But if you don't cut the cute shit with me, I'm gonna turn you off. Completely. You ain't gonna get a good mornin' outa me, you understand, because it's gettin' bad around here. I mean, I know how you think – how you keep lookin' out and seein' yourself, and that's what I'm tryin' to tell you because that's all that's happenin', Rich. That's all there is to it when you look out at me and think there's some kind of approval or whatever you see in my eyes – you're just seein' yourself. And I'm talkin' the simple quiet truth to you, Rich. I swear I am.

Billy *looks away from* **Richie** *now and tries to go back to the mopping.*
It is embarrassing for them all. **Roger** *has watched, has tried to keep*
working. **Richie** *has flopped back on his bunk. There is a silence.*

Richie   How . . . do . . . you want me to be? I don't know how else to be.

Billy   Ohhh, man, that ain't any part of it. (*The mop is clenched in his hands.*)

Richie   Well, I don't come from the same kind of world as you do.

Billy   Damn, Richie, you think Roger and I come off the same street?

Roger   Shit . . .

Richie   All right. Okay. But I've just done what I wanted all of my life. If I wanted to do something, I just did it. Honestly. I've never had to work or anything like that, and I've always had nice clothing and money for cab fare. Money for whatever I wanted. Always. I'm not like you are.

Roger   You ain't sayin' you really done that stuff, though, Rich.

Richie   What?

Roger   That fag stuff.

Richie (*continues looking at* **Roger** *and then he looks away*)   Yes.

Roger   Do you even know what you're sayin', Richie? Do you even know what it means to be a fag?

Richie   Roger, of course I know what it is. I just told you I've done it. I thought you black people were supposed to understand all about suffering and human strangeness. I thought you had depth and vision from all your suffering. Has someone been misleading me? I just told you I did it. I know all about it. Everything. All the various positions.

Roger   Yeh, so maybe you think you've tried it, but that don't make you it. I mean, we used to . . . in the old neighborhood, man, we had a couple dudes swung that way. But they was weird, man. There was this one little fella, he was a screamin' goddamn faggot . . . uh . . . (*He considers* **Richie** *wondering if perhaps he has offended him.*) Ohhh, ohhh,

you ain't no screamin' goddamn faggot, Richie, no matter
what you say. And the baddest man on the block was my
boy Jerry Lemon. So one day Jerry's got the faggot in one a
them ole deserted stairways and he's bouncin' him off the
walls. I'm just a little fella, see, and I'm watchin' the baddest
man on the block do his thing. So he come bouncin' back
into me instead of Jerry, and just when he hit, he gave his
ass this little twitch, man, like he thought he was gonna turn
me on. I'd never a thought that was possible, man, for a
man to be twitchin' his ass on me, just like he thought he
was a broad. Scared me to death. I took off runnin'. Oh, oh,
that ole neighborhood put me into all kinds a crap. I did
some sufferin', just like Richie says. Like this once, I'm
swingin' on up the street after school, and outa this phone
booth comes this man with a goddamned knife stickin' outa
his gut. So he sees me and starts tryin' to pull his
motherfuckin' coat out over the handle, like he's worried
about how he looks, man. 'I didn't know this was gonna
happen,' he says. And then he falls over. He was just all of a
sudden dead, man; just all of a sudden dead. You ever seen
anything like that, Billy? Any crap like that?

Billy, *sitting on* **Roger***'s bunk, is staring at* **Roger**.

Billy   You really seen that?

Roger   Richie's a big-city boy.

Richie   Oh, no; never anything like that.

Roger   'Momma, help me,' I am screamin'. 'Jesus, Momma,
help me.' Little fella, he don't know how to act, he sees
somethin' like that.

For a moment they are still, each thinking.

Billy   How long you think we got?

Roger   What do you mean?

Roger *is hanging up the mops;* **Billy** *is now kneeling on* **Roger***'s
bunk.*

Billy   Till they pack us up, man, ship us out.

Roger   To the war, you mean? To Disneyland? Man, I dunno; that up to them IBMs. Them machines is figurin' that. Maybe tomorrow, maybe next week, maybe never.

The war – the threat of it – is the one thing they share.

Richie   I was reading they're planning to build it all up to more than five hundred thousand men over there. Americans. And they're going to keep it that way until they win.

Billy   Be a great place to come back from, man, you know? I keep thinkin' about that. To have gone there, to have been there, to have seen it and lived.

Roger (*settling onto **Billy**'s bunk, lights a cigarette*)   Well, what we got right here is a fool, gonna probably be one a them five hundred thousand, too. Do you know I cry at the goddamn anthem yet sometimes? The flag is flyin' at a ball game, the ole Roger gets all wet in the eye. After all the shit been done to his black ass. But I don't know what I think about this war. I do not know.

Billy   I'm tellin' you, Rog – I've been doin' a lot a readin' and I think it's right we go. I mean, it's just like when North Korea invaded South Korea or when Hitler invaded Poland and all those other countries. He just kept testin' everybody and when nobody said no to him, he got so committed he couldn't back out even if he wanted. And that's what this Ho Chi Minh is doin'. And all these other Communists. If we let 'em know somebody is gonna stand up against 'em, they'll back off, just like Hitler would have.

Roger   There is folks, you know, who are sayin' L.B.J. is the Hitler, and not ole Ho Chi Minh at all.

Richie (*talking as if this is the best news he's heard in years*)   Well, I don't know anything at all about all that, but I am certain I don't want to go – whatever is going on. I mean, those Vietcong don't just shoot you and blow you up, you know. My God, they've got these other awful things they do: putting elephant shit on these stakes in the ground and then you step on 'em and you got elephant shit in a wound in your foot. The infection is horrendous. And then there's these caves they hide in and when you go in after 'em, they've got these snakes that they've tied by their tails to the ceiling. So it's dark and the snake is furious from having been hung by its tail and you crawl right into them – your face. My God.

Billy   They do not. (*Knows he has been caught; they all know it.*)

Richie   I read it, Billy. They do.

Billy (*completely facetious, yet the fear is real*)   That's bullshit, Richie.

Roger   That's right, Richie. They maybe do that stuff with the elephant shit, but nobody's gonna tie a snake by its tail, let ole Billy walk into it.

Billy   That's disgusting, man.

Roger   Guess you better get ready for the Klondike, my man.

Billy   That is probably the most disgusting thing I ever heard of. I DO NOT WANT TO GO! NOT TO NOWHERE WHERE THAT KINDA SHIT IS GOIN' ON! L.B.J. is Hitler; suddenly I see it all very clearly.

Roger   Billy got him a hatred for snakes.

Richie   I hate them, too. They're hideous.

Billy (*as a kind of apology to* **Richie**, *continues his self-ridicule far into the extreme*)   I mean, that is one of the most awful things I ever heard of any person doing. I mean, any person who would hang a snake by its tail in the dark of a cave in the hope that some other person might crawl into it and get bitten to death, that first person is somebody who oughta be shot. And I hope the five hundred thousand other guys that get sent over there kill 'em all – all them gooks – get 'em all driven back into Germany, where they belong. And in the meantime, I'll be holding the northern border against the snowmen.

Roger (*rising from* **Billy**'s *bed*)   And in the meantime, before that, we better be gettin' at the ole area here. Got to be strike troopers.

Billy Right.

Richie   Can I help?

Roger   Sure. Be good. (*And he crosses to his footlocker and takes out a radio.*) Think maybe I put on a little music, though it's gettin' late. We got time. Billy, you think?

Billy   Sure. (*Getting nervously to his feet.*)

Roger   Sure. All right. We can be doin' it to the music. (*He plugs the radio into the floor outlet as* **Billy** *bolts for the door.*)

Billy   I gotta go pee.

Roger   You watch out for the snakes.

Billy   It's the snowmen, man; the snowmen.

Billy *is gone and 'Ruby,' sung by Ray Charles, comes from the radio. For a moment, as the music plays,* **Roger** *watches* **Richie** *wander about the room, pouring little splashes of wax onto the floor. Then* **Richie** *moves to his bed and lies down, and* **Roger**, *shaking his head, starts leisurely to spread the wax, with* **Richie** *watching.*

Richie   How come you and Billy take all this so seriously – you know.

Roger   What?

Richie   This army nonsense. You're always shining your brass and keeping your footlocker neat and your locker so neat. There's no point to any of it.

Roger   We here, ain't we, Richie? We in the army. (*Still working the wax.*)

Richie   There's no point to any of it. And doing those push-ups, the two of you.

Roger   We just see a lot of things the same way is all. Army ought to be a serious business, even if sometimes it ain't.

Richie   You're lucky, you know, the two of you. Having each other for friends the way you do. I never had that kind of friend ever. Not even when I was little.

Roger (*after a pause during which he, while working, sort of peeks at* **Richie** *every now and then*)   You ain't really inta that stuff, are you, Richie? (*It is a question that is a statement.*)

Richie (*coyly looks at* **Roger**)   What stuff is that, Roger?

Roger   That fag stuff, man. You know. You ain't really into it, are you? You maybe messed in it a little is all – am I right?

Richie   I'm very weak, Roger. And by that I simply mean that if I have an impulse to do something, I don't know how to deny myself. If I feel like doing something, I just do it. I . . . will . . . admit to sometimes wishin' I . . . was a little more like you . . . and Billy, even, but not to any severe extent.

Roger   But that's such a bad scene, Rich. You don't want that. Nobody wants that. Nobody wants to be a punk. Not nobody. You wanna know what I think it is? You just got in with the wrong bunch. Am I right? You just got in with a bad bunch. That can happen. And that's what I think happened to you. I bet you never had a chance to really run with the boys before. I mean, regular normal guys like Billy and me. How'd you come in the army, huh, Richie? You get drafted?

Richie   No.

Roger   That's my point, see. (*He has stopped working. He stands, leaning on the mop, looking at* **Richie**.)

Richie   About four years ago, I went to this party. I was very young, and I went to this party with a friend who was older and . . . this 'fag stuff,' as you call it, was going on . . . so I did it.

Roger   And then you come in the army to get away from it, right? Huh?

Richie   I don't know.

Roger   Sure.

Richie   I don't know, Roger.

Roger   Sure; sure. And now you're gettin' a chance to run with the boys for a little, you'll get yourself straightened around. I know it for a fact; I know that thing.

From off there is the sudden loud bellowing sound of **Sergeant Rooney**.

Rooney THERE AIN'T BEEN NO SOLDIERS IN THIS CAMP BUT ME. I BEEN THE ONLY ONE – I BEEN THE ONLY ME!

And **Billy** *comes dashing into the room.*

Billy Oh, boy.

Roger Guess who?

Rooney FOR SO LONG I BEEN THE ONLY GODDAMN ONE!

Billy (*leaping onto his bed and covering his face with a* Playboy *magazine as* **Richie** *is trying to disappear under his sheets and blankets and* **Roger** *is trying to get the wax put away so he can get into his own bunk*) Hut who hee whor – he's got some yo-yo with him, Rog!

Roger Huh?

As **Cokes** *and* **Rooney** *enter. Both are in fatigues and drunk and big-bellied. They are in their fifties, their hair whitish and cut short. Both men carry whiskey bottles, beer bottles.* **Cokes** *is a little neater than* **Rooney**, *his fatigue jacket tucked in and not so rumpled, and he wears canvas-sided jungle boots.* **Rooney**, *very disheveled, chomps on the stub of a big cigar. They swagger in, looking for fun, and stand there side by side.*

Rooney What kinda platoon I got here? You buncha shit sacks. Everybody look sharp.

The three boys lie there, unmoving.

Off and on!

Cokes OFF AND ON! (*He seems barely conscious, wavering as he stands.*)

Roger What's happenin', Sergeant?

Rooney (*shoving his bottle of whiskey at* **Roger**, *who is sitting up*)

Shut up, Moore! You want a belt? (*Splashing whiskey on* **Roger**'s *chest.*)

Roger   How can I say no?

Cokes   My name is Cokes!

Billy (*rising to sit on the side of his bed*)   How about me, too?

Cokes   You wait your turn.

Rooney (*looks at the three of them as if they are fools. Indicates* **Cokes** *with a gesture*)   Don't you see what I got here?

Billy   Who do I follow for my turn?

Rooney (*suddenly, crazily petulant*)   Don't you see what I got here? Everybody on their feet and at attention!

Billy *and* **Roger** *climb from their bunks and stand at attention. They don't know what* **Rooney** *is mad at.*

Rooney   I mean it!

Richie *bounds to the position of attention.*

Rooney   This here is my friend, who in addition has just come back from the war! The goddamn war! He been to it and he come back.

He is patting **Cokes** *gently, proudly.*

The man's a fuckin' hero!

He hugs **Cokes**, *almost kissing him on the cheek.*

He's always been a fuckin' hero.

Cokes, *embarrassed in his stupor, kind of wobbles a little from side to side.*

Cokes   No-o-o-o-o-o . . .

And **Rooney** *grabs him, starts pushing him toward* **Billy**'s *footlocker.*

Rooney   Show 'em your boots, Cokes. Show 'em your jungle boots.

With a long, clumsy step, **Cokes** *climbs onto the footlocker,* **Rooney** *supporting him from behind and then bending to lift one of* **Cokes**'s *booted feet and display it for the boys.*

Lookee that boot. That ain't no everyday goddamn army boot. That is a goddamn jungle boot! That green canvas is a jungle boot 'cause a the heat, and them little holes in the bottom are so the water can run out when you been walkin' in a lotta water like in a jungle swamp. (*He is extremely proud of all this; he looks at them.*) The army ain't no goddamn fool. You see a man wearin' boots like that, you might as well see he's got a chestful a medals, 'cause he been to the war. He don't have no boots like that unless he been to the war! Which is where I'm goin' and all you slaphappy motherfuckers, too. Got to go kill some gooks. (*He is nodding at them, smiling.*) That's right.

Cokes (*bursting loudly from his stupor*)   Gonna piss on 'em. Old booze. 'At's what I did. Piss in the rivers. Goddamn G.I.'s secret weapon is old booze and he's pissin' it in all their runnin' water. Makes 'em yellow. Ahhhha ha, ha, ha! (*He laughs and laughs, and* **Rooney** *laughs, too, hugging* **Cokes**.)

Rooney   Me and Cokesy been in so much shit together we oughta be brown. (*And then he catches himself, looks at* **Roger**.) Don't take no offense at that, Moore. We been swimmin' in it. One Hundred and First Airborne, together. One-oh-one. Screamin' goddamn Eagles!

Looking at each other, face to face, eyes glinting, they make sudden loud screaming-eagle sounds.

This ain't the army; you punks ain't in the army. You ain't ever seen the army. The army is Airborne! Airborne!

Cokes (*beginning to stomp his feet*)   Airborne, Airborne! ALL THE WAY!

As **Richie**, *amused and hoping for a drink, too, reaches out toward* **Rooney**.

Richie   Sergeant, Sergeant, I can have a little drink, too.

Rooney *looks at him and clutches the bottle.*

Rooney   Are you kiddin' me? You gotta be kiddin' me. (*He looks to* **Roger**.) He's kiddin' me, ain't he, Moore? (*And then to*

Billy *and then to* **Cokes**.) Ain't he, Cokesy? (**Cokes** *steps forward and down with a thump, taking charge for his bewildered friend.*)

Cokes   Don't you know you are tryin' to take the booze from the hand a the future goddamn Congressional Honor winner . . . Medal . . . ? (*And he looks lovingly at* **Rooney**. *He beams*.) Ole Rooney, Ole Rooney. (*He hugs* **Rooney***'s head.*) He almost done it already.

And **Rooney**, *overwhelmed, starts screaming 'Agggggghhhhhhhhhh,' a screaming eagle sound, and making clawing eagle gestures at the air. He jumps up and down, stomping his feet.* **Cokes** *instantly joins in, stomping and jumping and yelling.*

Rooney   Let's show these shit sacks how men are men jumpin' outa planes. Agggggghhhhhhhhhh.

Stomping and yelling, they move in a circle, **Rooney** *followed by* **Cokes**.

A plane fulla yellin' stompin' men!

Cokes   All yellin' stompin' men!

They yell and stomp, making eagle sounds, and then **Rooney** *leaps up on* **Billy***'s bed and runs the length of it until he is on the footlocker,* **Cokes** *still on the floor, stomping.* **Rooney** *makes a gesture of hooking his rip cord to the line inside the plane. They yell louder and louder and* **Rooney** *leaps high into the air, yelling, '*GERONIMO-O-O-O!*' as* **Cokes** *leaps onto the locker and then high into the air, bellowing, '*GERONIMO-O-O-O!*' They stand side by side, their arms held up in the air as if grasping the shroud lines of open chutes. They seem to float there in silence.*

What a feelin' . . .

Rooney   Beautiful feelin' . . .

For a moment more they float there, adrift in the room, the sky, their memory. **Cokes** *smiles at* **Rooney**.

Cokes   Remember that one guy, O'Flannigan . . . ?

Rooney (*nodding, smiling, remembering*)   O'Flannigan . . .

Cokes   He was this one guy . . . O'Flannigan . . .

He moves now toward the boys, **Billy**, **Roger** *and* **Richie**, *who have gathered on* **Roger**'s *bed and footlocker.* **Rooney** *follows several steps, then drifts backward onto* **Billy**'s *bed, where he sits and then lies back, listening to* **Cokes**.

We was testing chutes where you could just pull a lever by your ribs here when you hit the ground – see – and the chute would come off you, because it was just after a whole bunch a guys had been dragged to death in an unexpected and terrible wind at Fort Bragg. So they wanted you to be able to release the chute when you hit if there was a bad wind when you hit. So O'Flannigan was this kinda joker who had the goddamn sense a humor of a clown and nerves, I tell you, of steel, and he says he's gonna release the lever midair, then reach up, grab the lines and float on down, hanging. (*His hand paws at the air, seeking a rope that isn't there.*) So I seen him pull the lever at five hundred feet and he reaches up to two fistfuls a air, the chute's twenty feet above him, and he went into the ground like a knife.

The bottle, held high over his head, falls through the air to the bed, all watching it.

Billy   Geezus.

Rooney (*nodding gently*)   Didn't get to sing the song, I bet.

Cokes (*standing, staring at the fallen bottle*)   No way.

Richie   What song?

Rooney (*rises up, mysteriously angry*)   Shit sack! Shit sack!

Richie   What song, Sergeant Rooney?

Rooney   'Beautiful Streamer,' shit sack.

Cokes, *gone into another reverie, is staring skyward.*

Cokes   I saw this one guy – never forget it. Never.

Billy   That's Richie, Sergeant Rooney. He's a beautiful screamer.

Richie   He said 'streamer,' not 'screamer,' asshole.

Cokes *is still in his reverie.*

Cokes   This guy with his chute goin' straight up above him in a streamer, like a tulip, only white, you know. All twisted and never gonna open. Like a big icicle sticking straight up above him. He went right by me. We met eyes, sort of. He was lookin' real puzzled. He looks right at me. Then he looks up in the air the chute, then down at the ground.

Rooney   Did HE sing it?

Cook   He didn't sing it. He started going like this. (*He reaches desperately upward with both hands and begins to claw at the sky while his legs pump up and down.*) Like he was gonna climb right up in the air.

Richie   Ohhhhhh, Geezus.

Billy   God.

Rooney *has collapsed backward on* **Billy**'s *bed and he lies there and then he rises.*

Rooney   Cokes got the Silver Star for rollin' a barrel a oil down a hill in Korea into forty-seven chinky Chinese gooks who were climbin' up the hill and when he shot into it with his machine gun, it blew them all to grape jelly.

Cokes, *rocking a little on his feet, begins to hum and then sing* '*Beautiful Streamer,*' *to the tune of Stephen Foster's* '*Beautiful Dreamer.*'

Cokes   'Beautiful streamer, open for me . . . The sky is above me . . .' (*And then the singing stops.*) But the one I remember is this little guy in his spider hole, which is a hole in the ground with a lid over it. (*And he is using* **Richie**'s *footlocker before him as the spider hole. He has fixed on it, is moving toward it.*) And he shot me in the ass as I was runnin' by, but the bullet hit me so hard – (*His body kind of jerks and he runs several steps.*) – it knocked me into this ditch where he couldn't see me. I got behind him. (*Now at the head of* **Richie**'s *bed, he begins to creep along the side of the bed as if sneaking up on the footlocker.*) Crawlin'. And I dropped a grenade into his hole. (*He jams a whiskey bottle into the footlocker, then slams down the lid.*)

Then sat on the lid, him bouncin' and yellin' under me.

Bouncin' and yellin' under the lid. I could hear him. Feel him.
I just sat there.

Silence. **Rooney** *waits, thinking, then leans forward.*

Rooney   He was probably singin' it.

Cokes (*sitting there*)   I think so.

Rooney   You think we should let 'em hear it?

Billy   We're good boys. We're good ole boys.

Cokes (*jerking himself to his feet, staggers sideways to join* **Rooney**
on **Billy***'s bed*)   I don't care who hears it, I just wanna be
singin' it.

Rooney *rises; he goes to the boys on* **Roger***'s bed and speaks to them
carefully, as if lecturing people on something of great importance.*

Rooney   You listen up; you just be listenin' up, 'cause if you
hear it right you can maybe stop bein' shit sacks. This is what
a man sings, he's goin' down through the air, his chute don't
open.

Flopping back down on the bunk beside **Cokes**, **Rooney** *looks at*
Cokes *and then at the boys. The two older men put their arms around
each other and they begin to sing.*

Rooney *and* **Cokes** (*singing*)
    Beautiful streamer,
    Open for me,
    The sky is above me,
    But no canopy.

Billy (*murmuring*)   I don't believe it.

Rooney *and* **Cokes**
    Counted ten thousand,
    Pulled on the cord.
    My chute didn't open,
    I shouted, 'Dear Lord.'

    Beautiful streamer,
    This looks like the end,

The earth is below me,
My body won't end.

Just like a mother
Watching o'er me,
Beautiful streamer,
Ohhhhh, open for me.

Roger   Un-fuckin'-believable.

Rooney (*beaming with pride*)   Ain't that a beauty.

And then **Cokes** *topples forward onto his face and flops limply to his side. The three boys leap to their feet.* **Rooney** *lunges toward* **Cokes**.

Richie   Sergeant!

Rooney   Cokie! Cokie!

Billy   Jesus.

Roger   Hey!

Cokes   Huh? Huh? (*He sits up.* **Rooney** *is kneeling beside him.*)

Rooney   Jesus, Cokie.

Cokes   I been doin' that; I been doin' that. It don't mean nothin'.

Rooney   No, no.

Cokes (*pushing at* **Rooney**, *who is trying to help him get back to the bed;* **Rooney** *agrees with everything* **Cokes** *is now saying, and the noises he makes are little animal noises*)   I told 'em when they wanted to send me back I ain't got no leukemia; they wanna check it. They think I got it. I don't think I got it. Rooney? Whata you think?

Rooney   No.

Cokes   My mother had it. She had it. Just 'cause she did and I been fallin' down.

Rooney   It don't mean nothin'.

Cokes (*lunges back and up onto the bed*)   I tole 'em I fall down 'cause I'm drunk. I'm drunk all the time.

Rooney You'll be goin' back over there with me, is what I know, Cokie (*He is patting* **Cokes**, *nodding, dusting him off.*) That's what I know.

Billy *comes up to them, almost seeming to want to be a part of the intimacy they are sharing.*

Billy That was somethin', Sergeant Cokes. Jesus.

Rooney *whirls on him, ferocious, pushing him.*

Rooney Get the fuck away, Wilson! Whata you know? Get the fuck away. You don't know shit. Get away! You don't know shit. (*And he turns to* **Cokes**, *who is standing up from the bed.*) Me and Cokes are goin' to the war zone like we oughta. Gonna blow it to shit. (*He is grabbing at* **Cokes**, *who is laughing. They are both laughing.* **Rooney** *whirls on the boys.*) Ohhh, I'm gonna be so happy to be away from you assholes; you pussies. Not one regular army people among you possible. I swear it to my mother who is holy. You just be watchin' the papers for doin' darin' deeds. 'Cause we're old hands at it. Makin' shit disappear. Goddamn whoosh!

Cokes Whoooosh!

Rooney Demnalitions. Me and . . . (*And then he knows he hasn't said it right.*) Me and Cokie . . . Demnal . . . Demnali . . .

Richie (*still sitting on* **Roger***'s bed*) You can do it, Sergeant.

Billy Get it. (*He stands by the lockers and* **Rooney** *glares at him.*)

Roger 'Cause you're cool with dynamite, is what you're tryin' to say.

Rooney (*charging at* **Roger**, *bellowing*) Shut the fuck up, that's what you can do; and go to goddamn sleep. You buncha shit . . . sacks. Buncha mothers – know-it-all motherin' shit sacks – that's what you are.

Cokes (*shoulders back, he is taking charge*) Just goin' to sleep is what you can do, 'cause Rooney and me fought it through two wars already and we can make it through this one more and leukemia that comes or doesn't come – who gives a shit? Not guys like us. We're goin' just pretty as pie. And it's lights-out time, ain't it, Rooney?

Rooney   Past it, goddammit. So the lights are goin' out.

There is fear in the room, and the three boys rush to their wall lockers, where they start to strip to their underwear, preparing for bed. **Rooney** *paces the room, watching them, glaring.*

Somebody's gotta teach you soldierin'. You hear me? Or you wanna go outside and march around awhile, huh? We can do that if you wanna. Huh? You tell me? Marchin' or sleepin'? What's it gonna be?

Richie (*rushing to get into bed*)   Flick out the ole lights, Sergeant; that's what we say.

Billy (*climbing into bed*)   Put out the ole lights.

Roger (*in bed and pulling up the covers*)   Do it.

Cokes   Shut up. (*He rocks forward and back, trying to stand at attention. He is saying good night.*)   And that's an order. Just shut up. I got grenades down the hall. I got a pistol. I know where to get nitro. You don't shut up, I'll blow . . . you . . . to . . . fuck.

Making a military left-face, he stalks to the wall switch and turns the lights out. **Rooney** *is watching proudly, as* **Cokes** *faces the boys again. He looks at them.*

That's right.

In the dark, there is only a spill of light from the hall coming in the open door. **Cokes** *and* **Roger** *put their arms around each other and go out the door, leaving it partly open.* **Richie**, **Roger** *and* **Billy** *lie in their bunks, staring. They do not move. They lie there. The sergeants seem to have vanished soundlessly once they went out the door. Light touches each of the boys as they lie there.*

Roger (*does not move*)   Lord have mercy, if that ain't a pair. If that ain't one pair a beauties.

Billy   Oh, yeh. (*He does not move.*)

Roger   Too much, man – too, too much.

Richie   They made me sad; but I loved them, sort of. Better than movies.

Roger   Too much. Too, too much. (*Silence.*)

Billy   What time is it?

Roger   Sleep time, men. Sleep time. (*Silence.*)

Billy   Right.

Roger   They were somethin'. Too much.

Billy   Too much.

Richie   Night.

Roger   Night. (*Silence.*) Night, Billy.

Billy   Night.

Richie *stirs in his bed.* **Roger** *turns onto his side.* **Billy** *is motionless.*

Billy   I . . . had a buddy, Rog – and this is the whole thing, this is the whole point – a kid I grew up with, played ball with in high school, and he was a tough little cat, a real bad man sometimes.

Used to have gangster pictures up in his room. Anyway, we got into this deal where we'd drive on down to the big city, man, you know, hit the bad spots, let some queer pick us up . . . sort of . . . long enough to buy us some good stuff. It was kinda the thing to do for a while, and we all did it, the whole gang of us. So we'd let these cats pick us up, most of 'em old guys, and they were hurtin' and happy as hell to have us, and we'd get a lot of free booze, maybe a meal, and we'd turn 'em on. Then pretty soon they'd ask us did we want to go over to their place. Sure, we'd say, and order one more drink, and then when we hit the street, we'd tell 'em to kiss off. We'd call 'em fag and queer and jazz like that and tell 'em to kiss off. And Frankie, the kid I'm tellin' you about, he had a mean streak in him and if they gave us a bad time at all, he'd put

'em down. That's the way he was. So that kinda jazz went on
and on for sort of a long time and it was a good deal if we
were low on cash or needed a laugh and it went on for a while.
And then Frankie – one day he come up to me – and he says
he was goin' home with the guy he was with. He said, what
the hell, what did it matter? And he's sayin' – Frankie's sayin'
– why don't I tag along? What the hell, he's sayin', what does
it matter who does it to you, some broad or some old guy, you
close your eyes, a mouth's a mouth, it don't matter – that's
what he's sayin'. I tried to talk him out of it, but he wasn't
hearin' anything I was sayin'. So the next day, see, he calls me
up to tell me about it. Okay, okay, he says, it was a cool scene,
he says; they played poker, a buck minimum, and he made a
fortune. Frankie was eatin' it up, man. It was a pretty way to
live, he says. So he stayed at it, and he had this nice little girl
he was goin' with at the time. You know the way a real bad
cat can sometimes do that – have a good little girl who's crazy
about him and he is for her, too, and he's a different cat when
he's with her?

Roger   Uh-huh.

*The hall light slants across **Billy**'s face.*

Billy   Well, that was him and Linda, and then one day he
dropped her, he cut her loose. He was hooked, man. He was
into it, with no way he knew out – you understand what I'm
sayin'? He had got his ass hooked. He had never thought he
would and then one day he woke up, and he was on it. He just
hadn't been told, that's the way I figure it; somebody didn't
tell him somethin' he shoulda been told and he come to me
wailin' one day, man, all broke up and wailin', my boy
Frankie, my main man, and he was a fag. He was a faggot,
black Roger, and I'm not lyin'. I am not lyin' to you.

Roger   Damn.

Billy   So that's the whole thing, man; that's the whole thing.

Silence. They lie there.

Roger   Holy . . . Christ. Richie . . . you hear him? You hear
what he said?

Richie   He's a storyteller.

Roger   What you mean?

Richie   I mean, he's a storyteller, all right; he tells stories, all right.

Roger   What are we into now? You wanna end up like that friend a his, or you don't believe what he said? Which are you sayin'?

The door bursts open. The sounds of machine guns and cannon are being made by someone, and **Carlyle**, *drunk and playing, comes crawling in.* **Roger**, **Richie**, *and* **Billy** *all pop up, startled, to look at him.*

Hey, hey, what's happenin'?

Billy   Who's happenin'?

Roger   You attackin' or you retreatin', man?

Carlyle (*looking up; big grin*)   Hey, baby . . . ? (*Continues shooting, crawling. The three boys look at each other.*)

Roger   What's happenin', man? Whatcha doin'?

Carlyle   I dunno, soul; I dunno. Practicin' my duties, my new abilities. (*Half-sitting, he flops onto his side, starts to crawl.*) The low crawl, man; like I was taught in basic, that's what I'm doin'. You gotta know your shit, man, else you get your ass blown so far away you don't ever see it again. Oh, sure, you guys don't care. I know it. You got it made. You got it made. I don't got it made. You got a little home here, got friends, people to talk to. I got nothin'. You got jobs they probably ain't ever gonna ship you out, you got so important jobs. I got no job. They don't even wanna give me a job. I know it. They are gonna kill me. They are gonna send me over there to get me killed, goddammit. WHATSAMATTER WITH ALL YOU PEOPLE?

The anger explodes out of the grieving, and **Roger** *rushes to kneel beside* **Carlyle**. *He speaks gently, firmly.*

Roger   Hey, man, get cool, get some cool; purchase some cool, man.

Carlyle   Awwwww . . . (*Clumsily, he turns away.*)

Roger   Just hang in there.

Carlyle   I don't wanna be no DEAD man. I don't wanna be
the one they all thinkin' is so stupid he's the only one'll go,
they tell him; they don't even have to give him a job. I got
thoughts, man, in my head; alla time, burnin' burnin'
thoughts a understandin'.

Roger   Don't you think we know that, man? It ain't the way
you're sayin' it.

Carlyle   It is.

Roger   No. I mean, we all probably gonna go. We all
probably gonna have to go.

Carlyle   No-o-o-o-o.

Roger   I mean it.

Carlyle (*as he suddenly nearly topples over*)   I am very drunk.
(*And he looks up at* **Roger**.) You think so?

Roger   I'm sayin' so. And I am sayin', 'No sweat.' No
point.

Carlyle *angrily pushes at* **Roger**, *knocking him backward.*

Carlyle   Awwwww, dammit, dammit, mother . . . shit . . .
it . . . ohhhhhhh. (*Sliding to the floor, the rage and anguish
softening into only breathing.*) I mean it. I mean it. (*Silence. He
lies there.*)

Roger   What . . . a you doin' . . . ?

Carlyle   Huh?

Roger   I don't know what you're up to on our freshly
mopped floor.

Carlyle   Gonna go sleep – okay? No sweat . . . (*Suddenly very
polite, he is looking up.*) Can I, soul? Izzit all right?

Roger   Sure, man, sure, if you wanna, but why don't you go
where you got a bed? Don't you like beds?

Carlyle Dunno where's zat. My bed. I can' fin' it. I can' fin' my own bed. I looked all over, but I can' fin' it anywhere. GONE!

Slipping back down now, he squirms to make a nest. He hugs his bottle.

Roger (*moving to his bunk, where he grabs a blanket*) Okay, okay, man. But get on top a this, man. (*He is spreading the blanket on the floor, trying to help* **Carlyle** *get on it.*) Make it softer. C'mon . . . get on this.

Billy *has risen with his own blanket, and is moving now to hand it to* **Roger**.

Billy Cat's hurtin', Rog.

Roger Ohhhhh, yeh.

Carlyle Ohhhhh . . . it was so sweet at home . . . it was so sweet, baby; so-o-o good. They doin' dances make you wanna cry . . . (*Hugging the blankets now, he drifts in a kind of dream.*)

Roger I know, man.

Carlyle So sweet . . .

Billy *is moving back to his own bed, where, quietly, he sits.*

Roger I know, man.

Carlyle So sweet . . . !

Roger Yeh.

Carlyle How come I gotta be here?

On his way to the door to close it, **Roger** *falters, looks at* **Carlyle**, *then moves on toward the door.*

Roger I dunno, Jim.

Billy *is sitting and watching, as* **Roger** *goes on to the door, gently closes it, and returns to his bed.*

Billy I know why he's gotta be here, Roger. You wanna know? Why don't you ask me?

Roger Okay. How come he gotta be here?

Billy (*smiling*)   Freedom's frontier, man. That's why.

Roger (*settled on the edge of his bed and about to lie back*)   Oh . . .
yeh . . .

As a distant bugle begins to play taps and **Richie**, *carrying a blanket, is
approaching* **Carlyle**. **Roger** *settles back;* **Billy** *is staring at*
Richie; **Carlyle** *does not stir; the bugle plays.*

Bet that ole sarge don't live a year, Billy. Fuckin' blow his own
ass sky high.

Richie *has covered* **Carlyle**. *He pats* **Carlyle**'*s arm, and then
straightens in order to return to his bed.*

Billy   Richie . . . !

His hissing voice freezes **Richie**. *He stands, and then he starts again to
move, and* **Billy**'*s voice comes again and* **Richie** *cannot move.*

Richie . . . how come you gotta keep doin' that stuff?

Roger *looks at* **Billy**, *staring at* **Richie**, *who stands still as a stone
over the sleeping* **Carlyle**.

Billy   How come?

Roger   He dunno, man. Do you? You dunno, do you, Rich?

Richie   No.

Carlyle (*from deep in his sleep and grieving*)   It . . . was . . . so . . .
pretty . . !

Richie   No.

The lights are fading with the last soft notes of taps.

Act Two

Scene One

*Lights come up on the cadre room. It is late afternoon and **Billy** is lying on his stomach, his head at the foot of the bed, his chin resting on his hands. He wears gym shorts and sweat socks; his T-shirt lies on the bed and his sneakers are on the floor. **Roger** is at his footlocker, taking out a pair of sweat socks. His sneakers and his basketball are on his bed. He is wearing his khakis.*

*A silence passes, and then **Roger** closes his footlocker and sits on his bed, where he starts lacing his sneakers, holding them on his lap.*

Billy Rog . . . you think I'm a busybody? In any way? (*Silence. **Roger** laces his sneakers.*) Roger?

Roger Huh? Uh-uh.

Billy Some people do. I mean, back home. (*He rolls slightly to look at **Roger**.*) Or that I didn't know how to behave. Sort of.

Roger It's time we maybe get changed, don't you think? (*He rises and goes to his locker. He takes off his trousers, shoes, and socks.*)

Billy Yeh. I guess. I don't feel like it, though. I don't feel good, don't know why.

Roger Be good for you, man; be good for you. (*Pulling on his gym shorts, he returns to his bed, carrying his shoes and socks.*)

Billy Yeh. (*He sits up on the edge of his bed. **Roger**, sitting, is bowed over, putting on his socks.*) I mean, a lot a people thought like I didn't know how to behave in a simple way. You know? That I overcomplicated everything. I didn't think so. Don't think so. I just thought I was seein' complications that were there but nobody else saw. (*He is struggling now to put on his T-shirt. He seems weary, almost weak.*) I mean, Wisconsin's a funny place. All those clear-eyed people sayin 'Hello' and lookin' you straight in the eye. Everybody's good, you think, and happy and honest. And then there's all of a sudden a neighbor who goes mad as a hatter. I had a neighbor who came out of his house one morning with axes in both hands. He started then attackin' the cars that were driving up and down in front of his house. An' we all knew why he did it, sorta. (*He pauses; he thinks.*) It made me wanna be a priest. I wanted to be a priest then. I was sixteen. Priests could help people. Could take away what hurt 'em. I wanted that, I thought. Somethin', huh?

Roger (*has the basketball in his hands*)   Yeh. But everybody's got feelin's like that sometimes.

Billy   I don't know.

Roger   You know, you oughta work on a little jump shot, my man. Get you some kinda fall-away jumper to go with that beauty of a hook. Make you tough out there.

Billy   Can't fuckin' do it. Not my game. I mean, like that bar we go to. You think I could get a job there bartendin', maybe? I could learn the ropes. (*He is watching* **Roger**, *who has risen to walk to his locker.*) You think I could get a job there off-duty hours?

Roger (*pulling his locker open to display the pinup on the inside of the door.*)   You don't want no job. It's that little black-haired waitress you wantin' to know.

Billy   No, man. Not really.

Roger   It's okay. She tough, man. (*He begins to remove his uniform shirt. He will put on an O.D. T-shirt to go to the gym.*)

Billy   I mean, not the way you're sayin' it, is all. Sure, there's somethin' about her. I don't know what. I ain't even spoke to her yet. But somethin'. I mean, what's she doin' there? When she's dancin', it's like she knows somethin'. She's degradin' herself, I sometimes feel. You think she is?

Roger   Man, you don't even know the girl. She's workin'.

Billy   I'd like to talk to her. Tell her stuff. Find out about her. Sometimes I'm thinkin' about her and I got a job there, I get to know her and she and I get to be real tight, man – close,

you know. Maybe we screw, maybe we don't. It's nice . . .
whatever.

Roger   Sure. She a real fine-lookin' chippy, Billy. Got nice
cakes. Nice little titties.

Billy   I think she's smart, too.

Roger *starts laughing so hard he almost falls into his locker.*

Billy   Oh, all I do is talk. 'Yabba-yabba.' I mean, my mom
and dad are really terrific people. How'd they ever end up
with somebody so weird as me?

Roger *moves to him, jostles him.*

Roger   I'm tellin' you, the gym and a little ball is what you
need. Little exercise. Little bumpin' into people. The soul is
tellin' you.

Billy *rises and goes to his locker, where he tarts putting on his sweat
clothes.*

Billy   I mean, Roger, you remember how we met in P
Company? Both of us brand new. You started talkin' to me.
You just started talkin' to me and you didn't stop.

Roger (*hardly looking up*)   Yeh.

Billy   Did you see somethin' in me made you pick me?

Roger   I was talkin' to everybody, man. For that whole day.
Two whole days. You was just the first one to talk back
friendly. Though you didn't say much, as I recall.

Billy   The first white person, you mean. (*Wearing his
sweatpants, he is now at his bed, putting on his sneakers.*)

Roger   Yeh. I was tryin' to come outa myself a little. Do like
the fuckin' headshrinker been tellin' me to stop them fuckin'
headaches I was havin', you know. Now let us do fifteen or
twenty push-ups and get over to that gymnasium, like I been
sayin'. Then we can take our civvies with us – we can shower
and change at the gym. (*He crosses to* **Billy**, *who flops down on his
belly on the bed.*)

Billy   I don't know . . . I don't know what it is I'm feelin'.
Sick like.

Roger *forces* **Billy** *up onto his feet and shoves him playfully
downstage, where they both fall forward into the push-up position, side by
side.*

Roger   Do 'em, trooper. Do 'em. Get it.

Roger *starts.* **Billy** *joins in. After five,* **Roger** *realizes that* **Billy**
has his knees on the floor. They start again. This time, **Billy** *counts in
double time. They start again. At about 'seven,'* **Richie** *enters. Neither*
Billy *nor* **Roger** *sees him. They keep going.*

Roger *and* **Billy**   . . . seven, eight, nine, ten . . .

Richie   No, no; no, no; no, no, no. That's not it; that's not it.

They keep going, yelling the numbers louder and louder.

Roger *and* **Billy**   . . . eleven, twelve, thirteen . . .

Richie *crosses to his locker and gets his bottle of cologne, and then
returning to the center of the room to stare at them, he stands there dabbing
cologne on his face.*

Roger *and* **Billy**   . . . fourteen, fifteen.

Richie   You'll never get it like that. You're so far apart and
you're both humping at the same time. And all that counting.
It's so unromantic.

Roger (*rising and moving to his bed to pick up the basketball*)   We
was exercisin', Richard. You heard a that?

Richie   Call it what you will, Roger.

With a flick of his wrist, **Roger** *tosses the basketball to* **Billy**.

Everybody has their own cute little pet names for it.

Billy   Hey!

And he tosses the ball at **Richie**, *hitting him in the chest, sending the
cologne bottle flying.* **Richie** *yelps, as* **Billy** *retrieves the ball and,
grabbing up his sweat jacket from the bed, heads for the door.* **Roger**, *at
his own locker, has taken out his suit bag of civilian clothes.*

You missed.

Richie   Billy, Billy, Billy, please, please, the ruffian approach will not work with me. It impresses me not even one tiny little bit. All you've done is spill my cologne. (*He bends to pick up the cologne from the floor.*)

Billy   That was my aim.

Roger   See you.

Billy *is passing* **Richie**. *Suddenly* **Richie** *sprays* **Billy** *with cologne, some of it getting on* **Roger**, *as* **Roger** *and* **Billy**, *groaning and cursing at* **Richie**, *rush to the door.*

Richie   Try the more delicate approach next time, Bill.

Having crossed to the door, he stands a moment, leaning against the frame. Then he bounces to **Billy**'s *bed, sings 'He's just my Bill,' and squirts cologne on the pillow. At his locker, he deposits the cologne, takes off his shirt, shoes, and socks. Removing a hardcover copy of Pauline Kael's* I Lost It at the Movies *from the top shelf of the locker, he bounds to the center of the room and tosses the book the rest of the way to the bed. Quite pleased with himself, he fidgets, pats his stomach, then lowers himself into the push-up position, goes to his knees, and stands up.*

Am I out of my fucking mind? Those two are crazy. I'm not crazy.

He pivots and strides to his locker. With an ashtray, a pack of matches, and a pack of cigarettes, he hurries to his bed and makes himself comfortable to read, his head propped up on a pillow. Settling himself, he opens the book, finds his place, thinks a little, starts to read. For a moment he lies there. And then **Carlyle** *steps into the room. He comes through the doorway looking to his left and right. He comes several steps into the room and looks at* **Richie**. **Richie** *sees him. They look at each other.*

Carlyle   Ain't nobody here, man?

Richie   Hello, Carlyle. How are you today?

Carlyle   Ain't nobody here? (*He is nervous and angrily disappointed.*)

Richie   Who do you want?

Carlyle   Where's the black boy?

Richie   Roger? My God, why do you keep calling him that? Don't you know his name yet? Roger. Roger. (*He thickens his voice at this, imitating someone very stupid.* **Carlyle** *stares at him.*)

Carlyle   Yeh. Where is he?

Richie   I am not his keeper, you know. I am not his private secretary, you know.

Carlyle   I do not know. I do not know. That is why I am asking. I come to see him. You are here. I ask you. I don't know. I mean, Carlyle made a fool outa himself comin' in here the other night, talkin' on and on like how he did. Lay on the floor. He remember. You remember? It all one hype, man; that all one hype. You know what I mean. That ain't the real Carlyle was in here. This one here and now the real Carlyle. Who the real Richie?

Richie   Well . . . the real Richie . . . has gone home. To Manhattan. I, however, am about to read this book. (*Which he again starts to try to do.*)

Carlyle   Oh. Shit. Jus' you the only one here, then, huh?

Richie   So it would seem. (*He looks at the air and then under the bed as if to find someone.*) So it would seem. Did you hear about Martin?

Carlyle   What happened to Martin? I ain't seen him.

Richie   They are shipping him home. Someone told about what he did to himself. I don't know who.

Carlyle   Wasn't me. Not me. I keep that secret.

Richie   I'm sure you did. (*Rising, walking toward* **Carlyle** *and the door, cigarette pack in hand.*) You want a cigarette? Or don't you smoke? Or do you have to go right away? (*Closing the door.*) There's a chill sometimes coming down the hall, I don't know from where. (*Crossing back to his bed and climbing in.*) And I think I've got the start of a little cold. Did you want the cigarette?

Carlyle *is staring at him. Then he examines the door and looks again* *at* **Richie**. *He stares at* **Richie**, *thinking, and then he walks toward him.*

Carlyle   You know what I bet? I been lookin' at you real close. It just a way I got about me. And I bet if I was to hang my boy out in front of you, my big boy, man, you'd start wantin' to touch him. Be beggin' and talkin' sweet to ole Carlyle. Am I right or wrong? (*He leans over* **Richie**.) What do you say?

Richie   Pardon?

Carlyle   You heard me. Ohhh. I am so restless, I don't even understand it. My big black boy is what I was talkin' about. My thing, man; my rope, Jim. HEY, RICHIE! (*And he lunges, then moves his fingers through* **Richie**'s *hair*.) How long you been a punk? Can you hear me? Am I clear? Do I talk funny? (*He is leaning close.*) Can you smell the gin on my mouth?

Richie   I mean, if you really came looking for Roger, he and Billy are gone to the gymnasium. They were –

Carlyle   No. (*He slides down on the bed, his arm placed over* **Richie**'s *legs*.) I got no athletic abilities. I got none. No moves. I don't know. HEY, RICHIE! (*Leaning close again.*) I just got this question I asked. I got no answer.

Richie   I don't know . . . what . . . you mean.

Carlyle   I heard me. I understood me. 'How long you been a punk?' is the question I asked. Have you got a reply?

Richie (*confused, irritated, but fascinated*)   Not to that question.

Carlyle   Who do if you don't? I don't. How'm I gonna?

Suddenly there is whistling in the hall, as if someone might enter, footsteps approaching, and **Richie** *leaps to his feet and scurries away toward the door, tucking in his undershirt as he goes.*

Man, don't you wanna talk to me? Don't you wanna talk to ole Carlyle?

Richie   Not at the moment.

Carlyle (*rising, starting after* **Richie**, *who stands nervously near* **Roger**'s *bed*)   I want to talk to you, man; why don't you want to talk to me? We can be friends. Talkin' back and forth, sharin' thoughts and bein' happy.

Richie   I don't think that's what you want.

Carlyle (*very near to* **Richie**)   What do I want?

Richie   I mean, to talk to me. (*As if repulsed, he crosses away. But it is hard to tell if the move is genuine or coy.*)

Carlyle   What am I doin'? I am talkin'. DON'T YOU TELL ME I AIN'T TALKIN' WHEN I AM TALKIN'! COURSE I AM. Bendin' over backwards. (*And pressing his hands against himself in his anger, he has touched the grease on his shirt, the filth of his clothing, and this ignites the anger.*) Do you know they still got me in that goddamn P Company? That goddamn transient company. It like they think I ain't got no notion what a home is. No nose for no home – like I ain't never had no home. I had a home. IT LIKE THEY THINK THERE AIN'T NO PLACE FOR ME IN THIS MOTHER ARMY BUT K.P. ALL SUDSY AND WRINKLED AND SWEATIN'. EVERY DAY SINCE I GOT TO THIS SHIT HOUSE, MISTER! HOW MANY TIMES YOU BEEN ON K.P.? WHEN'S THE LAST TIME YOU PULLED K.P.? (*He has roared down to where* **Richie** *had moved, the rage possessing him.*)

Richie   I'm E.D.

Carlyle   You E.D. ? You E.D. ? You Edie, are you? I didn't ask you what you friends call you, I asked you when's the last time you had K.P.?

Richie (*edging toward his bed; he will go there, get and light a cigarette*) E.D. is 'Exempt from Duty.'

Carlyle (*moving after* **Richie**)   You ain't got no duties? What shit you talkin' about? Everybody in this fuckin' army got duties. That what the fuckin' army all about. You ain't got no duties, who got 'em?

Richie   Because of my job, Carlyle. I have a very special job. And my friends don't call me Edie. (*Big smile.*) They call me Irene.

Carlyle   That mean what you sayin' is you kiss ass for somebody, don't it? Good for you. (*Seemingly relaxed and gentle, he settles down on* **Richie**'s *bed. He seems playful and charming.*) You know the other night I was sleepin' there. You know.

Richie   Yes.

Carlyle (*gleefully, enormously pleased*)   You remember that? How come you remember that? You sweet.

Richie   We don't have people sleeping on our floor that often, Carlyle.

Carlyle   But the way you crawl over in the night, gimme a big kiss on my joint. That nice.

Richie (*shocked, he blinks*)   What?

Carlyle   Or did I dream that?

Richie (*laughing in spite of himself*)   My God, you're outrageous!

Carlyle   Maybe you dreamed it.

Richie   What . . . ? No. I don't know.

Carlyle   Maybe you did it, then; you didn't dream it.

Richie   How come you talk so much?

Carlyle   I don't talk, man, who's gonna talk? YOU? (*He is laughing and amused, but there is an anger near the surface now, an ugliness.*) That bore me to death. I don't like nobody's voice but my own. I am so pretty. Don't like nobody else face. (*And then viciously, he spits out at* **Richie**.) You goddamn face ugly fuckin' queer punk! (*And* **Richie** *jumps in confusion.*)

Richie   What's the matter with you?

Carlyle   You goddamn ugly punk face. YOU UGLY!

Richie   Nice mouth.

Carlyle That's right. That's right. And you got a weird mouth. Like to suck joints.

As **Richie** *storms to his locker, throwing the book inside. He pivots, grabbing a towel, marching toward the door.*

Hey, you gonna jus' walk out on me? Where you goin'? You c'mon back. Hear?

Richie That's my bed, for Chrissake. (*He lunges into the hall.*)

Carlyle You'd best. (*Lying there, he makes himself comfortable. He takes a pint bottle from his back pocket.*) You come back, Richie, I tell you a good joke. Make you laugh, make you cry. (*He takes a big drink.*) That's right. Ole Frank and Jesse, they got the stagecoach stopped, all the peoples lined up – Frank say, 'All right, peoples, we gonna rape all the men and rob all the women.' Jesse say, 'Frank, no, no – that ain't it – we gonna –' And this one little man yell real loud, 'You shut up, Jesse; Frank knows what he's doin'.'

Loudly, he laughs and laughs. **Billy** *enters. Startled at the sight of* **Carlyle** *there in* **Richie**'s *bed,* **Billy** *falters, as* **Carlyle** *gestures toward him.*

Hey, man . . . ! Hey, you know, they send me over to that Vietnam, I be cool, 'cause I been dodgin' bullets and shit since I been old enough to get on pussy make it happy to know me. I can get on, I can do my job.

Billy *looks weary and depressed. Languidly he crosses to his bed. He still wears his sweat clothes.* **Carlyle** *studies him, then stares at the ceiling.*

Carlyle Yeh. I was just layin' here thinkin' that and you come in and out it come, words to say my feelin'. That my problem. That the black man's problem altogether. You ever considered that? Too much feelin'. He too close to everything. He is, man; too close his blood, to his body. It ain't that he don't have no good mind, but he BELIEVE in his body. Is . . . that Richie the only punk in this room, or is there more?

Billy What?

Carlyle   The punk; is he the only punk? (*Carefully he takes one of* **Richie**'s *cigarettes and lights it.*)

Billy   He's all right.

Carlyle   I ain't askin' about the quality of his talent, but is he the only one, is my question?

Billy (*does not want to deal with this; he sits there*)   You get your orders yet?

Carlyle   Orders for what?

Billy   To tell you where you work.

Carlyle   I'm P Company, man. I work in P Company. I do K.P. That all. Don't deserve no more. Do you know I been in this army three months and ten days and everbody still doin' the same shit and sayin' the same shit and wearin' the same green shitty clothes? I ain't been happy one day, and that a lotta goddamn misery back to back in this ole boy. Is that Richie a good punk? Huh? Is he? He takes care of you and Roger – that how come you in this room, the three of you?

Billy   What?

Carlyle (*emphatically*)   You and Roger are hittin' on Richie, right?

Billy   He's not queer, if that's what you're sayin'. A little effeminate, but that's all, no more; if that's what you're sayin'.

Carlyle   I'd like to get some of him myself if he a good punk, is what I'm sayin'. That's what I'm sayin'! You don't got no understandin' how a man can maybe be a little diplomatic about what he's sayin' sorta sideways, do you? Jesus.

Billy   He don't do that stuff.

Carlyle (*lying there*)   What stuff?

Billy   Listen, man. I don't feel too good, you don't mind.

Carlyle   What stuff?

Billy   What you're thinkin'.

Carlyle   What . . . am I thinkin'?

Billy   You . . . know.

Carlyle   Yes, I do. It in my head, that how come I know. But how do you know? I can see your heart, Billy boy, but you cannot see mine. I am unknown. You . . . are known.

Billy (*as if he is about to vomit, and fighting it.*)   You just . . . talk fast and keep movin', don't you? Don't ever stay still.

Carlyle   Words to say my feelin', Billy boy.

Richie *steps into the room. He sees* **Billy** *and* **Carlyle**, *and freezes.*

Carlyle   There he is. There he be.

Richie *moves to his locker to put away the towel.*

Richie   He's one of them who hasn't come down far out of the trees yet, Billy; believe me.

Carlyle   You got rudeness in your voice, Richie – you got meanness I can hear about ole Carlyle. You tellin' me I oughta leave – is that what you think you're doin'? You don't want me here?

Richie   You come to see Roger, who isn't here, right? Man like you must have important matters to take care of all over the quad; I can't imagine a man like you not having extremely important things to do all over the world, as a matter of fact, Carlyle.

Carlyle (*rises, begins to smooth the sheets and straighten the pillow; he will put the pint bottle in his back pocket and cross near to* **Richie**) Ohhhh, listen – don't mind all the shit I say. I just talk bad, is all I do; I don't do bad. I got to have friends just like anybody else. I'm just bored and restless, that all; takin' it out on you two. I mean, I know Richie here ain't really no punk, not really. I was just talkin', just jivin' and entertainin' my own self. Don't take me serious, not ever. I get on out and see you all later. (*He moves for the door,* **Richie** *right behind him, almost ushering him.*) You be cool, hear? Man don't do the jivin', he the one gettin' jived. That what my little brother Henry tell me and tell me.

Moving leisurely, **Carlyle** *backs out the door and is gone.* **Richie** *shuts the door. There is a silence as* **Richie** *stands by the door.* **Billy** *looks at him and then looks away.*

Billy   I am gonna have to move myself outa here, Roger decides to adopt that sonofabitch.

Richie   He's an animal.

Billy   Yeh, and on top a that, he's a rotten person.

Richie (*laughs nervously, crossing nearer to* **Billy**)   I think you're probably right.

Still laughing a little, **Richie** *pats* **Billy**'s *shoulder and* **Billy** *freezes at the touch. Awkwardly,* **Richie** *removes his hand and crosses to his bed. When he has lain down,* **Billy** *bends to take off his sneakers, then lies back on his pillow staring, thinking, and there is a silence.* **Richie** *does not move. He lies there, struggling to prepare himelf for something.*

Hey . . . Billy? (*Very slight pause.*) Billy?

Billy   Yeh.

Richie   You know that story you told the other night?

Billy   Yeh . . . ?

Richie   You know . . .

Billy   What . . . about it?

Richie   Well, was it . . . about you? (*Pause.*) I mean, was it . . . ABOUT you? Were you Frankie? (*This is difficult for him.*) Are . . . you Frankie? Billy? (**Billy** *is slowly sitting up.*)

Billy   You sonofabitch . . . !

Richie   Or was it really about somebody you knew . . . ?

Billy (*sitting, outraged and glaring*)   You didn't hear me at all!

Richie   I'm just asking a simple question, Billy, that's all I'm doing.

Billy   You are really sick. You know that? Your brain is really, truly rancid! Do you know there's a theory now it's genetic? That it's all a matter of genes and shit like that?

Richie   Everything is not so ungodly cryptic, Billy.

Billy   You. You, man, and the rot it's makin' outa your feeble fuckin' brain.

Roger, *dressed in civilian clothes, bursts in and* **Billy** *leaps to his feet.*

Roger   Hey, hey, anyone got a couple bucks he can loan me?

Billy   Rog, where you been?

Roger (*throwing the basketball and his sweat clothes into his locker*)   I need five. C'mon.

Billy   Where you been? That asshole friend a yours was here.

Roger   I know, I know. Can you gimme five?

Richie (*jumps to the floor and heads for his locker*)   You want five. I got it. You want ten or more, even?

Billy, *watching* **Richie**, *turns, and nervously paces down right, where he moves about, worried.*

Billy   I mean, we gotta talk about him, man; we gotta talk about him.

Roger (*as* **Richie** *is handing him two fives*)   'Cause we goin' to town together. I jus' run into him out on the quad, man, and he was feelin' real bad 'bout the way he acted, how you guys done him, he was fallin' down apologizin' all over the place.

Billy (*as* **Richie** *marches back to his bed and sits down*)   I mean, he's got a lotta weird ideas about us; I'm tellin' you.

Roger   He's just a little fucked up in his head is all, but he ain't trouble. (*He takes a pair of sunglasses from the locker and puts them on.*)

Billy   Who needs him? I mean, we don't need him.

Roger   You gettin' too nervous, man. Nobody said anything about anybody needin' anybody. I been on the street all my life; he brings back home. I played me a little ball, Billy; took me a shower. I'm feelin' good! (*He has moved down to* **Billy**.)

Billy   I'm tellin' you there's something wrong with him, though.

Roger (*face to face with* **Billy**, *he is a little irritated*)   Every black man in the world ain't like me, man; you get used to that idea. You get to know him, and you gonna like him. I'm tellin' you. You get to be laughin' just like me to hear him talk his shit. But you gotta relax.

Richie   I agree with Billy, Roger.

Roger   Well, you guys got it all worked out and that's good, but I am goin' to town with him. Man's got wheels. Got a good head. You got any sense, you'll come with us.

Billy   What are you talkin' about – come with you? I just tole you he's crazy.

Roger   And I tole you you're wrong.

Richie   We weren't invited.

Roger   I'm invitin' you.

Richie   No, I don't wanna.

Roger (*moves to* **Richie**; *it seems he really wants* **Richie** *to go*)   You sure, Richie? C'mon.

Richie   No.

Roger   Billy? He got wheels, we goin' in drinkin', see if gettin' our heads real bad don't just make us feel real good. You know what I mean. I got him right; you got him wrong.

Billy   But what if I'm right?

Roger   Billy, Billy, the man is waitin' on me. You know you wanna. Jesus. Bad cat like that gotta know the way. He been to D.C. before. Got cousins here. Got wheels for the weekend.

You always talkin' how you don't do nothin' – you just talk it.
Let's do it tonight – stop talkin'. Be cruisin' up and down the
strip, leanin' out the window, bad as we wanna be. True cool
is a car. We can flip a cigarette out the window – we can
watch it bounce. Get us some chippies. You know we can.
And if we don't, he knows a cathouse, it fulla cats.

Billy You serious?

Richie You mean you're going to a whorehouse? That's
disgusting.

Billy Listen who's talkin'. What do you want me to do? Stay
here with you?

Richie We could go to a movie or something.

Roger I am done with this talkin'. You goin', you stayin'?
(*He crosses to his locker, pulls into view a wide-brimmed black and shiny
hat, and puts it on, cocking it at a sharp angle.*)

Billy I don't know.

Roger (*stepping for the door*) I am goin'.

Billy (*turning, he sees the hat*) I'm going. Okay! I'm going!
Going, going, going! (*And he runs to his locker.*)

Richie Oh, Billy, you'll be scared to death in a cathouse
and you know it.

Billy BULLSHIT! (*He is removing his sweatpants and putting on a
pair of gray corduroy trousers.*)

Roger Billy got him a lion tamer 'tween his legs!

The door bangs open and **Carlyle** *is there, still clad in his filthy
fatigues, but wearing a going-to-town black knit cap on his head and
carrying a bottle.*

Carlyle Man, what's goin' on? I been waitin' like
throughout my fuckin' life.

Roger Billy's goin', too. He's gotta change.

Carlyle He goin', too! Hey! Beautiful! That beautiful! (*His
grin is large, his laugh is loud.*)

Roger   Didn't I tell you, Billy?

Carlyle   That beautiful, man; we all goin' to be friends!

Richie (*sitting on his bed*)   What about me, Carlyle?

Carlyle *looks at* **Richie**, *and then at* **Roger**, *and then he and* **Roger** *begin to laugh.* **Carlyle** *pokes* **Roger** *and they laugh as they are leaving.* **Billy**, *grabbing up his sneakers to follow, stops at the door, looking only briefly at* **Richie**. *Then* **Billy** *goes and shuts the door. The lights are fading to black.*

Scene Two

In the dark, taps begins to play. And then slowly the lights rise, but the room remains dim. Only the lamp attached to **Richie**'s *bed burns and there is the glow and spill of the hallway coming through the transom.* **Billy**, **Carlyle**, **Roger**, *and* **Richie** *are sprawled about the room.* **Billy**, *lying on his stomach, has his head at the foot of his bed, a half-empty bottle of beer dangling in his hand. He wears a blue oxford-cloth shirt and his sneakers lie beside his bed.* **Roger**, *collapsed in his own bed, lies upon his back, his head also at the foot, a* Playboy *magazine covering his face and a half-empty bottle of beer in his hands, folded on his belly. Having removed his civilian shirt, he wears a white T-shirt.* **Carlyle** *is lying on his belly on* **Richie**'s *bed, his head at the foot, and he is facing out.* **Richie** *is sitting on the floor, resting against* **Roger**'s *footlocker. He is wrapped in a blanket. Beside him is an unopened bottle of beer and a bottle opener.*

They are all dreamy in the dimness as taps plays sadly on and then fades into silence. No one moves.

Richie   I don't know where it was, but it was, but it wasn't here. And we were all in it – it felt like – but we all had different faces. After you guys left, I only dozed for a few minutes, so it couldn't have been long. Roger laughed a lot and Billy was taller. I don't remember all the details exactly, and even though we were the ones in it, I know it was about my father. He was a big man. I was six. He was a very big man when I was six and he went away, but I remember him.

He started drinking and staying home making model airplanes and boats and paintings by the numbers. We had money from Mom's family, so he was just home all the time. And then one day I was coming home from kindergarten, and as I was starting up the front walk he came out the door and he had these suitcases in his hands. He was leaving, see, sneaking out, and I'd caught him. We looked at each other and I just knew and I started crying. He yelled at me, 'Don't you cry; don't you start crying.' I tried to grab him and he pushed me down in the grass. And then he was gone. G-O-N-E.

Billy   And that was it? That was it?

Richie   I remember hiding my eyes. I lay in the grass and hid my eyes and waited.

Billy   He never came back?

Richie   No.

Carlyle   Ain't that some shit. Now, I'm a jive-time street nigger. I knew where my daddy was all the while. He workin' in this butcher shop two blocks up the street. Ole Mom used to point him out. 'There he go. That him – that your daddy.' We'd see him on the street, 'There he go.'

Roger   Man couldn't see his way to livin' with you – that what you're sayin'?

Carlyle   Never saw the day.

Roger   And still couldn't get his ass outa the neighborhood?

Richie *begins trying to open his bottle of beer.*

Carlyle   Ain't that a bitch. Poor ole bastard just duck his head – Mom pointin' at him – he git this real goddamn hangdog look like he don't know who we talkin' about and he walk a little faster. Why the hell he never move away I don't know, unless he was crazy. But I don't think so. He come up to me once – I was playin'. 'Boy,' he says, 'I ain't your daddy. I ain't. Your momma's crazy.' 'Don't you be callin' my momma crazy, Daddy,' I tole him. Poor ole thing didn't know what to do.

Richie (*giving up; he can't get the beer open*)   Somebody open this for me? I can't get this open.

Billy *seems about to move to help, but* **Carlyle** *is quicker, rising a little on the bunk and reaching.*

Carlyle   Ole Carlyle get it.

Richie *slides along the floor until he can place the bottle in* **Carlyle**'s *outstretched hand.*

Richie   Then there was this once – there was this T.V. documentary about these bums in San Francisco, this T.V. guy interviewing all these bums, and just for maybe ten seconds while he was talkin' . . .

Smiling, **Carlyle** *hands* **Richie** *the opened bottle.*

. . . to this one bum, there was this other one in the background jumpin around like he thought he was dancin' and wavin' his hat, and even though there wasn't anything about him like my father and I didn't really ever see his face at all, I just kept thinkin': That's him. My dad. He thinks he's dancin'.

They lie there in silence and suddenly, softly, **Billy** *giggles, and then he giggles a little more and louder.*

Billy   Jesus!

Richie   What?

Billy   That's ridiculous, Richie; sayin' that, thinkin' that. If it didn't look like him, it wasn't him, but you gotta be makin' up a story.

Carlyle (*shifting now for a more comfortable position, he moves his head to the pillow at the top of the bed*)   Richie first saw me, he didn't like me much nohow, but he thought it over now, he changed his way a thinkin'. I can see that clear. We gonna be one big happy family.

Richie   Carlyle likes me, Billy; he thinks I'm pretty.

Carlyle (*sitting up a little to make his point clear*)   No, I don't think you pretty. A broad is pretty. Punks ain't pretty. Punk – if he good-lookin' – is cute. You cute.

Richie   He's gonna steal me right away, little Billy. You're so slow, Bill. I prefer a man who's decisive. (*He is lying down now on the floor at the foot of his bed.*)

Billy   You just keep at it, you're gonna have us all believin' you are just what you say you are.

Richie   Which is more than we can say for you.

Now **Roger** *rises on his elbow to light a cigarette.*

Billy   Jive, jive.

Richie   You're arrogant, Billy. So arrogant.

Billy   What are you – on the rag?

Richie   Wouldn't it just bang your little balls if I were!

Roger (*to* **Richie**)   Hey, man. What's with you?

Richie   Stupidity offends me; lies and ignorance offend me.

Billy   You know where we was? The three of us? All three of us, earlier on? To the wrong side of the tracks, Richard. One good black upside-down whorehouse where you get what you buy, no jive along with it – so if it's a lay you want and need, you go! Or don't they have faggot whorehouses?

Roger   IF YOU GUYS DON'T CUT THIS SHIT OUT I'M GONNA BUST SOMEBODY'S HEAD! (*Angrily, he flops back on his bed. There is a silence as they all lie there.*)

Richie   'Where we was,' he says. Listen to him. 'Where we was.' And he's got more school, Carlyle, than you have fingers and . . . (*He has lifted his foot onto the bed; it touches, presses,* **Carlyle***'s foot.*) . . . toes. It's this pseudo-earthy quality he feigns – but inside he's all cashmere.

Billy   That's a lie. (*Giggling, he is staring at the floor.*) I'm polyester, worsted, and mohair.

Richie   You have a lot of school, Billy; don't say you don't.

Billy   You said 'fingers and toes'; you didn't say 'a lot.'

Carlyle   I think people get dumber the more they put their butts into some schoolhouse door.

Billy   It depends on what the hell you're talkin' about. (*Now he looks at* **Carlyle***, and sees the feet touching.*)

Carlyle   I seen cats back on the block, they knew what was shakin' – then they got into all this school jive and, man, every year they went, they come back they didn't know nothin'.

Billy *is staring at* **Richie***'s foot pressed against and rubbing* **Carlyle***'s foot.* **Richie** *sees* **Billy** *looking.* **Billy** *cannot believe what he is seeing. It fills him with fear. The silence goes on and on.*

Richie   Billy, why don't you and Roger go for a walk?

Billy   What? (*He bolts to his knees. He is frozen on his knees on the bed.*)

Richie   Roger asked you to go downtown, you went, you had fun.

Roger (*having turned, he knows almost instantly what is going on*)   I asked you, too.

Richie   You asked me; you BEGGED Billy. I said no. Billy said no. You took my ten dollars. You begged Billy. I'm asking you a favor now – go for a walk. Let Carlyle and me have some time. (*Silence.*)

Carlyle (*sits up, uneasy and wary*)   That how you work it?

Roger   Work what?

Carlyle   Whosever turn it be.

Billy   No, no, that ain't the way we work it, because we don't work it.

Carlyle   See? See? There it is – that goddamn education showin' through. All them years in school. Man, didn't we have a good time tonight? You rode in my car. I showed you a good cathouse, all that sweet black pussy. Ain't we friends? Richie likes me. How come you don't like me?

Billy   'Cause if you really are doin' what I think you're doin', you're a fuckin' animal!

Carlyle *leaps to his feet, hand snaking to his pocket to draw a weapon.*

Roger   Billy, no.

Billy   NO, WHAT?!

Roger   Relax, man; no need. (*He turns to* **Carlyle**; *patiently, wearily, he speaks.*) Man, I tole you it ain't goin' on here. We both tole you it ain't goin' on here.

Carlyle   Don't you jive me, nigger. You goin' for a walk like I'm askin', or not? I wanna get this clear.

Roger   Man, we live here.

Richie   It's my house, too, Roger; I live here, too. (*He bounds to his feet, flinging the blanket that has been covering him so it flies and lands on the floor near* **Roger**'s *footlocker.*)

Roger   Don't I know that? Did I say somethin' to make you think I didn't know that?

Standing, **Richie** *is removing his trousers and throwing them down on his footlocker.*

Richie   Carlyle is my guest.

Sitting down on the side of his bed and facing out, he puts his arms around **Carlyle**'s *thigh.* **Roger** *jumps to his feet and grabs the blanket from the foot of his bed. Shaking it open, he drops onto the bed, his head at the foot of the bed and facing off as he covers himself.*

Roger   Fine. He your friend. This your home. So that mean he can stay. It don't mean I gotta leave. I'll catch you all in the mornin'.

Billy   Roger, what the hell are you doin'?

Roger   What you better do, Billy. It's gettin' late. I'm goin' to sleep.

Billy   What?

Roger   Go to fucking bed, Billy. Get up in the rack, turn your back, and look at the wall.

Billy   You gotta be kiddin'.

Roger DO IT!

Billy Man . . . !

Roger Yeah . . . !

Billy You mean just . . .

Roger It been goin' on a long damn time, man. You ain't gonna put no stop to it.

Carlyle You . . . ain't . . . serious.

Richie (*both he and* **Carlyle** *are staring at* **Roger** *and then* **Billy**, *who is staring at* **Roger**)   Well, I don't believe it. Of all the childish . . . infantile . . .

Carlyle Hey! (*Silence.*) HEY! Even I got to say this is a little weird, but if this the way you do it . . . (*And he turns toward* **Richie** *below him.*) . . . it the way I do it. I don't know.

Richie With them right there? Are you kidding? My God, Carlyle, that'd be obscene. (*Pulling slightly away from* **Carlyle**.)

Carlyle Ohhh, man . . . they backs turned.

Richie No.

Carlyle What I'm gonna do? (*Silence. He looks at them, all three of them.*) Don't you got no feelin' for how a man feel? I don't understand you two boys. Unless'n you a pair of motherfuckers. That what you are, you a pair of motherfuckers? You slits, man. DON'T YOU HEAR ME!? I DON'T UNDERSTAND THIS SITUATION HERE. I THOUGHT WE MADE A DEAL!

Richie *rises, starts to pull on his trousers.* **Carlyle** *grabs him.*

Carlyle YOU GET ON YOUR KNEES, YOU PUNK, I MEAN NOW, AND YOU GONNA BE ON MY JOINT FAST OR YOU GONNA BE ONE BUSTED PUNK. AM I UNDERSTOOD?

He hurls **Richie** *down to the floor.*

Billy I ain't gonna have this going on here; Roger, I can't.

Roger   I been turnin' my back on one thing or another all my life.

Richie   Jealous, Billy?

Billy (*getting to his feet*)   Just go out that door, the two of you. Go. Go on out in the bushes or out in some field. See if I follow you. See if I care. I'll be right here and I'll be sleepin', but it ain't gonna be done in my house. I don't have much in this goddamn army, but HERE is mine. (*He stands beside his bed.*)

Carlyle   I WANT MY FUCKIN' NUT! HOW COME YOU SO UPTIGHT? HE WANTS ME! THIS BOY HERE WANTS ME! WHO YOU TO STOP IT?

Roger (*spinning to face* **Carlyle** *and* **Richie**)   THAT'S RIGHT, Billy. Richie one a those people want to get fucked by niggers, man. It what he know was gonna happen all his life – can be his dream come true. Ain't that right, Richie!

Jumping to his feet, **Richie** *starts putting on his trousers.*

Want to make it real in the world, how a nigger is an animal. Give 'em an inch, gonna take a mile. Ain't you some kinda fool, Richie? Hear me, Carlyle.

Carlyle   Man, don't make me no nevermind what he think he's provin' an' shit, long as I get my nut. I KNOW I ain't no animal, don't have to prove it.

Richie (*pulling at* **Carlyle**'s *arm, wanting to move him toward the door*)   Let's go. Let's go outside. The hell with it.

But **Carlyle** *tears himself free; he squats furiously down on the bunk, his hands seizing it, his back to all of them.*

Carlyle   Bull shit. Bullshit! I ain't goin' no-fuckin'-where – this jive ass ain't runnin' me. Is this you house or not? (*He doesn't know what is going on; he can hardly look at any of them.*)

Roger (*bounding out of bed, hurling his pillow across the room*)   I'm goin' to the fuckin' john, Billy. Hang it up, man; let 'em be.

Billy   No.

Roger   I'm smarter than you – do like I'm sayin'.

Billy   It ain't right.

Roger   Who gives a big rat's ass!

Carlyle   Right on, bro! That boy know; he do. (*He circles the bed toward them.*) Hear him. Look into his eyes.

Billy   This fuckin' army takin' everything else away from me, they ain't takin' more than they got. I see what I see – I don't run, don't hide.

Roger (*turning away from* **Billy**, *stomps out the door, slamming it*) You fuckin' well better learn.

Carlyle   That right. Time for more schoolin'. Lesson number one. (*Stealthily he steps and snaps out the only light, the lamp clamped to* **Richie***'s bed.*) You don't see what you see so well in the dark. It dark in the night. Black man got a black body – he disappear.

The darkness is so total, they are all no more than shadows.

Richie   Not to the hands; not to the fingers. (*Moving from across the room toward* **Carlyle**.)

Carlyle   You do like you talk, boy, you gonna make me happy. (*As* **Billy**, *nervously clutching his sneaker, is moving backward.*)

Billy   Who says the lights go out? Nobody goddamn asked me if the lights go out.

Billy *lunging to the wall switch, throws it. The overhead lights flash on, flooding the room with light.* **Carlyle** *is seated on the edge of* **Richie***'s bed.* **Richie** *kneeling before him.*

Carlyle   I DO, MOTHERFUCKER, I SAY! (*And the switchblade seems to leap from his pocket to his hand.*) I SAY! CAN'T YOU LET PEOPLE BE?

Billy *hurls his sneaker at the floor at* **Carlyle***'s feet. Instantly* **Carlyle** *is across the room, blocking* **Billy***'s escape out the door.*

Carlyle   Goddamn you, boy! I'm gonna cut your ass, just to show you how it feel – and cuttin' can happen. This knife true.

Richie   Carlyle, now c'mon.

Carlyle   Shut up, pussy.

Richie   Don't hurt him, for chrissake.

Carlyle   Goddamn man throw a shoe at me, he don't walk around clean in the world thinkin' he can throw another. He get some shit come back at him.

Billy *doesn't know which way to go, and then* **Carlyle**, *jabbing the knife at the air before* **Billy**'s *chest, has* **Billy** *running backward, his eyes fixed on the moving blade. He stumbles, having run into* **Richie**'s *bed. He sprawls backward and* **Carlyle** *is over him.*

Carlyle   No, no; no, no. Put you hand out there. Put it out. (*Slight pause;* **Billy** *is terrified.*) DO THE THING I'M TELLIN'!

Billy *lets his hand rise in the air and* **Carlyle** *grabs it, holds it.*

Carlyle   That's it. That's good. See? See?

The knife flashes across **Billy**'s *palm; the blood flows.* **Billy** *winces, recoils, but* **Carlyle**'s *hand still clenches and holds.*

Billy   Motherfucker.

Again the knife darts, cutting, and **Billy** *yelps.* **Richie**, *on his knees beside them, turns away.*

Richie   Oh, my God, what are you –

Carlyle (*in his own sudden distress, he flings the hand away*) That you blood. The blood inside you, you don't ever see it there. Take a look how easy it come out – and enough of it come out, you in the middle of the worst goddamn trouble you ever gonna see. And know I'm the man can deal that kinda trouble, easy as I smile. And I smile . . . easy. Yeah.

Billy *is curled in upon himself, holding the hand to his stomach as* **Richie** *now reaches tentatively and shyly out as if to console* **Billy**, *who repulses the gesture.* **Carlyle** *is angry and strangely depressed. Forlornly he slumps onto* **Billy**'s *footlocker as* **Billy** *staggers up to his wall locker and takes out a towel.*

Carlyle Bastard ruin my mood, Richie. He ruin my mood.
Fightin' and lovin' real different in the feelin's I got. I see
blood come outa somebody like that, it don't make me feel
good – hurt me – hurt on somebody I thought was my friend.
But I ain't supposed to see. One dumb nigger. No mind, he
thinks, no heart, no feelings a gentleness. You see how that
ain't true, Richie. Goddamn man threw a shoe at me. A lotta
people woulda cut his heart out. I gotta make him know he
throw shit, he get shit. But I don't hurt him bad, you see what
I mean?

Billy's *back is to them, as he stands hunched at his locker, and suddenly
his voice, hissing, erupts.*

Billy Jesus . . . H . . . Christ . . . Do you know what I'm
doin'? Do you know what I'm standin' here doin'? (*He
whirls now; he holds a straight razor in his hand. A bloody towel is
wrapped around the hurt hand.* **Carlyle** *tenses, rises, seeing the
razor.*) I'm a twenty-four-year-old goddamn college
graduate – intellectual goddamn scholar type – and I got a
razor in my hand. I'm thinkin' about comin' up behind one
black human being and I'm thinkin' nigger this and nigger
that – I wanna cut his throat. THAT IS RIDICULOUS. I
NEVER FACED ANYBODY IN MY LIFE WITH
ANYTHING TO KILL THEM. YOU UNDERSTAND
ME? I DON'T HAVE A GODDAMN THING ON THE
LINE HERE!

The door opens and **Roger** *rushes in, having heard the yelling.* **Billy**
flings the razor into his locker.

Look at me, Roger, look at me. I got a cut palm – I don't
know what happened. Jesus Christ, I got sweat all over me
when I think a what I was near to doin'. I swear it. I mean, do
I think I need a reputation as a killer, a bad man with a knife?
(*He is wild with the energy of feeling free and with the anger at what these
others almost made him do.* **Carlyle** *slumps down on the footlocker, he
sits there.*) Bullshit! I need shit! I got sweat all over me. I got the
mile record in my hometown. I did four forty-two in high
school, and that's the goddamn record in Windsor County. I
don't need approval from either one of the pair of you. (*And he*

rushes at **Richie**.) You wanna be a goddamn swish – a goddamn faggot-queer – GO! Suckin' cocks and takin' it in the ass, the thing of which you dream – GO! AND YOU – (*Whirling on* **Carlyle**.) You wanna be a bad-assed animal, man, get it on – go – but I wash my hands. I am not human as you are. I put you down, I put you down – (*He almost hurls himself at* **Richie**.) – you gay little piece a shit cake – SHIT CAKE. AND YOU – (*Hurt, confused,* **Richie** *turns away, nearly pressing his face into the bed beside which he kneels, as* **Billy** *has spun back to tower over the pulsing, weary* **Carlyle**.) – you are your own goddamn fault, SAMBO! SAMBO!

And the knife flashes up in **Carlyle**'s *hand into* **Billy**'s *stomach, and* **Billy** *yelps.*

Ahhhhhhhh. (*And pushes at the hand.* **Richie** *is still turned away.*)

Richie Well, fuck you, Billy.

Billy (*backs off the knife*) Get away, get away.

Richie (*as* **Roger**, *who cannot see because* **Billy**'s *back is to him, is approaching* **Carlyle**, *and* **Billy** *goes walking up toward the lockers as if he knows where he is going, as if he is going to go out the door and to a movie, his hands holding his belly*) You're so-o messed up.

Roger (*to* **Carlyle**) Man, what's the matter with you?

Carlyle Don't nobody talk that weird shit to me, you understand?

Roger You jive, man. That's all you do – jive!

Billy, *striding swiftly, walks flat into the wall lockers; he bounces, turns. They are all looking at him.*

Richie Billy! Oh, Billy!

Roger *looks at* **Richie**.

Billy Ahhhhhhh. Ahhhhhhh.

Roger *looks at* **Carlyle**, *as if he is about to scream, and beyond him,* **Billy** *turns from the lockers, starts to walk again, now staggering and moving toward them.*

Richie   I think . . . he stabbed him. I think Carlyle stabbed Billy. Roger!

Roger *whirls to go to* **Billy**, *who is staggering downstage and angled away, hands clenched over his belly.*

Billy   Shut up! It's just a cut, it's just a cut. He cut my hand, he cut my gut. (*He collapses onto his knees just beyond* **Roger**'s *footlocker.*) It took the wind out of me, scared me, that's all. (*Fiercely he tries to hide the wound and remain calm.*)

Roger   Man, are you all right?

He moves to **Billy**, *who turns to hide the wound. Till now no one is sure what happened.* **Richie** *only 'thinks'* **Billy** *has been stabbed.* **Billy** *is pretending he isn't hurt. As* **Billy** *turns from* **Roger**, *he turns toward* **Richie** *and* **Richie** *sees the blood.* **Richie** *yelps and they all begin talking and yelling simultaneously.*

Carlyle (*overlapping*)   You know what I was learnin', he was learnin' to talk all that weird shit, cuttin', baby, cuttin', the ways and means a shit, man, razors.

Roger (*overlapping*)   You all right? Or what? He slit you?

Billy (*overlapping*)   Just took the wind outa me, scared me.

Richie   Carlyle, you stabbed him; you stabbed him.

Carlyle   Ohhhh, pussy, pussy, pussy, Carlyle know what he do.

Roger (*trying to lift* **Billy**)   Get up, okay? Get up on the bed.

Billy (*irritated, pulling free*)   I am on the bed.

Roger   What?

Richie   No, Billy, no, you're not.

Billy   Shut up!

Richie   You're on the floor.

Billy   I'm on the bed. I'm on the bed. (*Emphatically. And then he looks at the floor.*) What?

Roger   Let me see what he did.

Billy's *hands are clenched on the wound.*

Roger   Billy, let me see where he got you.

Billy (*recoiling*)   NO-O-O-O-O, you nigger!

Roger (*leaps at* **Carlyle**)   What did you do?

Carlyle (*hunching his shoulders, ducking his head*)   Shut up.

Roger   What did you do, nigger – you slit him or stick him?
(*And then he tries to get back to* **Billy**.) Billy, let me see.

Billy (*doubling over till his head hits the floor*)   NO-O-O-O-O!
Shit, shit, shit.

Richie (*suddenly sobbing and yelling*)   Oh, my God, my God,
ohhhh, ohhhh, ohhhh. (*Bouncing on his knees on the bed.*)

Carlyle   FUCK IT, FUCK IT, I STUCK HIM. I
TURNED IT. This mother army break my heart. I can't be
out there where it pretty, don't wanna live! Wash me clean,
shit face!

Richie   Ohhhh, ohhhhh, ohhhhhhhhhhh. Carlyle stabbed
Billy, oh, ohhhh, I never saw such a thing in my life.
Ohhhhhh.

As **Roger** *is trying gently, fearfully, to straighten* **Billy** *up.*

Don't die, Billy; don't die.

Roger   Shut up and go find somebody to help. Richie, go!

Richie   Who? I'll go, I'll go. (*Scrambling off the bed.*)

Roger   I don't know. JESUS CHRIST! DO IT!

Richie   Okay. Okay. Billy, don't die. Don't die. (*Backing for
the door, he turns and runs.*)

Roger   The sarge, or C.Q.

Billy (*suddenly doubling over, vomiting blood;* **Richie** *is gone*)
Ohhhhhhhhhhh. Blood. Blood.

Roger   Be still, be still.

Billy (*pulling at a blanket on the floor beside him*)   I want to stand up. I'm – vomiting – (*Making no move to stand, only to cover himself.*) – blood. What does that mean?

Roger (*slowly standing*)   I don't know.

Billy   Yes, yes, I want to stand up. Give me blanket, blanket. (*He rolls back and forth, fighting to get the blanket over him.*)

Roger   RIICCHHHIIIEEEE!

As **Billy** *is furiously grappling with the blanket.*

No, no. (*He looks at* **Carlyle**, *who is slumped over, muttering to himself. He runs for the door.*) Wait on, be tight, be cool.

Billy   Cover me. Cover me.

At last he gets the blanket over his face. The dark makes him grow still. He lies there beneath his blanket. Silence. No one moves. And then **Carlyle** *senses the quiet; he turns, looks. Slowly, wearily, he rises and walks to where* **Billy** *lies. He stands over him, the knife hanging loosely from his left hand as he reaches with his right to gently take the blanket and lift it slowly from* **Billy**'s *face. They look at each other.* **Billy** *reaches up and pats* **Carlyle**'s *hand holding the blanket.*

I don't want to talk to you right now, Carlyle. All right? Where's Roger? Do you know where he is? (*Slight pause.*) Don't stab me anymore, Carlyle, okay? I was dead wrong doin' what I did. I know that now. Carlyle, promise me you won't stab me anymore. I couldn't take it. Okay? I'm cold . . . my blood . . . is . . .

From off comes a voice.

Rooney   Cokesy? Cokesy wokesy? (*And he staggers into the doorway, very drunk, a beer bottle in his hand.*) Ollie-ollie oxen-freeee. (*He looks at them.* **Carlyle** *quickly, secretly, slips the knife into his pocket.*) How you all doin'? Everybody drunk, huh? I los' my friend. (*He is staggering sideways toward* **Billy**'s *bunk, where he finally drops down, sitting.*) Who are you, soldier?

Carlyle *has straightened, his head ducked down as he is edging for the door.*

Rooney   Who are you, soldier?

And **Richie**, *running, comes roaring into the room. He looks at* **Rooney** *and cannot understand what is going on.* **Carlyle** *is standing.* **Rooney** *is just sitting there. What is going on?* **Richie** *moves along the lockers, trying to get behind* **Rooney**, *his eyes never off* **Carlyle**.

Richie   Ohhhhhh, Sergeant Rooney, I've been looking for you everywhere – where have you been? Carlyle stabbed Billy, he stabbed him.

Rooney (*sitting there*)   What?

Richie   Carlyle stabbed Billy.

Rooney   Who's Carlyle?

Richie   He's Carlyle.

As **Carlyle** *seems about to advance, the knife again showing in his hand*

Carlyle, don't hurt anybody more!

Rooney (*on his feet, he is staggering toward the door*)   You got a knife there? What's with the knife? What's goin' on here?

Carlyle *steps as if to bolt for the door, but* **Rooney** *is in the way, having inserted himself between* **Carlyle** *and* **Richie**, *who has backed into the doorway.*

Rooney   Wait! Now wait!

Richie (*as* **Carlyle** *raises the knife*)   Carlyle, don't! (*He runs from the room.*)

Rooney   You watch your step, you understand. You see what I got here? (*He lifts the beer bottle, waves it threateningly.*) You watch your step, motherfucker. Relax. I mean, we can straighten all this out. We –

Carlyle *lunges at* **Rooney**, *who tenses.*

Rooney   I'm just askin' what's goin' on, that's all I'm doin'. No need to get all –

And **Carlyle** *swipes at the air again;* **Rooney** *recoils.*

Motherfucker. Motherfucker. (*He seems to be tensing, his body gathering itself for some mighty effort. And he throws his head back and gives the eagle yell.*) Eeeeeeeeeeeaaaaaaaaaaaaaaaaaahhhhhh! Eeeeaaaaaaaaaaaaaahhhhhhhhhhhhhh!

Carlyle *jumps; he looks left and right.*

Rooney   Goddammit, I'll cut you good. (*He lunges to break the bottle on the edge of the wall lockers. The bottle shatters and he yelps, dropping everything.*) Ohhhhhhhh! Ohhhhhhhhhhhhhh!

Carlyle *bolts, running from the room.*

Rooney   I hurt myself, I cut myself. I hurt my hand. (*Holding the wounded hand, he scurries to* **Billy**'s *bed, where he sits on the edge, trying to wipe the blood away so he can see the wound.*) I cut –

Hearing a noise, he whirls, looks; **Carlyle** *is plummeting in the door and toward him.* **Rooney** *stands.*

I hurt my hand, goddammit!

The knife goes into **Rooney**'s *belly. He flails at* **Carlyle**.

I HURT MY HAND! WHAT ARE YOU DOING? WHAT ARE YOU DOING? WAIT! WAIT! (*He turns away, falling to his knees and the knife goes into him again and again.*) No fair. No fair!

Roger, *running, skids into the room, headed for* **Billy**, *and then he sees* **Carlyle** *on* **Rooney**, *the leaping knife.* **Roger** *lunges, grabbing* **Carlyle**, *pulling him to get him off* **Rooney**. **Carlyle** *leaps free of* **Roger**, *sending* **Roger** *flying backward. And then* **Carlyle** *begins to circle* **Roger**'s *bed. He is whimpering, wiping at the blood on his shirt as if to wipe it away.* **Roger** *backs away as* **Carlyle** *keeps waving the knife at him.* **Rooney** *is crawling along the floor under* **Billy**'s *bed and then he stops crawling, lies there.*

Carlyle   You don't tell nobody on me you saw me do this, I let you go, okay? Ohhhhhhhhh. (*Rubbing, rubbing at the shirt.*) Ohhhhhh, how'm I gonna get back to the world now, I got all this mess to –

Roger   What happened? That you – I don't understand that you did this! That you did –

Carlyle YOU SHUT UP! Don't be talkin' all that weird shit to me – don't you go talkin' all that weird shit!

Roger Nooooooooooooo!

Carlyle I'm Carlyle, man. You know me. You know me.

He turns, he flees out the door. **Roger***, alone, looks about the room.* **Billy** *is there.* **Roger** *moves toward* **Billy***, who is shifting, undulating on his back.*

Billy Carlyle, no; oh, Christ, don't stab me anymore. I'll die. I will – I'll die. Don't make me die. I'll get my dog after you. I'LL GET MY DOG AFTER YOU!

Roger *is saying, 'Oh, Billy, man, Billy.' He is trying to hold* **Billy***. Now he lifts* **Billy** *into his arms.*

Roger Oh, Billy; oh, man. GODDAMMIT, BILLY!

As a **Military Police Lieutenant** *comes running in the door, his .45 automatic drawn, and he levels it at* **Roger***.*

Lieutenant Freeze, soldier! Not a quick move out of you. Just real slow, straighten your ass up.

Roger *has gone rigid; the* **Lieutenant** *is advancing on him. Tentatively,* **Roger** *turns, looks.*

Roger Huh? No.

Lieutenant Get your ass against the lockers.

Roger Sir, no. I –

Lieutenant (*hurling* **Roger** *away toward the wall lockers*) MOVE!

As another **M.P, PFC Hinson***, comes in, followed by* **Richie***, flushed and breathless.*

Hinson, cover this bastard.

Hinson (*drawing his .45 automatic, moving on* **Roger**) Yes, sir.

The **Lieutenant** *frisks* **Roger***, who is spreadeagled at the lockers.*

Richie What? Oh, sir, no, no. Roger, what's going on?

Lieutenant   I'll straighten this shit out.

Roger   Tell 'em to get the gun off me, Richie.

Lieutenant   SHUT UP!

Richie   But, sir, sir, he didn't do it. Not him.

Lieutenant (*fiercely he shoves* **Richie** *out of the way*)   I told you, all of you, to shut up. (*He moves to* **Rooney***'s body.*) Jesus, God, this SFC is cut to shit. He's cut to shit. (*He hurries to* **Billy***'s body.*) This man is cut to shit.

As **Carlyle** *appears in the doorway, his hands cuffed behind him, a third* **M.P.***, **PFC Clark***, shoving him forward.* **Carlyle** *seems shocked and cunning, his mind whirring.*

Clark   Sir, I got this guy on the street, runnin' like a streak a shit.

He hurls the struggling **Carlyle** *forward and* **Carlyle** *stumbles toward the head of* **Richie***'s bed as* **Richie***, seeing him coming, hurries away along* **Billy***'s bed and toward the wall lockers.*

Richie   He did it! Him, him!

Carlyle   What is going on here? I don't know what is going on here!

Clark (*club at the ready, he stations himself beside* **Carlyle**)   He's got blood all over him, sir. All over him.

Lieutenant   What about the knife?

Clark   No, sir. He must have thrown it away.

As a fourth **M.P.** *has entered to stand in the doorway, and* **Hinson***, leaving* **Roger***, bends to examine* **Rooney***. He will also kneel and look for life in* **Billy***.*

Lieutenant   You throw it away, soldier?

Carlyle   Oh, you thinkin' about how my sister got happened, too. Oh, you ain't so smart as you think you are! No way!

Roger   Jesus God almighty.

Lieutenant   What happened here? I want to know what happened here.

Hinson (*rising from* **Billy**'s *body*)   They're both dead, sir. Both of them.

Lieutenant (*confidential, almost whispering*)   I know they're both dead. That's what I'm talkin' about.

Carlyle   Chicken blood, sir. Chicken blood and chicken hearts is what all over me. I was goin' on my way, these people jump out the bushes be pourin' it all over me. Chicken blood and chicken hearts. (*Thrusting his hands out at* **Clark**.) You goin' take these cuffs off me, boy?

Lieutenant   Sit him down, Clark. Sit him down and shut him up.

Carlyle   This my house, sir. This my goddamn house.

Clark *grabs him, begins to move him.*

Lieutenant   I said to shut him up.

Clark   Move it; move! (*Struggling to get* **Carlyle** *over to* **Roger**'s *footlocker as* **Hinson** *and the other* **M.P.** *exit*)

Carlyle   I want these cuffs taken off my hands.

Clark   You better do like you been told. You better sit and shut up!

Carlyle   I'm gonna be thinkin' over here. I'm gonna be thinkin' it all over. I got plannin' to do. I'm gonna be thinkin' in my quietness; don't you be makin' no mistake.

He slumps over, muttering to himself **Hinson** *and the other* **M.P.** *return, carrying a stretcher. They cross to* **Billy**, *chatting with each other about how to go about the lift. They will lift him; they will carry him out.*

Lieutenant (*to* **Richie**)   You're Wilson?

Richie   No, sir. (*Indicating* **Billy**.) That's Wilson. I'm Douglas.

Lieutenant (*to* **Roger**)   And you're Moore. And you sleep here.

Roger   Yes, sir.

Richie   Yes, sir. And Billy slept here and Sergeant Rooney was our platoon sergeant and Carlyle was a transient, sir. He was a transient from P Company.

Lieutenant (*scrutinizing* **Roger**)   And you had nothing to do with this? (*To* **Richie**). He had nothing to do with this?

Roger   No, sir, I didn't.

Richie   No, sir, he didn't. I didn't either. Carlyle went crazy and he got into a fight and it was awful. I didn't even know what it was about exactly.

Lieutenant   How'd the SFC get involved?

Richie   Well, he came in, sir.

Roger   I had to run off to call you, sir. I wasn't here.

Richie   Sergeant Rooney just came in – I don't know why – he heard all the yelling, I guess – and Carlyle went after him. Billy was already stabbed.

Carlyle (*rising, his manner that of a man who is taking charge*)   All right now, you gotta be gettin' the fuck outa here. All of you. I have decided enough of the shit has been goin' on around here and I am tellin' you to be gettin' these motherfuckin' cuffs off me and you be gettin' me a bus ticket home. I am quittin' this jive-time army.

Lieutenant   You are doin' what?

Carlyle   No, I ain't gonna be quiet. No way. I am quittin' this goddamn –

Lieutenant   You shut the hell up, soldier. I am ordering you.

Carlyle   I don't understand you people! Don't you people understand when a man be talkin' English at you to say his mind? I have quit the army!

Hinson *returns*.

Lieutenant   Get him outa here!

Richie   What's the matter with him?

Lieutenant   Hinson! Clark!

They move, grabbing **Carlyle**, *and they drag him, struggling, toward the door.*

Carlyle   Oh, no. Oh, no. You ain't gonna be doin' me no more. I been tellin' you. To get away from me. I am stayin' here. This my place, not your place. You take these cuffs off me like I been tellin' you! My poor little sister Lin Sue understood what was goin' on here! She tole me! She knew! (*He is howling in the hallway now.*) You better be gettin' these cuffs off me!

Silence. **Roger**, **Richie**, *and the* **Lieutenant** *are all staring at the door. The* **Lieutenant** *turns, crosses to the foot of* **Roger**'*s bed.*

Lieutenant   All right now. I will be getting to the bottom of this. You know I will be getting to the bottom of this. (*He is taking two forms from his clipboard.*)

Richie   Yes, sir.

Hinson *and the fourth* **M.P.** *return with another stretcher. They walk to* **Rooney**, *talking to one another about how to lift him. They drag him from under the bed. They will roll him onto the stretcher, lift him and walk out.* **Roger** *moves, watching them, down along the edge of* **Billy**'*s bed.*

Lieutenant   Fill out these forms. I want your serial number, rank, your MOS, the NCOIC of your work. Any leave coming up will be canceled. Tomorrow at 0800 you will report to my office at the provost marshal's headquarters. You know where that is?

Roger (*as the two* **M.P.**'*s are leaving with the stretcher and* **Rooney**'*s body*)   Yes, sir.

Richie   Yes, sir.

Lieutenant (*crossing to* **Roger**, *he hands him two cards*)   Be prepared to do some talking. Two perfectly trained and primed strong pieces of U.S. Army property got cut to shit up here. We are going to find out how and why. Is that clear?

Richie   Yes, sir.

Roger   Yes, sir.

The **Lieutenant** *looks at each of them. He surveys the room. He marches out.*

Richie   Oh, my God. Oh. Oh.

He runs to his bed and collapses, sitting hunched down at the foot. He holds himself and rocks as if very cold. **Roger***, quietly, is weeping. He stands and then walks to his bed. He puts down the two cards. He moves purposefully up to the mops hanging on the wall in the corner. He takes one down. He moves with the mop and the bucket to* **Billy***'s bed, where* **Rooney***'s blood stains the floor. He mops.* **Richie***, in horror, is watching.*

Richie   What . . . are you doing?

Roger   This area a mess, man.

Dragging the bucket, carrying the mop, he moves to the spot where **Billy** *had lain. He begins to mop.*

Richie   That's Billy's blood, Roger. His blood.

Roger   Is it?

Richie   I feel awful.

Roger (*keeps mopping*)   How come you made me waste all that time talkin' shit to you, Richie? All my time talkin' shit, and all the time you was a faggot, man; you really was. You shoulda jus' tole ole Roger. He don't care. All you gotta do is tell me.

Richie   I've been telling you. I did.

Roger   Jive, man, jive!

Richie   No!

Roger   You did bullshit all over us! ALL OVER US!

Richie   I just wanted to hold his hand, Billy's hand, to talk to him, go to the movies hand in hand like he would with a girl or I would with someone back home.

Roger   But he didn't wanna; HE didn't wanna.

Finished now, **Roger** *drags the mop and bucket toward the corner.*
Richie *is sobbing; he is at the edge of hysteria.*

Richie   He did.

Roger   No, man.

Richie   He did. He did. It's not my fault.

Roger *slams the bucket into the corner and rams the mop into the*
bucket. Furious, he marches down to **Richie**. *Behind him* **Sergeant**
Cokes, *grinning and lifting a wine bottle, appears in the doorway.*

Cokes   Hey!

Richie, *in despair, rolls onto his belly.* **Cokes** *is very, very happy.*

Cokes   Hey! What a day, gen'l'men. How you all doin'?

Roger (*crossing up near the head of his own bed*)   Hello, Sergeant
Cokes.

Cokes (*affectionate and casual, he moves near to* **Roger**)   How
you all doin'? Where's ole Rooney? I lost him.

Roger   What?

Cokes   We had a hell of a day, ole Rooney and me, lemme,
tell you. We been playin' hide-and-go-seek, and I was hidin',
and now I think maybe he started hidin' without tellin' me he
was gonna and I can't find him and I thought maybe he was
hidin' up here.

Richie   Sergeant, he –

Roger   No. No, we ain't seen him.

Cokes   I gotta find him. He knows how to react in a tough
situation. He didn't come up here looking for me?

Roger *moves around to the far side of his bed, turning his back to*
Cokes. *Sitting,* **Roger** *takes out a cigarette, but he does not light it.*

Roger   We was goin' to sleep, Sarge. Got to get up early.
You know the way this mother army is.

Cokes (*nodding, drifting backward, he sits down on* **Billy**'s *bed*)
You don't mind I sit here a while. Wait on him. Got a little
wine. You can have some. (*Tilting his head way back, he takes a big
drink and then, looking straight ahead, corks the bottle with a whack of
his hand.*) We got back into the area – we had been downtown
– he wanted to play hide-and-go-seek. I tole him okay, I was
ready for that. He hid his eyes. So I run and hid in the bushes
and then under his jeep. 'Cause I thought it was better. I hid
and I hid and I hid. He never did come. So finally, I got tired
– I figured I'd give up, come lookin' for him. I was way over
by the movie theater. I don't know how I got there. Anyway, I
got back here and I figured maybe he come up here lookin'
for me, figurin' I was hidin' up with you guys. You ain't seen
him, huh?

Roger   No, we ain't seen him. I tole you that, Sarge.

Cokes   Oh.

Richie   Roger!

Roger   He's drunk, Richie! He's blasted drunk. Got a brain
turned to mush!

Cokes (*in deep agreement*)   That ain't no lie.

Roger   Let it be for the night, Richie. Let him be for the
night.

Cokes   I still know what's goin' on, though. Never no worry
about that. I always know what's goin' on. I always know.
Don't matter what I drink or how much I drink. I always still
know what's goin on. But . . . I'll be goin' maybe and look for
Rooney. (*But rising, he wanders down center.*) But . . . I mean, we
could be doin' that forever. Him and me. Me under the jeep.
He wants to find me, he goes to the jeep. I'm over here. He
comes here. I'm gone. You know, maybe I'll just wait a little
while more I'm here. He'll find me then if he comes here. You
guys want another drink? (*Turning, he goes to* **Billy**'s *footlocker,
where he sits and takes another enormous guzzle of wine.*) Jesus, what a
goddamn day we had. Me and Rooney started drivin' and we
was comin' to this intersection and out comes this goddamn

Chevy. I try to get around her, but no dice. BINGO! I hit her
in the left rear. She was furious. I didn't care. I gave her my
name and number. My car had a headlight out, the fender
bashed in. Rooney wouldn't stop laughin'. I didn't know what
to do. So we went to D.C. to this private club I know. Had ten
or more snorts and decided to get back here after playin' some
snooker. That was fun. On the way, we picked up this kid
from the engineering unit, hitchhiking. I'm starting to feel real
clearheaded now. So I'm comin' around this corner and all of
a sudden there's this car stopped dead in front of me. He's not
blinkin' to turn or anything. I slam on the brakes, but it's like
puddin' the way I slide into him. There's a big noise and we
yell. Rooney starts laughin' like crazy and the kid jumps outa
the back and says he's gonna take a fuckin' bus. The guy from
the other car is swearin' at me. My car's still workin' fine, so I
move it off to the side and tell him to do the same, while we
wait for the cops. He says he wants his car right where it is and
he had the right of way 'cause he was makin' a legal turn. So
we're waitin' for the cops. Some cars go by. The guy's car is
this big fuckin' Buick. Around the corner comes this little red
Triumph. The driver's this blond kid got this blond girl next
to him. You can see what's gonna happen. There's this fuckin'
car sittin' there, nobody in it. So the Triumph goes crashin'
into the back of the Buick with nobody in it. BIFF-BANG-
BOOM. And everything stops. We're staring. It's all still. And
then that fuckin' Buick kinda shudders and starts to move.
With nobody in it. It starts to roll from the impact. And it rolls
just far enough to get where the road starts a downgrade. It's
driftin' to the right. It's driftin' to the shoulder and over it and
onto this hill, where it's pickin' up speed 'cause the hill is steep
and then it disappears over the side, and into the dark, just
rollin' real quiet. Rooney falls over, he's laughin' so hard. I
don't know what to do. In a minute the cops come and in
another minute some guy comes runnin' up over the hill to tell
us some other guy had got run over by this car with nobody in
it. We didn't know what to think. This was fuckin'
unbelievable to us. But we found out later from the cops that
this wasn't true and some guy had got hit over the head with a
bottle in a bar and when he staggered out the door it was just

at the instant that this fuckin' Buick with nobody in it went by. Seein' this, the guy stops cold and turns around and just goes back into the bar. Rooney is screamin' at me how we been in four goddamn accidents and fights and how we have got out clean. So then we got everything all straightened out and we come back here to play hide-and-seek 'cause that's what ole Rooney wanted. (*He is taking another drink, but finding the bottle empty.*) Only now I can't find him.

Near **Richie**'s *footlocker stands a beer bottle, and* **Cokes** *begins to move toward it. Slowly he bends and grasps the bottle; he straightens, looking at it. He drinks. And settles down on* **Richie**'s *footlocker.*

I'll just sit a little.

Richie, *lying on his belly, shudders. The sobs burst out of him. He is shaking.* **Cokes**, *blinking, turns to study* **Richie**.

Cokes   What's up? Hey, what're you cryin' about, soldier? Hey?

Richie *cannot help himself.*

Cokes   What's he cryin' about?

Roger (*disgustedly, he sits there*)   He's cryin' 'cause he's a queer.

Cokes   Oh. You a queer, boy?

Richie   Yes, Sergeant.

Cokes   Oh. (*Pause.*) How long you been a queer?

Roger   All his fuckin' life.

Richie   I don't know.

Cokes (*turning to scold* **Roger**)   Don't be yellin' mean at him. Boy, I tell you it's a real strange thing the way havin' leukemia gives you a lotta funny thoughts about things. Two months ago – or maybe even yesterday – I'da called a boy who was a queer a lotta awful names. But now I just wanna be figurin' things out. I mean, you ain't kiddin' me out about ole Rooney, are you, boys, 'cause of how I'm a sergeant and you're enlisted men, so you got some idea a vengeance on me? You ain't doin' that, are you, boys?

Roger   No.

Richie   Ohhhh. Jesus. Ohhhh. I don't know what's hurtin' in me.

Cokes   No, no, boy. You listen to me. You gonna be okay. There's a lotta worse things in this world than bein' a queer. I seen a lot of 'em, too. I mean, you could have leukemia. That's worse. That can kill you. I mean, it's okay. You listen to the ole sarge. I mean, maybe I was a queer, I wouldn't have leukemia. Who's to say? Lived a whole different life. Who's to say? I keep thinkin' there was maybe somethin' I coulda done different. Maybe not drunk so much. Or if I'd killed more gooks, or more Krauts or more dinks. I was kindhearted sometimes. Or if I'd had a wife and I had some kids. Never had any. But my mother did and she died of it anyway. Gives you a whole funny different way a lookin' at things, I'll tell you. Ohhhhh, Rooney, Rooney. (*Slight pause.*) Or if I'd let that little gook outa that spider hole he was in, I was sittin' on it. I'd let him out now, he was in there. (*He rattles the footlocker lid under him.*) Oh, how'm I ever gonna forget it? I see him and dive, goddamn bullet hits me in the side, I'm midair, everything's turnin' around. I go over the edge of this ditch and I'm crawlin' real fast. I lost my rifle. Can't find it. Then I come up behind him. He's half out of the hole. I bang him on top of his head, stuff him back into the hole with a grenade for company. Then I'm sittin' on the lid and it's made outa steel. I can feel him in there, though, bangin' and yellin' under me, and his yelling I can hear is beggin for me to let him out. It was like a goddamn Charlie Chaplin movie, everybody fallin' down and clumsy, and him in there yellin' and bangin' away, and I'm just sittin' there lookin' around. And he was Charlie Chaplin. I don't know who I was. And then he blew up. (*Pause.*) Maybe I'll just get a little shut-eye right sittin' here while I'm waitin' for ole Rooney. We figure it out. All of it. You don't mind I just doze a little here, you boys?

Roger   No.

Richie   No.

Roger *rises and walks to the door. He switches off the light and gently closes the door. The transom glows.* **Cokes** *sits in a flower of light.* **Roger** *crosses back to his bunk and settles in, sitting.*

Cokes   Night, boys.

Richie   Night, Sergeant.

Cokes *sits there, fingers entwined, trying to sleep.*

Cokes   I mean, he was like Charlie Chaplin. And then he blew up.

Roger (*suddenly feeling very sad for this old man*)   Sergeant . . . maybe you was Charlie Chaplin, too.

Cokes   No. No. (*Pause.*) No. I don't know who I was. Night.

Roger   You think he was singin' it?

Cokes   What?

Roger   You think he was singin' it?

Cokes   Oh, yeah. Oh, yeah; he was singin' it.

Slight pause. **Cokes**, *sitting on the footlocker, begins to sing a makeshift language imitating Korean, to the tune of 'Beautiful Streamer.' He begins with an angry, mocking energy that slowly becomes a dream, a lullaby, a farewell, a lament.*

> Yo no som lo no
> Ung toe lo knee
> Ra so me la lo
> La see see oh doe.
> Doe no tee ta ta
> Too low see see
> Ra mae me lo lo
> Ah boo boo boo eee.
> Boo boo eee booo eeee
> La so lee lem
> Lem lo lee da ung
> Uhhh so ba booooo ohhhh.

Boo booo eee ung ba
Eee eee la looo
Lem lo lala la
Eeee oohhh ohhh ohhh ohhhhh.

In the silence, he makes the soft, whispering sound of a child imitating an explosion, and his entwined fingers come apart. The dark figures of **Richie** *and* **Roger** *are near. The lingering light fades to black.*

The Orphan

For the teachers and students of Villanova Theatre, 1967–1972

Let no one think for an instant that we, in our vaunted modern civilization, have gone 'beyond the primitive human sacrifice'.

– Rollo May
Power and Innocence

The Orphan was first produced professionally by Joseph Papp on 18 April 1973. The cast was as follows:

The Speaker	Jeanne Hepple
Orestes	Cliff DeYoung
Clytemnestra One	Marcia Jean Kurtz
Clytemnestra Two	Rae Allen
Agamemnon	W. B. Brydon
Aegisthus	John Harkins
The Girl	Mariclaire Costello
Calchas	Tom Aldredge
Apollo	Richard Lynch
Iphigenia	Laurie Heineman
Electra	Carol Williard
Pylades	Peter Maloney
Family 1	Annemarie Zinn
Family 2	Janet Sarro
Family 3	Joanne Nail

Directed by Jeff Bleckner
Set by Santo Loquasto
Costumes by Theoni V. Aldredge
Lighting by Tharon Musser
Music by Peter Link

The Orphan was first performed in its current and final form at the Manning Street Actors' Theater of Philadelphia in association with the New York Shakespeare Festival on 13 March 1974. The cast was as follows:

The Figure	Jon Thomson
The Speaker	Cindy Winkler
Orestes	Tommy Hulce
Clytemnestra One	Annemarie Zinn
Clytemnestra Two	Norma Orazi
Agamemnon	Richard Fancy
Aegisthus	Mark McGovern
The Girl	Nancy Mette
Electra	Bonnie Cavanaugh
Iphigenia	Maureen McFadden
Pylades	Alkis Papoutsis
Becky	Susan Payne
Sally	Pamela Sindaco
Jenny	Maureen McFadden

Directed by Barnet Kellman
Set by Debbe Hale
Costumes by A Christina Ciannini
Lighting by James Leitner
Music by Elizabeth Myers

Act One

Darkness: we hear a rhythmic breathing, an eerie rattle, and then the lights rise to show us: A large rope cargo net hangs vertically upstage. Behind it and stretching downstage on either side of the cargo net are a series of ramps and platforms with rope wound around the ramps, the railings, the struts, the beams, their texture echoing that of the net. The lights rise slowly and we see **Sally**, **Becky**, *and* **Jenny** *scattered about and seeming to sleep. With them is* **Pylades**, *a young man in a dark jumpsuit. Eight white heads hang from the ceiling, a planetary swirl amid which other white fragments are strewn, as if a giant statue has broken apart.* **Clytemnestra One** *and* **Clytemnestra Two** *sit behind the large hanging cargo net. They wear identical costumes, elegant silky gowns. They are the same person at two different points of time in her life.*

Clytemnestra Two *is ten years older than* **Clytemnestra One**. *A single shawl is spread across their shoulders. One is young, thoughtful, hopeful; the other violent, sensual, bitter. Under the stage left scaffold stands* **Iphigenia**, *a girl dressed in white. Upstage and off to the side is* **Agamemnon**, *wearing a dark shirt, trousers, and dress shoes. On the top level of the scaffold stands* **The Girl**. *She wears a blouse and jeans and beads. Her feet are bare. Downstage is* **The Figure**, *a man with a thick black beard; he wears a T-shirt, Levi's jacket and jeans, and boots. He is lean and agile. He has long dark hair but it is now tied up, or held in a ponytail. Beside him stands* **The Speaker**, *a young woman dressed elegantly, a sexy satin gown, lush and form-fitting, her eyes closed as if she dozes on her feet; in her hands, hanging at her side, she holds a flashlight and a microphone.*

Now **The Figure** *leans close to* **The Speaker**'s *ear.*

The Figure   Say 'Good Evening.'

The Speaker (*eyes open as she speaks into her mike*)   Good evening.

As **The Figure** *is retreating.*

In a place like this we all begin. Deep within the dark of another's belly. The smallest and largest cells collide and multiplying ten thousand times possess one beating heart. Think of time as a pool. Do we speak to the past? Or merely look at it? Is it right? Left? Up? Down?

She shines her light in many directions, hitting **Orestes** *as he comes running in. He wears a T-shirt, trousers.*

Here comes Orestes.

Becky *kisses him.*

Orestes   I have been told I am Orestes.

Becky   It is written that you kill your mother.

The Figure (*high in the scaffolding*)   You want to kill your mother. You want Clytemnestra dead.

Orestes   I have been told I kill my mother. I want some time to have my mother dead.

As he draws a sword from his belt, **Electra** *wanders across the stage.*

The Speaker   There is Electra.

Orestes *moves toward her, and she seems to flee him. He is grabbed and spun by* **Jenny**. *Other* **Family Members** *push him.*

Clytemnestra One   And all is mist.

Clytemnestra Two   When there is a thing that I must touch, I reach.

They strain forward against the net.

Clytemnestra One   I am dirt.

Clytemnestra Two   It flees.

The Speaker   She is as you see, One and Two. Ten years older. Ten years younger.

Her flashlight hits each of them.

Clytemnestra. Clytemnestra.

Clytemnestra One   I –

Clytemnestra Two   I –

They rise and spin off from one another, whirling in opposite directions.

The Speaker   She splits like an atom. Divides like a cell. Multiplying into the future.

The Figure (*high in the scaffolding*)   And all is like a strange impossible Monday when you must kill and kill your mother.

Orestes   And all is like a strange impossible Monday when I must kill . . . and kill my mother.

Orestes *moves toward* **Clytemnestra One**, *his sword pointing at her as she backs away in fear, and* **Becky** *plucks the sword from his hand and gives it to someone else. Off the sword goes, passing from hand to hand across the space behind him as he stands there dazed, watching.*

The Speaker   Before the advent of the special theory of relativity –

Becky   No one ever thought there could be any ambiguity in the statement –

Sally   – that two events in different places happened at the same time –

Jenny   – or that two events in different places happened at different times –

The Speaker *and* **Family**   Science found, however, that two events in different places may appear simultaneous to one observer –

Becky   While another may judge that the second event preceded the first –

Jenny   – and still a third may say –

The Speaker   – that the first event preceded the second.

Sally   This would occur when the three observers were moving rapidly relative to one another.

The Speaker   May this not also mean the opposite?

The Speaker *and* **Family** (*as they spin off into new positions*) May it not be that events thought to be in sequence, are in fact, simultaneous?

And the sword is put back into the hand of **Orestes**.

Orestes   She fills the corners of my room. She fills the corners of my room.

Behind **Orestes** *fire flares.* **Agamemnon** *stands as he strides forward.*

Agamemnon   Curious, how the smell of incense is sweeter than the bones of Troy burning. In this flickering, I see the way a face can change with fear or flame. I am tired. I am home. I have seen the sleeping face of my child.

Clytemnestra Two *is moving from behind the net to approach him.*

Clytemnestra Two   You shall bathe. We will bathe together.

He laughs warmly.

The tub is prepared with scented water. The sheets of our bed are fresh. Wine and fruit await us.

She sighs, touching him, as **Aegisthus** *enters, wheeling out the tub. The tub is a laundry basket on wheels with a towel draped over the side.*

Go to the tub.

Agamemnon   I will. And you will join me. (*Reaching to remove the strap of her dress.*) Who is the servant?

Aegisthus *bows.*

Agamemnon   And my Trojan slave – the girl, Cassandra, my prize of war, where is she?

Clytemnestra Two   I have sent her to the kitchens.

Agamemnon   It is said she knows the future.

Aegisthus *smashes down a club upon the head of* **Agamemnon**, *who, crying out, falls to the floor.*

Clytemnestra Two   Whoring in your foreign bed, did she tell you of this moment in the future? Or of the moment only minutes ago, when her own throat was cut in the kitchens? Put him in the tub. He is important in the tub.

Agamemnon *groans as they work to lift him.*

Clytemnestra Two   You smell of time gone, Agamemnon. It's time that you bathe. Let it begin that you bathe. You are filth and filth must bathe.

They have dumped his slack body in the tub. Now she is looking about.

Where's the net? We must have the net.

Aegisthus   I see no net.

Agamemnon *is stirring.*

Clytemnestra Two   He moves; already he starts to awaken. Where is the net? We must have the net and knife!

The Figure   Clytemnestra! (*In the scaffolding high above them he stands, waving the net.*) Clytemnestra! . . .

Aegisthus   Who's that?

Clytemnestra Two   He has the net.

Aegisthus   Who is it?

The Figure   I have the net.

Aegisthus   It is Apollo!

Clytemnestra Two   Apollo?

Aegisthus   Apollo, God of Reason, has the net. (*And slowly* **The Figure** *is descending the ladder toward them.*) Born on the little island of Delos, he is a master musician, the God of Truth from whom no lie can come, the God of Light and Reason in whom there is no dark at all.

The Figure   Your thighs are white and perfect, Clytemnestra. What is he, Agamemnon, always poking and seeking in the air outside himself, his feeble seed desolate on sand or stone, till he can enter the rich earth of your belly. He rises into emptiness, stands obvious and simple. You are a clever, subtle cavern, deep and jeweled within.

Clytemnestra Two   Apollo, am I chosen? Have you chosen me?

The Figure   What other life have we but you?
Clytemnestra, you are all. (*He has put the net around her shoulders.
Now he is backing away from her.*) All!

Clytemnestra Two   Oh, Apollo, no; I worship you.

The Figure   I worship you.

Clytemnestra Two   I have the net, Aegisthus!

Aegisthus *reaches to take an end of the net.*

Clytemnestra Two   Look, I have the net!

They move to spread the net above **Agamemnon** *in the tub.*

And when we drop the net upon him.

Aegisthus   We drop the net upon him.

Clytemnestra Two   We drop the net upon him.

And they fling the net down upon **Agamemnon** *and then leap
backward.*

Agamemnon (*slowly, carefully, a little perplexed, takes hold of the
net*)   What's this? What's this?

Orestes (*rushing forward, raging, sword in hand*)   She fills the
corners of my room!

Clytemnestra One   I am –

Clytemnestra Two   – dirt! (*This is with revulsion.*)

Clytemnestra One   Dirt!

*And the telephone begins to ring loudly, spreading fear through everyone.
They scurry back and forth, looking upward.*

The Speaker   We call to one another across space – our
voices pass through distance – may we not call through time,
also – down and up, let us say, through time.

Iphigenia   Hello, hello.

The Speaker   May we not also call through time.

Orestes   Hello.

Agamemnon   Hello.

Aegisthus   Hello.

Clytemnestra One   Hello.

Clytemnestra Two   Hello.

The Girl (*standing in a far corner of the scaffolding*)   Well, I was just the kinda person who would groove, see, just flow with the moment. Because I knew society was not worthy of my respect, I made up my own, only my justice was just, unlike the regular one. I had this man offer to marry me and he was older so I fled, and shortly thereafter, on acid, I saw down into the center of the earth, and I said, 'Oh, God, just take me now for yours.' And the next day, I met this man . . .

The Figure *moves behind her to embrace her.*

The Girl   . . . and he sang for me and knew my heart and he was Abaddon, the angel, and I was in his Army.

The ringing stops.

Clytemnestra Two (*moving sadly to* **Orestes**, *who raises his sword as she moves on past him toward* **Clytemnestra One**) And now I see Orestes, and the thing I am seeking is a knife of silver in his fingers.

Clytemnestra One (*moving to sadly embrace* **Clytemnestra Two**)   Having fallen to him.

The Figure   Through the flesh of the father to the hand of the son falls the sword.

And **Orestes** *has moved to stand beside* **Clytemnestra One** *and* **Clytemnestra Two**, *holding the sword pointed at them, as* **Electra** *comes wandering by.*

Electra   I was so important, so important.

Clytemnestra One *and* **Clytemnestra Two**   Who will help us?

The Figure   I am here.

Pylades   Apollo is a God.

The Girl   Oh, wow.

Aegisthus   I was the most important person in the world and they killed me.

Everyone   What time is it? What time is it?

The Speaker   It passes; goes by.

Aegisthus   Bubbles mark the ocean for a moment where we drown.

Clytemnestra One   I hold the infant of my son, Orestes, in my arms.

Clytemnestra Two   I hold the infant of my killer in my arms.

Both are happy as they sit side by side, rocking invisible infants.

The Figure   Keep your son an infant, she believes, and you will never die.

Aegisthus   What about Orestes?

The Speaker   He kills you, Aegisthus.

Clytemnestra One   I don't.

They look at **Aegisthus**, *then at each other.*

Clytemnestra Two   I don't.

The Speaker   And you, Clytemnestra.

Clytemnestra Two   Nooo.

Clytemnestra One   Nooo.

Clytemnestra Two   I am not Agamemnon.

Clytemnestra One   I live.

Agamemnon (*reaching up in the tub, presses tentatively against the net*)   I want to be Aegisthus!

The Speaker   You are Agamemnon.

Aegisthus   I want to be Agamemnon.

The Speaker   You are Aegisthus.

Agamemnon   What is this net? What is it? It smells of fish. I can smell the sea. (*Now he is struggling in the net.*) It holds me whatever way I go. What is this net? I'll tear the threads. I'll tear them. It doesn't tear. I'll rip them. I'll rip and tear. I'll bite them. I'll bite. They taste of salt. Fish and salt. I'll pull them off. I'll pull. (*Now his struggle is frantic.*) I'll bite them. Bite and throw. Bite it, throw it, tear it. It doesn't! It doesn't! I'll rip and tear! I'll – I'll – CASSANDRAAAAAAAA! WHAT IS THIS NET?

The Speaker   (*walking up, shining the light on him in the tub*)   He, Agamemnon, at one point, killed a young king and stole his wife. He killed their infant son and took the young queen to be his own, and she was Clytemnestra.

Flashlight on **Clytemnestra One**, *who moves to kneel on the floor in front of* **Agamemnon**, *who still struggles slowly, wearily in the tub.*

At another point, he Agamemnon . . .

Flashlight on **Agamemnon**.

sacrificed the life of his daughter, Iphigenia . . .

Flashlight on **Iphigenia** *as she moves to kneel beside* **Clytemnestra One**, *putting her head into her mother's lap.*

born of Clytemnestra in order that the wind would arise and power his ships to Troy. At still another point, she . . .

Flashlight on **Clytemnestra Two**, *who moves to kneel beside* **Clytemnestra One**.

and he . . .

Flashlight on **Aegisthus**, *who moves to stand behind the kneeling* **Clytemnestra Two** *and beside* **Agamemnon**.

murdered him. They put down upon Agamemnon a fish net and stabbed . . .

Lights on **Agamemnon**, *as* **Orestes** *moves near, looking for a place in this family portrait.*

with a haunted knife of eight inches and imperfect alloy. And she –

Flashlight on **The Girl**. *They all look.*

The Girl (*leaping to her feet and bounding down from one level to the next, joyous, exuberant*)　I mean, one a the things about great Abaddon, our leader, that anybody woulda admired was how he knew about people and he says, 'Be kind to 'em; don't be tellin' 'em how you're gonna kill 'em. Let 'em go in peace into eternity,' he says. 'Cause the last thing you're doin' when you die, you just keep doin' it – just, oh, wow, screamin' the whole way a eternity.

Iphigenia　He makes me think of dogs. They lick my breasts. They suck my tongue. He fills my sweating brain with dogs. I do not know I die. Iphigenia does not know she dies. What is his name?

And behind her **The Figure** *is moving toward her. He wears a toga woven with bones over the white T-shirt; he wears a bone necklace and a half-mask molded to the contours of his own face.*

Aegisthus (*hurrying downstage with a portfolio from which he pulls various items*)　I have maps that show all we own. They indicate the length and breadth of things, the up and down, this and that; they show the top and bottom, both sides, trees and ocean.

The Figure (*grabs* **Iphigenia** *from behind*)　Calchas! Calchas! Mask of God made manifest in man, Priest, and prophet.

Agamemnon　I kill a thousand Trojans.

Clytemnestra Two　I kill Agamemnon.

Clytemnestra One　I kill a man; a husband.

Agamemnon　I kill a daughter.

Orestes　I kill my mother.

There is a curious note of music. The characters are spread about the stage. **Iphigenia** *is near her father.* **Clytemnestra One** *is beside her husband.* **Clytemnestra Two** *is between* **Aegisthus** *and* **Agamemnon**. **Orestes** *is alone. The music rises and together they all sing, except for* **The Speaker** *who moves about observing.*

All

> The sand in an hourglass, measuring time, is more or less accurate,
> which is to say, more or less inaccurate.
> We say 'Monday,' we say 'Tuesday.
> I must do this, I must do that
> Help, hello, I drown, I drown.'
> We say 'Monday,' we say 'Tuesday
> I must do this, I must do that
> Help, hello, I drown, I drown.'
> The sand in an hourglass, measuring time, is more or less accurate,
> which is to say, more or less inaccurate.
> Bubbles mark the ocean for a moment where we drown.
> Bubbles mark the ocean for a moment where we drown.
> Bubbles mark the ocean for a moment where we drown.
> Bubbles mark the ocean for a moment where we drown.

The Speaker (*as all are exiting*)   They come and go; there have been the Greeks and Romans, the Serbs and Greco-Romans; there have been the Croatians, the Chinese, the Assyrians, Arabs, Jews. Today there are the Arabs, Russians, Jews, the Americans, Arabs, Chinese, Serbs, Croatians and Japanese and others.

It has been a spinning of activity, all leaving. **Becky** *hands* **Agamemnon** *a message as he climbs from the tub and* **The Figure** *puts on the mask of Calchas and they are priest and king.*

The Figure   It is my burden to know what I know, Agamemnon. You must do as I say.

Agamemnon   No.

The Figure   You must send for your daughter.

Agamemnon (*angrily turning to face Calchas*)   I should have been told of your plan before you spoke at council. There is no time now. Think of the weeks as she travels; the wind could come before she arrived and we would seem foolish.

The Figure   Artemis has dreamed in lust of your child.

Agamemnon   The Goddess said this to you, used the name of Iphigenia, spoke my name?

The Figure   They confer about you, Agamemnon. They analyze your thoughts, discuss your deeds. All you do is written in scrolls of smoke they read and murmur about among themselves.

Agamemnon   I please the Gods; I pay them homage.

The Figure   But only with your words. Let your deeds obey the Gods, or by your own example, you will teach mutiny to the army you want to rule.

Agamemnon   We are chained to this place, Priest! The most powerful army in the world.

The Figure   And Iphigenia is the key. In smoke and the moon and the innards of a blessed and God-sent bird, I have read Iphigenia must die.

Agamemnon   Why do I not hear them? It is my daughter.

The Figure   I feel in my pulse the movement of each star. Am I not the priest of Apollo? Apollo made manifest in man, the issue of wisdom begotten by knowledge! (*Pause.*) Send for the child, The wind must have her.

Agamemnon   What am I to say to her? 'Come, my child. Journey to us so that we may kill you.'

The Figure   No, no, lie to her. Trick her. Write a letter. Send the letter now. (*He hands a scroll to* **Agamemnon**.) Pray to God Apollo if you have need.

As a **Servant** *runs up and snatches the scroll from* **Agamemnon**, *and running off the* **Servant** *hands the note to* **Becky**, *who puts it in an envelope and crosses away with it.*

Pray. God is here. Call out to him. Call to Apollo. God is
good.

The Figure *is leaving as* **Jenny** *takes the letter from* **Becky**.
Agamemnon *is following after* **The Figure**, *the letter passing
from the hands of* **Jenny** *to those of* **Sally**.

Agamemnon   I will beg her not to die. I will beg the knife
not to kill her – her skin not to open, her heart to go on
beating, though you, Priest, hold it in your hand. She is my
child! Iphigenia!

Iphigenia   Who calls me? Who calls? Hello.

*High in the scaffolding, she stands, having heard her name. She looks
about and starts climbing down as still the letter travels from one person to
another across the space and* **Clytemnestra One** *stands behind the
cargo net, waiting.*

The Speaker   Sound consists of waves that need air to
travel. Sounds wiggle through the fabric of the air.
Experimenters have sent out signals and gotten back echoes
from two million miles beyond the moon.

Iphigenia   What does the letter say, Mother?

Clytemnestra One, *reading the letter, looks up in surprise to see
both* **Iphigenia** *and* **Electra**.

Iphigenia   You have a letter. May I know what it says?

Clytemnestra One   This and that. It says this and that.
(*She turns away from them.*)

Iphigenia   I know it's from Father.

Iphigenia *and* **Electra** *look at each other.*

Electra   Is he well? Does he mention us?

Iphigenia   Does he mention me as a this or that?

Clytemnestra One (*turns, smiling*)   There is some trouble,
but he seems in good spirits, and he mentions you.

Iphigenia   Is there love in his mentioning? Oh, let me see.

Clytemnestra One   Your father has made plans. We are to pack and travel to Aulus.

Iphigenia   To visit? Me?

Electra   And me, Mother?

Clytemnestra One   Only Iphigenia. To marry.

Iphigenia *looks at* **Electra**, *then* **Clytemnestra One**.

Iphigenia   Oh, Mother, is it true? (*She runs to* **Clytemnestra One**, *taking the letter*.) It says I am to marry Achilles. But he is a God – a half-God, Achilles. Have you seen him? Is he as beautiful as they say?

Clytemnestra One   He is beautiful and strong – a great warrior and man.

Iphigenia (*runs to kneel and throws herself in her mother's lap*) You must help me, Mother, to get ready – to plan colors and clothing, and you must explain to me what I have done to make a man such as him, a God, love me, so that I may never stop doing it. (*She runs to embrace* **Electra**.) I am to marry.

Clytemnestra One   Do you feel only eagerness to leave your poor mother alone?

Iphigenia   No, no. It is you he loves, Mother. You and Electra – you are in me and he loves you. We will make it so he never thinks to leave. I will plan menus and parties. How is it that I laugh and cry? Am I really to be given to a God?

And the tub, pushed by **Aegisthus**, *comes rushing out from the dimness behind the net,* **Clytemnestra Two**, *knife in hand, raging at the figure in the tub played by the actor who will be* **Orestes**.

Clytemnestra Two   Like a fish he gapes and breathes. I will strike and suck from you the mystery of your life, Agamemnon.

Aegisthus   I've never done this before.

Clytemnestra Two   There is a passion in our fingers, this handle, Aegisthus. (*And she is putting the knife into his hands*.) Our

flesh; this steel. I saw a man once with a snake put into his
hand. Up he came from sleep, this hissing creature in his grip.
He clutched it for fear that if he let it go, it would strike and
kill him. And yet, could he hold it forever? What could he do?

Aegisthus   I hate snakes.

Clytemnestra Two   I love you, I love you. (*She kisses him.*)
Kill him.

Aegisthus *backs up and she whirls away.*

Clytemnestra Two   No, no, Clytemnestra is not coy, and
that is her cunning. A blunt request is honest and fair; how
else could it be made so openly? His lean muscled body shall
be soft as a woman's.

She has moved back to **Aegisthus**. *Together, gripping the knife, they
have moved to stand over the tub. And there is thrashing from the tub, a
muffled cry. She breaks away, yelling down into the tub.*

No longer have your wishes any meaning. We are here now.
Down ten years of roads and maps, ships and pathways, you
have traveled to this tub. You have fled Aulus, triumphed at
Troy, come back to me. I have seen too much of killing not to
know the ways of doing it well. As you stuffed the mouth of
my daughter using rags, I will stuff your mouth with blood.
Aegisthus is my little husband now. Remember him?
Uninterested in any war, he worries over papers and numbers.
He tabulates and scribbles. (*And grabbing the end of the tub, she
whirls it.*) He sits in candlelight. And where will you stab,
Aegisthus? How many times?

Aegisthus   As many as you wish.

Clytemnestra Two   Will you cut off a hand, let us say; or
pluck out an eye?

Aegisthus   Of course.

Clytemnestra Two   And will you make speeches, my love?
Will you tell him of the honor, the glory for him to have his
foot cut off because, as a result, the wind will rise, the fleet will
sail, as if the wind could have an interest in feet burning or

children . . . burning. (*Now she is bellowing to the figure in the tub.*) The wind has no feet, Agamemnon; it has no children. It does not know that they are valuable.

And the telephone begins to ring. In a kind of panic, all look about and upward. Like **Agamemnon**, *they paw the air above them.*

Clytemnestra One　Agamemnon!

Iphigenia　Father?

Clytemnestra One　I'm here.

Aegisthus　I'm here.

Iphigenia　Answer.

Clytemnestra Two　ANSWER!

The Girl　Well, one of the more interesting facets of ourselves was our sneakies, these special uniforms which were all black so in the dark nobody could see us hardly at all. For lots of times we just wore 'em and went into people's houses for the fear of it, just to feel the fear of bein' in somebody's house – they didn't know you were there – they might come home any second – what would happen, oh, wow. So anyway, we had our sneakies on and the Angel says he wants Tex, who's from Texas, and us girls to be goin' out in this rich neighborhood and kill some gooks. I'm from Pennsylvania.

The ringing stops. **Clytemnestra One** *stands looking toward* **Agamemnon**, *who is some distance from her, testing his knee. He pokes it, bends it. On the uppermost scaffolding,* **Iphigenia** *stands reading a letter.* **Aegisthus** *and* **Clytemnestra Two** *are with the tub behind the hanging cargo net.* **Becky**, **Jenny**, *and* **Sally** *are scattered around the platforms.*

Iphigenia　I think, Father, that I understand. Father?

Clytemnestra One *steps toward* **Agamemnon**.

Clytemnestra One　Hello.

Agamemnon　Clytemnestra, Clytemnestra, my knee is strange.

Clytemnestra One   What?

Agamemnon   Walking last night to speak to the sentries, my foot went between two rocks in the dark. I fell sideways.

Clytemnestra One   Let me see. (*Moving forward to examine the knee.*)

Agamemnon   Now it aches. Why should that be? My knee is a bendable thing. I had never wondered about it before. What is in a knee to make it work? It bends but one way.

Clytemnestra One   I don't know. How are you otherwise? I go through the encampment, but nowhere do I find signs of our daughter's wedding. When I ask about the preparations, I am met with glances that frighten me.

Agamemnon   Clytemnestra, I have thought to tell you this a hundred ways, but my lips and tongue can manage none of them. I have written what I cannot say. (*He hands her the letter and goes to lean against the scaffold while* **Clytemnestra One** *reads.*) I don't understand it. But they talk about me. They are here now. One of them – they're everywhere, listening, judging. They have dreamed of her – the Gods. It is their will, their desire. They brood in lust of our daughter. They talk of taking their love from me.

Clytemnestra One   Agamemnon, what is this?

Agamemnon (*gesturing to* **Pylades** *who marches forward to hand a book, perhaps a copy of the* Iliad, *to* **Clytemnestra One**) Helen, wife of my good brother Menelaus, has been kidnapped by conniving Trojans and their hearts must adorn my sword!

Clytemnestra One (*hurling the book away*)   I know the troubles that brought you to this shore, but –

Agamemnon   I thought you would send her. (*He moves to touch her.*) I did not think you would be here to share this pain.

Clytemnestra One   What pain? You wrote me a letter promising a joyous day of marriage. I am here for her wedding.

Agamemnon (*seizes her shoulders*)   I need only your faith in me.

Clytemnestra One   You say you did not know I would be here. But you summoned me.

Agamemnon (*still holding her*)   I want your trust, Clytemnestra. I ask only for your trust.

Clytemnestra One   If this letter is true, there is no such thing as trust! There is no such word! (*She thrusts his hands aside.*) I am no fool, Agamemnon!

Agamemnon   You are unfair. You burden me with unjust blame. I am not blameless, but I am no monster. (*He is moving around her.*) What is it in you that you must call your husband monster? Yes, I am your husband, our daughter's father, but I am also a king and general. This kidnapping is more than the disappearance of one woman. We have been violated and threatened. This venture on the part of the barbarians is not accidental, but it is a probe to test our will. One man sent into our midst to steal one woman, and now they await our reaction, which must come. Our sudden towering sails shall turn their shoreline black with shadow; and they will sue for peace at the sight of us. They cannot truly wish to fight unless they find some pulse of weakness beating in us, some sweet softness corrosive in our blood. Then our danger will have begun. No woman nor anything in Greece will be safe, and it will not be just one man who disgraces and robs us, but bands of raiders, and then small fleets until one day an armada closes in upon the sea around us and we are lost. (*From a distance, he faces her.*) You do not believe this because it is of the kind of knowledge that men have that I am speaking. (*He is crossing to her.*) But there are nations in this world – these eyes have seen them – men who have no grace nor mercy – they plunder for no reason but their own hungers. From these inhuman creatures we must protect ourselves. And even if it were not so simple – if it were more complicated, which it could be – because there are times when the people who threaten you do it without validity – not without true grievance. But is that any reason to allow them to kill you? Because it is possible they have the right.

Clytemnestra One   Agamemnon, you must –

Agamemnon   Answer my question. Is there any reason to allow them to kill us?

Clytemnestra One   No. Of course not. But –

Agamemnon   Then go from this place.

Clytemnestra One   But these papers declare that my child must die!

Agamemnon   We are chained here. The most powerful army in the world, and Iphigenia is the key. In smoke and the moon, in the innards of a blessed and God-sent bird, Calchas has read that Iphigenia, though she be innocent, must die.

Iphigenia (*standing with her father's letter in her hand. Yet she speaks upward as if her father is somewhere high above her*)   Father, I tremble when I think of it.

Agamemnon   The Goddess of this place demands a virgin's death.

Iphigenia   When in love he holds me, Father – Achilles, who is of the blood of a Goddess – when we are one in love, will I be also, as he, divine?

Clytemnestra Two   AGAMEMNON!

The phone begins to ring.

Clytemnestra One (*to **Agamemnon***)   The wind has no children!

Clytemnestra Two   The wind has no feet or children!

Clytemnestra One (*moving forward as **Clytemnestra Two** is moving backward, ripping up **Agamemnon**'s letter*)   The wind has no children. It does not know that they are valuable.

Clytemnestra Two   Who takes my time away from me?

*As **Clytemnestra One** tosses the paper at **Agamemnon** and runs to embrace **Clytemnestra Two**.*

Clytemnestra One   Who takes my time away from me? Who takes my time?

The Speaker   For not only are the systems of space large, but they are becoming continually larger. Every thirteen hundred million years, space doubles its linear dimensions, so that already there is eight times as much space as when the first radioactive rock solidified and there is perhaps more than one hundred times as much as when the earth itself was torn out of the sun. With every tick of the clock, the distance of the width of space increases by hundreds and hundreds of thousands of miles. With every tick of the clock. It is a black immensity in which we float like singular particles of dust . . . bits of air . . . molecules in peculiar exile.

Agamemnon (*kneeling, praying to the Godheads*)   I say to you, Gods, if your word is cruel, is it any less your holy and blessed word? I don't know, but I think we have no right to resist when, if this price were being asked of some other, we would compel that payment. I believe we have no choice, though once I thought we did, and though it is the cruelty of our natures to make it seem we do – and so the pain in me – though it is Clytemnestra who makes all the noises of suffering – my pain is monstrous. Do you hear me? Do you hear me, Gods? This child's death torments me! Who hears me? (*He opens his eyes, looks about.*) Who hears me?

The Speaker   I hear you, Agamemnon.

Agamemnon   Who hears me?

Clytemnestra Two (*at the tub*)   Our knife, Aegisthus, will sever the threads that lock in his life. Since he wishes to speak of monstrous pain, we will teach it to him. Hold his arm to begin the lesson.

Aegisthus *seizes the arm of the man in the tub.*

Clytemnestra Two   To have your skin cut deep and quickly, Agamemnon . . . (*She lunges.*) . . . is that monstrous pain? Or to have straight, slow slices. Or is it simply to know the knife is near? Can you define it? In terms of your own flesh, I mean. (*She moves to the end of the tub.*) Do you know for instance that a man is all strings, all bits of hair, and an eye and knife deft and quick enough could sever him apart thread by string. Would that be monstrous?

The man in the tub groans.

You mutter, you murmur. What is monstrous pain?!

And she thrusts into the tub, her own voice a scream that is joined by the cry of the man in the tub, one loud wail that ends as a yelp from **Agamemnon**, *sitting poking at his knee.*

Agamemnon   I have indeed hurt my knee. I did not bend it out of the ordinary trying to kick a guard. A trivial thing – yet it hurts. I have done a drawing of it. (*As* **The Speaker** *holds up a drawing of the knee.*) In order to try and see what might have happened inside it when I fell among the rocks the other night. It is so odd, bending so extremely in one way and so little in the others. Also it has made me curious about . . . the elbow . . . which bends only in the opposite direction. (*Now he demonstrates how the knee bends one way while the elbow bends the other. This stands him on one leg, his right leg and right elbow bending.*)

Clytemnestra One   I have been looking for you.

Agamemnon   Do you see the way I suspect they work? I'm curious to learn more of them.

Clytemnestra One   They have told Iphigenia. Her eyes, agleam as if with love, let loose tears. Where were you, Agamemnon? You must stop this thing.

Agamemnon   I can not.

Clytemnestra One   You do not even hesitate.

Agamemnon   Because the truth is not elusive, I do not hesitate. (*He is pacing away.*)

Clytemnestra One   What truth? Where is this truth, and where is Iphigenia in any of it? Like dogs you do the tricks of foolish Menelaus, who can not keep his wife – but between this departure of Helen and our daughter's death, nothing real exists – do you see – unless you put it there.

Agamemnon   I put nothing. No. It is Calchas.

Under the booth, **Clytemnestra Two** *leans against the net, watching.*

Clytemnestra One   It happens within you. All within you – that is what I am saying.

Agamemnon   She will be given to a God.

Clytemnestra One   I will damn you to that same God, Agamemnon. (*Her hands are moving to his face.*) I swear it. His bones will hold you. He will kiss you at the rim of hell.

Agamemnon   Don't . . . touch me!

Clytemnestra Two   Aegisthus, do you know me where I am an animal? (*Entwining herself on the ropes of the net.*)

Aegisthus (*moves behind her, hands around her waist*)   I have loved you, yes . . . touched you.

Agamemnon *is trying to remove* **Clytemnestra One***'s hands from his face. But it is as if she is enormously strong.*

Clytemnestra Two   I am an animal.

Aegisthus   Flesh. So are we all.

Clytemnestra Two   I am full within myself. I paint my body. (*She takes* **Aegisthus***' hand to her breast.*) I decorate not my clothing, but my skin. I am water and oil, sea salt. I crawl up, thinking, from the sea.

Iphigenia   Father, where are you?

She runs to **Agamemnon***, who breaks free from* **Clytemnestra One** *and grabs* **Iphigenia***.*

I dreamed of you: monkeys carried snakes. They murdered you. There were many corridors of shelves of bottles and in one of them, in a greenish-yellow liquid, you were sealed. I beat upon the glass. They said I could not speak to you. You have been cut in battle, Father, what is the feeling?

Agamemnon   It is not the same. No, no.

Iphigenia   And will I be given wine? I must have wine.

Agamemnon Of course.

Iphigenia Good, good. And will it be far to walk? I fear
the walking. I would like to know whose hands will hold the
knife. Will it tear my clothing? Will my wrists be bound? Will
I be naked? I don't want to be naked. If it could be arranged
that I could be carried, I would feel much better. There is
nothing I can think of to want but dignity – I have thought
and thought and it is dignity that I want. Not clothes or
perfume. Clean water. All seem foolish. I could sit correctly,
Father, I am sure. Properly. Erect as a queen. Or resting
softly, if I were carried there. All would cheer and think me
beautiful.

Pylades, *wearing the half-mask, comes running in and*
Agamemnon *leaps to his feet.*

Pylades Sir!

Agamemnon I must go.

Pylades Sir, there's trouble, the man –

Agamemnon All right, all right!

Pylades It's urgent!

Yet **Iphigenia** *grabs* **Agamemnon** *as he moves to go.*

Iphigenia No. Please. And I know you are busy, and you
are all good fine men who will only do what is right, but when
I've been cut, will I be dead? I know I will no longer live, but
when the knife is in me and I am no longer as I am . . . now
. . . will I be merely changed or will I be nothing? Emptiness
. . . or as I thought I would be joined to Achilles? I have fear,
Father. Fear that is not ceremony, not burial, but
disappearance. I fear, Father, that I shall vanish.

Clytemnestra One She loves you, Agamemnon.

Agamemnon Is this your curse?

Clytemnestra One She loves you more than I have ever
loved you. And I do not say that to hurt or surprise you, but
only to make you see the thing you say you must destroy.

Agamemnon   But what of the inevitable and terrible losses to come if she is spared?

Clytemnestra One   There is no reason for this war. Helen loved the foreigner. Your brother is a dull, cold man and Helen left him. Dare you not acknowledge that she could long for a man from another land?

Agamemnon (*whirls to face her*)   I have reports – proofs of kidnapping.

Clytemnestra One   Lies.

Agamemnon   Eyewitnesses saw her bound and gagged. Sentries were bribed; others murdered.

Clytemnestra One   It is only your pride.

Agamemnon   I would kill my daughter for pride?

Clytemnestra One   You have forgotten her.

Agamemnon (*taking* **Iphigenia**'s *shoulder, he looks at her*)   She is my child, whom I love and whom I will love even more in death.

Man in Tub   Father.

Iphigenia   What about my clothing? Will I be naked?

Agamemnon's *hands are still on his daughter.*

Clytemnestra One   Her bones shall hold you as no daughter should a father!

Iphigenia   And I would be carried.

Clytemnestra One   Gagged with rot, her mouth shall press around your tongue.

Iphigenia   Have you nothing to tell me?

Clytemnestra One   What clothing will she wear?

Pylades   Sir, we must go!

Clytemnestra One   Will she be carried or dragged?

Man in Tub   Father!

Clytemnestra One   Answer!

Clytemnestra Two   Answer!

Agamemnon   Ohhh, God Apollo. Help me! (*He runs from them all.*)

Iphigenia   I dare not walk!

Man in Tub (*screaming*)   FATHER!

As **Clytemnestra One** *and* **Iphigenia** *are embracing, leaving.*

Clytemnestra Two (*crouching with* **Aegisthus** *beside the man flailing in the tub*)   He comes to life. Our netted, incredulous fish, in order that he might die. Ohh, no. This knife is your knife, Agamemnon. Stabbing gently. Kindly. The death it gives is meaningful. What is there to fear in this good, kind knife of sacrifice?

Aegisthus   Oh, my God.

Clytemnestra Two   It's true.

Aegisthus   No, no – I dreamed – I just remembered – I dreamed that you dreamed of giving birth to a snake. Green and cruel, it came out of you. It looked like him. (*Gesturing at the tub.*) It wanted to embrace us. You nurtured it. I said, 'Kill it.'

Clytemnestra Two (*laughing, moving toward him*)   I had no such dream.

Aegisthus   No! I did. I did. I had it (*As he starts to flee.*) It looked like him.

Clytemnestra Two   Aegisthus! (*Moving after him.*)

The Speaker (*alone on the empty stage*)   The activity of the brain is mainly electrical. Yet surprisingly enough, a thin section of brain tissue under a microscope looks like garden weeds.

As **Agamemnon** *enters and picks up a bottle of whiskey sitting on the scaffolding. He starts drinking.*

An electrochemical change in a single neuron – and there are some thirteen trillion in the body – institutes a series of changes all along the nerves so that an electrical impulse flows along its fiber like a spark along a fuse toward an explosion . . . At each instant of our lives, in all the different parts of our body, some millions of neurons are firing, all the impulses leaping to the brain.

Agamemnon   A . . . ga . . . num . . . non. Aga . . . min . . . nom. (*He moves a step forward, trying very hard to concentrate.*) Aga . . . num . . . num! Aga . . . num . . . num? Shit. I . . . have a name, that when I get drunk, I can't say it. I didn't ask to have such a name and be . . . me. Did anyone ever hear Agamum . . . nun . . . drunk or sober, request that he be me? But I am. I'm going to let my daughter die. (*Reeling to his feet.*) I get drunk. I fall down. I pour wine in my ear. I pour it in my hair. (*Having staggered center stage, his back to the audience, he urinates.*) I piss on rocks, and still she is going to die. (*A* **Soldier** *races up to him, whispers in his ear and flees.*) Soldiers run up to me and say this has occurred, or that. I don't give a fuck. A man has fallen off his horse and landed on his sword. Am I to explain that? Take the man off the sword and give the horse to someone else. I don't know. And there are platoons of men at one far part of this island dividing the terrain into sectors and preparing to fight because one believes the other stole its aluminum tent poles.

The Speaker   There are no aluminum tent poles.

Agamemnon   They are fighting over them. Who am I talking to? (*He looks about.*) Who hears me?

The Girl   I hear you.

The Speaker   I hear you, Agamemnon. (*As he drinks.*)

Agamemnon   I am here! I AM HERE! I see the surf destroying itself on the shore, and I think, 'Be like that. Be like that.' (*Whirling away from them.*) Oh, my God, I will make myself hard and let the world destroy itself against me. What is a daughter? If I took off running with my wine – now – how far would I get? I so love my power. Would I feel it in the dark

behind me to draw me back? People do as I say. 'Come here,'
I say, and they do. 'Go. Stand. Sit.' It's amazing. So amazing.
(*He crosses back, sits down on the floor, staring outward.*) As a child,
my brother and I would play games of our father and uncle.
(*Pause. He sits, remembering.*) Uncle Thyestes would seduce his
sister-in-law, our mother. And then Atreus, our father, would
make a dinner of our cousins, the sons of Thyestes, and feed
them to him. He would eat and vomit them up. We would
laugh. (*He laughs aloud, the sound trailing off.*) I wanted to be
Atreus, but Menelaus managed always to be our father and I
was foolish Thyestes, forever foolish and vomiting. But now I
am . . . Aga . . . num . . . num.

Pylades   Agamemnon. (*He enters without the half-mask and
carrying* **Agamemnon**'s *armor.*)

Agamemnon   Yes. YES!

Pylades   It's time to get started.

Agamemnon   What? I know, I know.

Pylades (*beginning to put the armor on* **Agamemnon**)   Soon
they will come for you. The great events of morning will be a
storm to hurl us from this place. The men are excited. They
know we leave soon. They talk of learning more of the wild
beasts and men that fill the unknown world.

Agamemnon   I have never been to Asia Minor, but the
people I have seen from Troy made little impression on me,
though they are cunning. In six weeks we'll tack their tails to
the wall.

Behind them **Clytemnestra One** *has come to stand, watching.*

Pylades   To get some Trojan whores, Agamemnon. To
drink wine in another man's land. Think of it. To leave their
wives and sisters fat with seed. How can he ever drive us out
when the children of his women belong in blood to us and
they are there amid his people like little spies with faces that
show forever what we have done to him?

Agamemnon   Buckle it tighter. It is good to feel this old
skin of leather. Soon we go beyond the rim of this familiar sea.

Pylades *stands, smiling broadly.*

Clytemnestra One   Look at you!

Agamemnon *whirls, startled.*

Clytemnestra One   My God, I think we learn of one another, and I am not a fool to care for you. When I awoke to find you gone from our bed, I imagined you alone and heartsick somewhere in the night. I set out to console you, but –

Agamemnon   I need no consolation!

Clytemnestra One   I find you preening with this jackass, your brain lost in the glories of ruin and blood.

Agamemnon   Why do you never speak of survival? (*To* **Pylades**.) Why does she never mention honor? (*And back to her.*) Why does this army mean nothing to you, these tens of thousands who languish here day after day eating half-rotten food so they may go finally into battle where they must risk their pride, their youth, their lives? Should only Clytemnestra risk nothing?

Clytemnestra One   I am losing my child.

Agamemnon   And so you must go on with dignity as I will in her honor.

Clytemnestra One   You cannot make me do this again! It cannot happen!

Agamemnon   We have other children. Last night, I put another into you – we drew him to this world. In my sleep, I saw him – a son. We must call him Orestes. Devote yourself to Electra.

Clytemnestra One   I have seen your unhappy face when for some small mischief you had to punish Iphigenia, simply scold her, and now you will kill her with pride. What am I to do?

Agamemnon   Go home, Clytemnestra! A ship can be readied within the hour to –

Clytemnestra One   But I am haunted! Already, I am –

Agamemnon   – Spare yourself this –

Clytemnestra One   You have killed my infant boy and now you will kill my girl. There are times already, Agamemnon, when that dead child torments me that I sleep in the arms of his killer.

Agamemnon   I have no fear of such a mewing little ghost.

Clytemnestra One   But what shall I do when both my children who are dead come back to sit on either side of our bed and you sleep and I sit, seeing the wishes of their eyes?

Agamemnon   I took you from a land of poverty and barbarism. Our land is a land of wealth. The Gods blessed and chose us. Your husband paid no tribute. He was a little man who fell sideways before my sword had even touched him and he knelt there panting until I clubbed him as I would a dog. I have no fear for his son who isn't even here.

Clytemnestra One   Again and again, I forget what you are!

Agamemnon   Then look at me! See me!

Clytemnestra One   Just as you have forgotten what you did.

Agamemnon (*whirling to stride away*)   I haven't time for this.

Clytemnestra One   Even now I think of killing you, Agamemnon! My dead and squalling children demand it! (*Her words have stopped him.*) Like the knife they urge me to use, they shred all other hopes.

Agamemnon   I have not forgotten what I did, what we –

Clytemnestra One   But you have! And so you think that I have, too. I was a girl, though already a queen and a wife and mother. And one morning my husband runs to tell me barbarians have crossed our sacred borders. He is the king, but barely more than a boy. His cheeks are flushed, his eyes hot with fear. And by dusk you are there before me, his poor corpse strung through the heels on strips of leather, whose ends wrap round your fist. I watched you, my baby, mewing and sightless as a puppy in my arms, as you strode across that courtyard toward me.

Agamemnon   Women in captured towns huddle in shadows, Clytemnestra. They hold their children to them, they stare at the ground, you knelt in sunlight in the middle of that courtyard, your eyes –

Clytemnestra One   I know where I was. I know what I did. I told myself if I didn't move, you would not see me and I was trembling. I thought that if I did not look at you, you would pass me by and I could not take my eyes off you. I handed my son up to you to show our helplessness, to beg for mercy, his small mouth open to cry. You stood over me, like a beast dreaming that his prey adores him, my two men dangling from your hands. And then the child cried out, moving through the air, and I saw that you would kill him.

Agamemnon   I simply tossed him aside. I did not know his head would crack open on that wall. Seeing the look in your eye, I simply threw him in a kind of joy at what you would give me.

Clytemnestra One   But I reached to stop you – how could you not see that I reached to stop you!

Agamemnon   No. No.

As he reaches toward her and she knocks his hands away.

Clytemnestra One   It was impossible. I could not hold him. And then his little body was gone, and I held only your empty hands. Far behind me, there was a sound like teeth biting into an apple.

Agamemnon   You reached to bring me to you, as you draw me even now with your eyes and breath. You wanted me. (*He has her now.*)

Clytemnestra One   No.

Agamemnon (*as they struggle*)   And now you lie, seeking to order the past by deceiving the present. (*Forcing her to the ground.*) You gave your permission.

Clytemnestra One   No!

Agamemnon   It was your wish in your eye.

Clytemnestra One   Kill no more that I love! Your name will come to mean no more than blood to me. I beg you!

Agamemnon   You held that child up like a gift.

Clytemnestra One (*flailing wildly against him*)   Could I have wanted you pumping your filth into me with my dead husband and child beside me in the dirt? Is that what you think? It isn't possible! Agamemnon!

Agamemnon   What are we talking about? (*Breaking free of the embrace, struggling to stand.*)

Clytemnestra One   It is not possible!

Agamemnon   I don't know what we're talking about. Because none of this matters. None of it is of any consequence at all.

Clytemnestra One   But it is all that matters. It's everything. Think. Please find a way to lift us from this fate. I beg you, Agamemnon, think! Think!

His hands are clutching his head and **The Speaker** *eases up beside him, pointer in hand.*

The Speaker   Recent scientific brain experimentation has led – among other things – to the fact that the left lobe of the brain is verbal while the right lobe is mute, along with the knowledge that even when the left doesn't know what the right is doing, it persists in explaining the activities in which it finds itself involved. The more an anatomist, scalpel in hand, explores, the more he destroys that which he seeks to understand. Unlike the human heart which betrays its action by beating, the brain, laboring to solve the most complex of problems, is totally, utterly silent.

Agamemnon   But there is no wind, Clytemnestra. What am I to do when there is no wind and there must be? It is a common thing, yet it is not here. Where is it when it is not here? (*He looks about at the air.*)

The Speaker (*whispering*)   He's thinking.

Agamemnon   It is impossible. And I am a king and a general, and what if not to confront and make common the impossible is the purpose of a man who bears those names?

Clytemnestra One   It is not your motive.

Agamemnon   I swear it.

Clytemnestra One (*as he comes moving toward her*)   Pride is your motive – vanity and power. The wind is your alibi and excuse.

Agamemnon   Nooooo! (*And he pivots from her, ferocious in his denial.*)

The Speaker (*pointing her pointer at his head*)   An electro-chemical change in a single neuron – say, here – (*And the pointer skips to his hand.*) institutes a series of changes so that an electrical impulse flows along its fiber (*The pointer darts back to his head.*) like a spark toward an explosion.

Agamemnon *wheels about to face* **Clytemnestra One**.

Agamemnon   You don't see the difficulty of every move, every decision, and all the while the petty considerations of the age rave at my heels like poor dumb dogs.

The Speaker   It is the task of the brain . . . (*She points to his head.*) to sort these billions of impulses, to establish priorities amid this popping.

Agamemnon   Always there are a thousand alternatives to every decision – each an unknown road whose end I ache to glimpse before I take our land forward upon it, so that I may know with certainty that it is the way most right for us. A thing I can not ever know. (*As he moves,* **The Speaker** *follows, pointing to his head.*)

The Speaker   It is the task of the brain to pronounce decisions amid these explosions. To deliver insights within this crackling, hissing skull.

Agamemnon   And this happens endlessly! Because there are moments whose dimensions demand the eye of a God to comprehend them when there are only men alive within them. And so I make decisions that in a God would be humane, but because I am a man, they are unnatural.

The Figure (*appearing in the mask, the netted toga, beads, and bones of Calchas*)   They are not unnatural. You do not speak of the reasons. You do not speak of the issues. I am Calchas, the prophet. I will tell the reasons.

Agamemnon   Priest, she torments me.

The Figure   I will bring peace and harmony. (*He moves forward, carrying a briefcase.*)

Clytemnestra One   Calchas, I honor you; I know your name.

The Figure   Little else but my name. Not of the secrets these figures spread now before your eyes can read. There are things to be seen by touching. (*He places his briefcase on the ground.*)

Agamemnon   Forgive me, Priest, if I offended you. For a moment, I could see nothing but the wish of my child to live.

The Figure   It is only love of one another that confuses you.

Clytemnestra One   Priest, I beg you – let me understand.

The Figure (*gently*)   You seek to change him, Clytemnestra, and because he cares for you, he feels weakness. I am not a cold man. I understand. Believe that I understand. And believe that I feel, after your large grief, something that is mine alone. I am mystery to you, a voice come to tell you that your daughter must die. You would demand, 'By what right? What authority?' And because I respect you, because I want no human pain to exist if there is a way it can be avoided, I will refuse the temptation to feel dishonored by your request, which I know, if it is made at all, must be made in doubt of my word and power. I will explain. We are creatures of reason. I will make of this meeting a moment in which words and goodwill shared among men make mystery less mystery. There is peace to be given by reason. Please, Agamemnon, kneel also.

Agamemnon   Yes. (*He kneels while* **The Figure** *opens his briefcase and takes out a small object wrapped in cloth.*)

The Figure   Clytemnestra, listen. (*Beginning to spread on the cloth the many small hunks of bone wrapped in the cloth.*)

Clytemnestra One   Priest, know that I wish to hear you. I ache for the rest you offer.

The Figure   Then listen. There are lines of blood on the small bones of a bird, and they have meaning. A triangular bit of stone can alter the importance of a winglike pattern of sinew. My fingers read these signs, these many intricate signs. The bird is brushed against me and then put into flight. He soars to touch against the cloud citadels of heaven to eavesdrop upon the whispering Gods within. Returned, slit open, his warm birdheart beats between these fingers I now thrust toward you, and they learn of his journey. There are colors and hidden sounds, deep pockets of mucus that, looked into, have voice. Purple is a cry for help. Scarlet mucus means innocence. Amber is royalty. (*He rises.*) Three successive days I read it, Clytemnestra: our ships frozen on a summer sea, and nothing possible to free them but the blood of a girl. Blood, do you see? To melt all ice and unleash our imprisoned ships. Because of our outrageous numbers in this harbor, the Goddess of this place has grown offended, and so she has hidden the wind. Consequently, it is her wish – the wish of Artemis – that before we can depart, a recompense be paid, a recompense of blood, the blood of royalty and innocence, the royal and innocent blood of Iphigenia.

Agamemnon (*kneeling and bowed over*)   Did you see? It is as I told you: she is and has been the price from the beginning. (*He* *straightens*.) Our ships do not shiver with the smallest breeze. All rot in the degradation of lacking a thing so common as wind, a thing so common as children. (*He rises to his feet*.) I do not fear the truth. She is a child and the world teems with them. All put here for the use of the Gods, and now Calchas in wisdom and goodness has told us that use.

Clytemnestra One   Priest, could you say it again?

Agamemnon   She belongs to the Gods.

The Figure   The Gods shall have her.

Clytemnestra One   I feel the rocks shall drink her blood.

Agamemnon   Woman, be careful that you –

Clytemnestra One   I feel dirt will have her.

The Figure   Do not refuse the peace I offer.

Clytemnestra One   Her dried blood will look like moss upon the stones.

The Figure (*his hand on* **Clytemnestra One**'s *head*)   I am the final authority, offering peace and rest. The tongue with which I speak is rooted in the mouth of God. I am His lips and tongue.

Clytemnestra One   You are His vomit!

Agamemnon (*slapping her*)   He is the power that guides us through the world!

Clytemnestra One (*rising up and backing away*)   No, I deny!

The Figure   It does no good to deny. You will have no rest till you accept my words.

Clytemnestra One (*covering her face*)   I deny.

The Figure (*outraged*)   You must accept my words! Only then will her name and yours, also, and mine and Agamemnon's be sung with reverence into time, for to make possible the sailing of these ships will be to make possible the beginning of a miracle!

Agamemnon   Priest, humble yourself no further. She blames us because the Gods kill her children.

Clytemnestra One   The entrails of a bird are garbage.

The Figure   Only when we see beyond ourselves do we truly begin to see. We must see the concerns of others. (*He crosses away, taking the briefcase and bones with him.*)

Agamemnon   You are consumed with yourself. (*He follows* **The Figure** *away, leaving her.*)

Clytemnestra One   No, it is you. All of you. In postures of mourning, you will gather together, and you will look at the sky as if the sky could be pertinent while she dies at your feet, a gagging, butchered girl.

As **Sally**, **Becky**, **Pylades**, *and* **Jenny** *enter. They lower the cargo net and spread it on the floor.*

All because you are kings and generals and priests to whom even the wind you believe must bow if only you can find the means to tempt it. Why can you not understand that a thing in this universe can be deaf to you? Not unconcerned, or opposed, but deaf beyond response.

The Figure *as Calchas returns carrying a bowl of blood, as he moves to stand on the net spread on the floor.*

Clytemnestra One   You trade my daughter for your delusions!

Iphigenia   Priest, I honor you. I honor you.

Moving to stand before **The Figure**, *she kneels, he kneels facing her, suddenly tearing open the front of her dress. He begins to paint her body and murmur.*

The Speaker   Even the briefest consideration of uncivilized people everywhere and in all ages shows that terror lurked down the primeval street, in the primeval forest, over the primeval sea, terror and magic, and the most common defense of all – the human sacrifice – some awesome ritual by which bodies are piled up to the invisible and monuments are built to the bodies.

Iphigenia   Father, he paints me. Calchas paints me. The ropes are tight.

Agamemnon (*rushing forward to her*)   Child, I have outrage at what has been done to us, at time and this life and how they have conspired to make it impossible for us to know one another as we should, through all the changes of many years.

Clytemnestra One   Give him nothing for his lies! (*Bending to* **Iphigenia** *from the opposite side.*)

Agamemnon   Take her! Guards!

Clytemnestra One (*as* **Pylades** *in a mask rushes forward to grab her and drag her back*)   No! Don't listen.

Agamemnon   Iphigenia, forgive me.

The Figure *pushes* **Iphigenia** *backward to lie on the net. He rises, the bowl of blood in hand.*

Clytemnestra One   See how he lies to make you think of your death as more his suffering than your own! You are to return to him his innocence because he suffers for his crime even as he does it. And yet he does it.

Agamemnon (*rushing to* **Clytemnestra One**)   You are a pit, Clytemnestra!

Clytemnestra One   He lies to make your death seem a gift you give rather than a deceit and robbery done to you!

As the net with **Iphigenia** *lying in it begins to rise, Calchas with her.*

Iphigenia   I will give you children, Father; grandsons!

Clytemnestra One   Look into hatred of him, Iphigenia!

Agamemnon   You are a pit. You think forever in terms of that cell inside you. You would hold the world there and lock it in that darkness! (*Whirling, he runs back to kneel beneath the risen net.*) Iphigenia, look to the Goddess! The Goddess will guide you!

Iphigenia (*singing*)
Will I circle in the air?

Will I tremble as a smaller start?
Birds pass by like boats in the water.
I am the sound of snow afar.
I fall and wonder
How I am more, more than I, can explain
Am I the perfect smallness of the rain?

High above them, **The Figure** *kneels astride* **Iphigenia**, *the knife and beaker of blood in his hands above her.*

Clytemnestra One (*as* **Pylades** *releases her, now that the net has risen*)   Why is it that the Gods have always the minds of old men hungry for the bodies of young girls? Why is that, Agamemnon? I swear it to you – had I known the prize her purity was to win for her, I would have coupled her with a dog – the first passing cur.

Agamemnon   I am your king and husband, Clytemnestra; know that and be still.

Clytemnestra One   But I say you are murdering our daughter.

Agamemnon   I am twice your ruler!

Clytemnestra One   And if you slaughter a child –

Agamemnon   I do not murder –

Clytemnestra One   – you are no king or husband.

As **Aegisthus** *comes rushing forward with the tub while* **Clytemnestra Two** *comes storming toward the tub, dagger poised.*

Agamemnon   I do not slaughter! I sacrifice! I sacrifice! (*He is fleeing.*)

Clytemnestra Two   I SACRIFICE!

And **Clytemnestra Two** *plunges her knife into the tub, and* **Iphigenia** *screams as the figure in the tub writhes.*

Clytemnestra One   I SACRIFICE!

Clytemnestra Two   You have murdered children that I loved . . .

Clytemnestra One   You have murdered children that I loved . . .

Clytemnestra Two   You have murdered love in me.

Clytemnestra One   You have murdered love in me.

Clytemnestra Two   You have hurt and left me lonely, but for none of these reasons . . .

Clytemnestra One   For none of these reasons . . .

Clytemnestra Two   For no reason you can ever name or know, I am going to cut your life out of you. There is a tree, Agamemnon, that I wish to see grow. I am told your blood will give it life. And so, because I wish this tree to grow, and because it is my whim and appetite at this moment to see you die, I make this thrust into your flesh.

As she thrusts fiercely into the tub, **Aegisthus** *is backing away.*

Do you know, if I were to think of this as cruelty, I could not do it. But it is not, and there is dignity in it. And so, because to kill you is a pointless thing, and a pointless thing is what I wish to do, I will make this final thrust . . . (*The knife is rising.*) . . . into your flesh and you . . . in some few seconds will be also a bride of Achilles. He will kiss you at the rim of hell! (*She stabs.*)

Iphigenia (*in the net above the tub as* **The Figure** *leaves her*) They stood in rows along the pathway, eating bread and cheese, drinking wine. One tried to lie beside me. Guards pushed him off. I did not understand. And then I did and I felt separate from everything. They were an army gathered to await their war. I was a young girl put out before them. They had thronged there piled among the rocks and I heard the roaring vulgar sound they made until I heard nothing.

Clytemnestra Two (*staring into the tub*)   Look at him.

Aegisthus (*cannot bear the sight*)   My God.

Clytemnestra Two   Look at him.

Aegisthus (*reels backward*)   They are screaming in the streets.

Clytemnestra Two   Do you know, Aegisthus, I have let the life run out of a king? A king's dying is larger than a daughter's. It is impossible – impossible that I could marry a man who would kill our children. I could not kill my husband. I am not such a woman.

The Figure   It is time for Orestes. Time that Orestes come. (*High in the scaffolding, he wears his Levi's jacket, boots, trousers.*)

Clytemnestra Two   Apollo!

The Figure (*coming down*)   It is time that Orestes arrive with his story . . . understanding nothing.

Aegisthus (*backing away*)   Understanding nothing?

The Figure   With his story and hatred and knife. And it will not be his story that will matter, nor will it be his hatred, but only the knife.

Clytemnestra Two   Aegisthus . . . ! (*She looks toward him.*)

The Figure (*moving to the side of the tub, looking down into it*) When you have it, you live.

Clytemnestra Two   Aegisthus! The knife! What is he saying?

The Figure   You live until you lose it.

Clytemnestra Two   I struck. Where is it?

She is seeking the knife in the tub, plunging her arms in again and again, and though she grows bloody, she cannot find the knife, not even the body.

The knife, the knife! It entered into him. You are not fair, Apollo.

The Figure   I know.

Clytemnestra Two   Vanished into him . . .

The Figure   Through the flesh of the father . . .

Clytemnestra Two   Fell through him. I could not hold it.

Clytemnestra One (*off to the side, staring at* **Clytemnestra**

Two *struggling in the tub*)   It sank as if he were enormous.

Clytemnestra Two   Falling past my groping hands a hundred times.

The Figure   To the hand of the son.

Clytemnestra Two   Apollo, no!

The Figure   If I am Apollo, should I not then hate the dark and the dark conjuring incantations of the Pythian Princess whom I adore? I feel I am Dionysus, Apollon of the pit, prince of light and bearer of darkness. I feel I should lift men, though they call me Apollo. I love the pitiful small reeds of their bones. I wish the earth to spin faster, and men to learn of the universe until they uncover their natures and drown in madness. I must have Orestes. I embrace you. I must have Orestes! (*Touching her face with his fingertips.*) I embrace you in my embrace of dear love, Clytemnestra. (*He is so gentle with her.*) And the weaker you grow, the tinier your cries, the greater my loss of you. Where is Orestes?

Clytemnestra Two (*sinking to her knees*)   Apollo! I did not mean to lose it!

The Figure   I KNOW. WHERE IS ORESTES? I MUST HAVE HIM!

Clytemnestra One (*from off to the side*)   He shall not be born!

Clytemnestra Two   Oh, my God!

The Figure   Oh, yes. There. (*He looks at* **Clytemnestra One**.) He is there. My Orestes. (*He moves to* **Clytemnestra One** *as* **Clytemnestra Two** *collapses.*) I had forgotten, but he is . . . (*Kneeling in worship before* **Clytemnestra One**, *his hands on her belly.*) . . . here. Put here by good Agamemnon. And he will arrive, my Orestes, to see me and use me to rid the world of all Clytemnestras. What friends we will be! Apollo and Orestes. (*His hands are caressing her belly.*)

Clytemnestra One (*she pushes at the hands, trying feebly to remove them*)   No. I say, no. (*Yet she cannot resist them. Her struggle ceases.*)

The Figure (*holds her as* **The Speaker** *is approaching*)   Yet we shall. Yet we shall. Oh, belly, we await you. I embrace you. Oh, belly. Oh, beautiful, beautiful belly.

All (*singing from wherever they are, a minor key*)
  Bubbles mark the ocean for a moment where we drown.
  Bubbles mark the ocean for a moment where we drown.

The Speaker (*touching* **Clytemnestra One**'s *belly with the pointer*)   In a place like this, we all begin. Deep within the body of another.

As the lights fade to black.

Act Two

On the scaffolding, a statue of **Aegisthus** *lies on its side. The tub is midstage left with* **Clytemnestra Two** *near it. Downstage left,* **The Figure** *kneels before* **Clytemnestra One**, *his hands on her belly, as she is sinking down onto the floor.* **Becky**, **Sally**, **Jenny**, *and* **Pylades** *are scattered about the stage.* **The Speaker** *steps forward.*

The Speaker   As we travel along now, moving here and there in space and time and time and space, shall we see our earth come into being as a burning ball of gas which gradually cools? In due time, shall we see life appear?

Now both **Clytemnestra One** *and* **Clytemnestra Two** *begin to move and pant with the throes of giving birth,* **The Figure** *tending* **Clytemnestra One**.

Grass and weeds, fish and frogs, apes and mice and trees appear. Lizards, dogs, ticks, flowers, acorns, horses, spiders, whales, orchids, robins, leeches, snails, daisies, fox, cats, stallions, stickbugs, cardinals, crows, pythons and monarch butterflies. And finally, shall there be among them, man!

Orestes *peeps out from the tub, as both* **Clytemnestras** *scream and collapse. Startled, he ducks back down into the tub.* **The Figure** *pulls the knife from between the legs of* **Clytemnestra One**. *Leaving the knife on the floor,* **The Figure** *backs away.*

The Speaker   Shall he arrive at last to take possession of his tiny buzzing bee in space . . . the hissing, humming thing on which he finds himself adrift and starboard of the moon.

Orestes *slowly reappears, wary and wrapped in the placentalike gory net in which his father died.*

The Speaker   Is it with astonishment and terror that he views the cold stellar reaches of his future, the earth, and himself?

As **Orestes** *steps out of the tub.*

Is it with rage and venom that he steps into his world? Is it with love or dread that he arrives?

Orestes *is staring at the knife lying on the floor. He is wrapped in gore, covered in blood. Both* **Clytemnestras** *stare at him.*

Clytemnestra One (*backing toward* **Clytemnestra Two**) What . . . do you want?

Clytemnestra Two   What?

Orestes (*to* **Clytemnestra One** *and* **Clytemnestra Two** *who are together, as he moves toward them*)   Life. To breathe, To breathe.

Clytemnestra One   Who are you?

Orestes (*to* **Clytemnestra One** *and* **Clytemnestra Two**) I don't know. For sure. I think I know.

Clytemnestra Two   Who?

The Figure (*from under the scaffold*)   Orestes!

Both **Clytemnestras** *are retreating as* **Orestes**, *moving after them, has come upon the knife.*

Clytemnestra One   No.

Clytemnestra Two   No.

Orestes (*following* **Clytemnestra One** *and* **Clytemnestra Two**, *he gestures with the knife as he would with a stick as he speaks*) I have been in exile.

They scream and run from the stage, leaving **Orestes** *staring in bafflement.* **The Figure**, *dressed in Levi's, a Levi's jacket, and boots is approaching. His hair is still up, or in a ponytail.*

The Figure   I know who you are.

Orestes   Hello.

Becky, *in Levi's and a blouse tied at her belly, enters with a towel to clean the blood of birth from* **Orestes**.

The Figure   Hello. Don't be worried or afraid. You are Orestes.

Orestes   Oh, I know. Of course.

The Figure   It's good to be Orestes.

Orestes   I feel . . . it is good. I feel it is great. Am I not great? I am here now. At last my exile is over.

The Figure   Son of Agamemnon, Atreus, Tantalus.

Orestes *faces* **The Figure**.

The Figure   You move away from them, up from them. You progress.

Orestes (*to Becky*)   I have never been here before.

The Figure   But you are now. Are you hungry?

Orestes   What?

The Figure   What do you know of your mother and father?

Orestes   Who are you? May I ask?

The Figure (*approaching* **Orestes**, *in a conspiratorial manner*)   I feel I must speak to you of your mother – I must speak to you of your father – yet it is complex – who am I to tell you? Your father is dead, Orestes.

Orestes   What? What did she do? What did my good mother do to my good father?

The Figure (*unveiling a kind of bust of* **Agamemnon**; *it is a fragment of what was once a larger statue*)   There's nothing left of him but this!

Orestes   This is not my father. No, no – not this cold stone. (*Taking the stone into his hands.*)

The Figure   It is his likeness – a shell, nothing more. But even in this fragment, do you not see the inherent honor of his gaze, the nobility of those matchless eyes. Once this statue stood atop his grave and was a shrine that aroused in many a huge devotion. He seemed to gesture toward the horizon that had once held the limitless vista of his ideals.

Orestes   Shall I put a lock of hair upon his grave? Where is it? I want to pray for him.

The Figure (*indicating the tub*)   Over there.

Orestes (*moves to the tub*)   I will.

The Figure   Beware of Tantalus, however. Or have you no concern for him?

Orestes   Who?

The Figure   Tantalus – your great-great-grandfather. Do you wish to put a lock of hair upon his ancient dirt, also? Even though he suffers at this very moment deep at the center of the earth in Hell.

Orestes   I have a relative in Hell?

He looks down into the tub.

The Figure   Do you not feel his eyes looking up through all the layers of the earth to you? Peer down the hole.

Orestes   I have no wish to acknowledge a relative in Hell.

Trying to back away.

The Figure   Peer down the hole.

Forcing him to look into the tub.

Orestes   This . . . you said . . . was my father's grave.

The Figure   It is all one.

Orestes   I think not. (*Pulling free, backing away.*) And there is a chill. Something icy rising from it.

The Figure   Are you cold – you look uncomfortable.

Orestes   A little. (*As* **Becky** *enters with clothing for* **Orestes**. *She helps him dress.*)

The Figure   Here's some clothing, trousers and a shirt with the face of Tantalus upon the front. Wear it with pride.

Quickly, **Orestes** *examines the face upon his shirt.*

Orestes   Tantalus? But his eyes are kind. How can he be in Hell if his eyes are so kind?

The Figure Wear it to show you have no shame – to show you understand that shame is a negative, pointless thing. He is your ancestor, your roots.

Becky *is helping* **Orestes** *dress at tub's edge.*

The Figure I feel him looking up, don't you? His grief and confusion arise like starving dogs. How is it possible, he wonders, that his descendant has grown to such perfection as you? Poor Tantalus. He cooked and fed his son to the Gods, yearning blindly to trick their divine bellies into filling with the flesh and blood of Tantalus. He loved his son. He loved himself.

Orestes (*disgusted*) That's a terrible thing.

The Figure It was a darkness that moved in him.

Orestes It no longer moves in me.

The Figure Of course not.

Orestes I don't understand it.

The Figure He is the oldest of your house, however, so he is often discussed. You should know of him. There are those who say he leapt full-grown from the lip of God. Others say he lived as a half-beast for many, many years, and then, touched by a God, he became man.

Orestes I suspect not.

The Figure Oh?

Orestes It is just my feeling, but I would guess he only looked like a man, seemed one – and was more the beast until a longer time went by, and many others were born, each becoming more and more nearly as I am.

Music begins softly, an introduction.

The Figure The culmination.

Orestes I feel I am.

Becky (*to* **Orestes**) Sing to me, won't you sing to me?

Sally   Do you sing?

The Figure   Oh, yes; do sing. Sing.

He backs away as **Orestes** *quickly kisses* **Sally**, *and begins to sing.*

Orestes
I wake up in the morning
The morning's aflame
Lines of wonder mark my brain.

And as **Orestes** *sings, his audience,* **The Family**, *waves lighted Zippo lighters back and forth, as they listen and back farther and farther away.*

In the morning sun awakening
I wear a lion's mane,
In some magic corner of my brain.
I feel taller than before
And in the mellow air
I hear how I am so much more.
Oooorestes. Ooooorestes
Great, great, great Orestes.
Great, great, great Orestes.

Singing, his eyes closed, he is now alone except for **The Girl** *leaning against an upstage bit of scaffolding.*

The Girl   We didn't know how many people or what kind of weapons, and we went around looking to see how many people while meanwhile Tex, Sally, and Sissie were tying people up – and Becky, oh, wow, was yelling terrible because the girl she was fighting was so strong and biting her and Tex came running in to stab the girl in the stomach, I guess, because I saw her grab down there.

Orestes (*startled by this stranger*)   Are you . . . talking to me? (*He crosses toward her.*)

The Girl   Hi.

Orestes   Did you hear my song and came to speak to me? And those terrible things you were talking about – were they what was done to my good father?

But she turns, leaving him.

Wait!

He is puzzled, looking after her, as behind him **Becky**, **Sally**, *and* **Jenny** *rush on carrying books and papers, a book bag.*

Becky   Orestes, hello.

They all say 'Hello, hello,' as **The Speaker**, *smiling, enters. The girls all wear Levi's and blouses, yet they have on their half-masks.*

Orestes   You know my name. (*He recognizes* **Becky** *and moves toward her.*) You heard my song. I saw you before.

Sally (*stopping him*)   Apollo sent us to help you.

Jenny   Abbadon.

Becky   We have been sent by your friend, God of Reason and the pit.

Jenny (*handing him books, papers, pencils*)   To help you learn. We're here to help you learn.

Becky (*opening a book*)   It is written in the journal of Aegisthus that you are dead. 'The infant of Orestes was killed by me,' he has written. (*Referring to her book.*)

Orestes   But I am here.

Sally (*coming to his side*)   Yet other things are written. And you are here.

Becky   Of course he is.

Jenny   He's here.

Orestes   I'm here.

Sally   It is written that you're here because at the time your father returned from Troy, your mother saved you from murderous Aegisthus. (*She is referring to another book.*)

Becky   On page ninety-nine she sent you off to Phocis to live with your grandparents. See. (*She points.*)

Sally   But there are difficulties, contradictions.

Jenny   Yes, yes, because it is also written on one hundred twelve that on the day of your father's murder, it was not your mother who saved you but a certain good and gracious nurse named Arsinoe that let you live.

Becky   Do you want to take some notes? You ought to take some notes.

Jenny, **Sally** *and* **Becky** (*shouting*)   Take some notes!

Sally   It is written that the nurse was named Laodomaia!

Becky   Gellissa is also written!

Jenny   Aegisthus killed somebody.

Orestes   How is Laodomaia spelled?

Becky (*as* **Sally** *starts spelling names*)   Arsinoe is very probable.

Orestes   Laodomaia, Arsinoe, Gell –

Sally   Clytemnestra could have done it!

Becky   Someone put an infant in your cradle for Aegisthus! Who did Aegisthus kill?

Jenny   It is written in his journal that it was Orestes!

Orestes   Nooooo!

Sally   Of course not.

Jenny   Into whose infant skull did Aegisthus crash his sword!

Orestes *is trying to write all this down.*

Becky   It is written that your mother killed your father to avenge the death of your sister, Iphigenia.

Orestes   My sister is dead?

Jenny   It is said your mother wanted to screw Aegisthus!

Orestes (*to* **Jenny**)   Who is Aegisthus?

Jenny   It is said that she lusts only after political power for herself!

Sally   It is claimed Aegisthus is a man she can rule. It is said that he is a man she worships.

Orestes   Who is he? I don't know who he is.

Becky   Your father is dead. Kill his killers.

Sally   If you hurt your good mother, your brain will rot and blacken with sores.

Jenny   You must avenge your father or scales will close your eyes and blacken your brain with sores.

Orestes   I can't write this fast.

Becky (*handing him books as she goes*)   Read these books. It's so beautiful here in the park.

Sally (*handing him more books as she goes*)   Read these books. It's so lovely here in the park.

Jenny (*piling more books in his arms as she turns and, with the others, leaves*)   Read these books in the lovely, beautiful park.

As **Orestes** *is left with his pile of books and flowers around his neck, he tries to study.* **The Speaker**, *having observed all this, steps closer to him.*

The Speaker   Every day we live, Orestes, we learn more and more. We know things we did not know for millions of years about the height of the universe; life on the largest moon of Saturn is possible; we know of transistor radios, cars, and how the lobes of our brains, when photographed, seem netting or moonscape. We know of the biochemical compounds in the fluids of our brains.

Orestes (*hurling the books down on the floor*)   This is written, that is written. Who is doing all this writing? I must talk to someone! (*He kicks a book.*) Yet I must remain calm. I will remain calm. For it is my belief that the truth, if pursued with patience, reveals itself. It is my belief that there are great good lessons in the sky, and the wise know them while all others struggle throughout their lives to move toward some understanding of these great good lessons. I will move toward them. (*He packs his books into the book bag.*) I will move to find them, to find my sister, Electra. She is here. She has been here while Father and Iphigenia are dead. There has been much pain and ruin without me. But where will I find her? Which way shall I go? (*He looks about a little puzzled.*) That way . . . or . . . that way . . . ? (*Pause: He thinks.*) I don't know what way any way is. (*And then, with great exhilaration, he points to his right.*) That way! I feel it!

Off he goes as **Pylades** *comes rushing in from behind him.*

Pylades (*yelling*)   You! You!

Orestes *stops and turns back toward* **Pylades**, *who looks around furtively.*

Pylades   Come here. I have something for you.

As **Orestes** *starts back,* **Pylades** *moves to meet him.*

I have found these locks of hair upon the grave of Agamemnon. Do you know them? They are the colors of your own.

Orestes   I am looking for his daughter.

Pylades (*taking a piece of parchment from his pocket*)   This message is for his son.

Orestes   I'm very busy.

Pylades (*conspiratorially*)   Are you friend enough to read?

Orestes (*turning to leave*)   I haven't time for any more reading! I've been reading and reading! I've too many questions!

Pylades (*grabbing* **Orestes,** *shoving the paper into his hands*) LOOK AT THIS!

And then the voice of **Electra** *is heard. She is on the scaffolding behind the cargo net.*

Electra   Orestes, they keep me in little light!

Orestes   It is addressed to me. Who sent this? Who is kept in little light?

Electra (*her hands wrapped in the links of rope like the bars of a cage as* **Orestes** *scans the note*)   High above the city streets I am in jail. I am looking at a flaw near the corner that is like a pockmarked face. The walls of the cell are gray.

Orestes   I have no friends in jail.

Pylades   She is in jail.

Orestes   Who?

Pylades   Electra.

Orestes   My sister? She is a princess.

Pylades   Two days ago there was a great gathering on a hillside in the park. There was a platform with Aegisthus upon it.

Orestes   Was that two days ago?

Pylades   Did you see? Were you part of the mob?

Orestes   No, no. I was in the park to do my reading – I was studying under a tree. I have so many books. An important man was making speeches. Foolish people went running forward at him, screaming, throwing rocks and eggs. I told them to stop; it was terrible.

Pylades   Electra was among them; your sister was arrested for befouling the name of Aegisthus.

Orestes *is horrified*.

Orestes   But the only girl among them spit at me.

Pylades   She was the only girl among them.

Orestes   She ran to me where I stood. 'Pretend I'm with you,' she said. Guards were running up. 'No,' I told her. 'You take your punishment. I saw what you did.' She spit at me. Could she have been Electra and not known I was Orestes?

Jenny *comes running in to hand another message to* **Pylades**.

Pylades   You did not know she was Electra. And you have another message.

Orestes   What?

Electra (*standing, pressing against the net*)   Aegisthus fears me.
He fears that I will seduce some guard and lie in secret with
him, that I will deliver a son possessed of the rage of our father
buried without libations. I take men into the dark corners of
this place. I whisper. I hold – I fuck them until they scream.
But I know I can not conceive.

Aegisthus *enters carrying a stool,* **Clytemnestra One** *and*
Clytemnestra Two *both with him wearing royal gowns. He has a
suitcoat over his net toga, medallion and T-shirt.*

Electra   It is my only cry. Nothing happens but that the
guards all hurry off to tell one another what Electra has done
to them.

Aegisthus (*standing atop the stool, begins to speak in the manner of a
politician among cronies as* **Orestes** *receives and reads a newspaper*)
Sometimes I have fun. I have so much fun. I get drunk and go
to Agamemnon's grave. I jump all over it. Up and down. I
kick the dirt. I piss upon it.

Electra (*screaming at* **Aegisthus**)   Abomination!

Aegisthus (*laughing, happy*)   Aegisthus!

Electra   Murderous adulterer!

Aegisthus (*happy, laughing as* **Orestes** *is very confused, another
messenger running up to him*)   Aegisthus! Aegisthus!

Orestes (*rejecting this last message, he turns to* **Pylades**)   What is
all this reading and reading? Are there no people? This is not
enough. (*He throws down the papers.*)

Pylades   I will take you. I will show you. Follow me. Follow
me!

And he grabs the startled **Orestes** *and leads him to the right and they
duck, they weave. They press against a wall in shadows.*

Shhhhhhh. Wait here. You can speak to her through the bars.

Looking up to the scaffolding where **Electra** *sits brooding, he calls
quietly.*

Electra. I have Orestes with me.

Orestes *moves to where he can see* **Electra** *and she can see him.*

Electra (*pressing against the ropes*)   You have abandoned me.

Orestes   No.

Electra   I forgive you.

Orestes   I haven't abandoned you!

Electra   A daughter loves a father, a son, a mother, and so you abandon me.

Orestes (*straining up to be nearer to her*)   My interest is justice – goodness – virtue and understanding. I will be fair.

Electra   Is it fair that I sit in jail? Is it good, is it virtuous? Is it just?

Pylades   You have been away, Orestes. What do you know, living as you did in wealth and exile, while your sister was a slave to Aegisthus, mending clothes, polishing plates?

Electra   Mother must die!

Orestes   What?

Electra   Only in Mother's death is there hope!

Orestes   No, no, I disagree, I –

Electra   Think of our poor, good father struggling always for honor and virtue in our land and they butcher him. Our mother and Aegisthus slaughter him!

Orestes   There is some question of who did what to –

Electra   I was there!

Orestes   I have a plan; it is my own. I am not as rash as you.

Electra   I am Electra!

Orestes   I will go to the marble statue of Aegisthus in the park, where the flag of Clytemnestra waves before the temple

on which the ideals of our land are carved. I will destroy the
flag of our mother; I will shatter the stone likeness of
Aegisthus. Upon the monument to the ideals of our land
which they have abandoned, I will put flowers.

Electra   What good will that do?

Orestes   Just wait and see! You'll be surprised!

Electra   Because you want ideals, you think you must
perform in that same manner which is to not perform at all.
You do nothing!

Orestes (*moving backward in frustration*)   I have only just
arrived, but you act like –

Electra   You think to speak in subtle signs and gestures
when they are blunt, crude people!

Orestes   She is my mother.

Electra   Because of you I am locked away! (*Angrily she strains
against the ropes that cage her.*)

Orestes   I didn't know that was you in the park.

Electra   My degradation is a price I pay to you.

Orestes   I'll get you out!

Reaching to touch her hands with his, he stretches; she crouches.

Electra (*pleading, demanding*)   Free me!

Orestes   I will, I will. I promise!

He pivots away, and sees on an upper level the large statue of
Aegisthus *that has been lying on its side, now being raised.* **Orestes**
pulls his sword.

I will break into the mind of Aegisthus and sweep aside the
ignorance encrusting his heart and soul, which are not unlike
my own, for we are both men, both human!

Aegisthus (*taking the microphone from* **The Speaker** *and talking
into it, while* **Orestes** *scurries to the scaffold and the statue*)   One of
the things most necessary at the moment is a decision as to

whether or not to start higher rediscount rates or begin the sale of our royal securities.

Orestes (*sword poised above the head of the statue*)   Aegisthus, my message for you is as follows: With the shattering of this stone, I will break into your mind. You are a petty, shameful man who has brought corruption all through our land. In your heart you know this. You long for confession and expiation. In the shattering of this statue you will see your shame and guilt and ruin revealed. You will understand my purpose, goodness, and seriousness. You will thank me and beg my help.

He smashes his sword into the head of the statue, as a **Messenger** *runs up and hands a document to* **Aegisthus**. **Orestes** *confronts the shattered statue.*

What do you have to say to me?

Aegisthus   Vandalism is spreading all across our land. Sacrilege. Wanton, petty, psychotic vandalism.

Orestes *is pushing the statue over.*

The Speaker (*leaning in to use the microphone in* **Aegisthus**' *hand.*)   You do not know the word 'psychotic.'

The statue topples now.

Aegisthus   It is everywhere! Sick, demented people are going about destroying the beautiful, wonderful shrines to our wisdom and virtue all across the land.

As a message is delivered to **Aegisthus**.

Orestes (*standing over the fallen statue*)   Free my sister!

Pylades *and* **Others**   Free Electra!

Aegisthus   This is the work of Electra!

And **Pylades** *comes dashing on with a document for* **Orestes**.

Pylades   Orestes! Orestes! He wars against the Persians – he diverts our resources into a pointless struggle with the Peloponnesians. He slaughters the Vietnamese.

Orestes   Who are they?

Pylades   Good, gentle people! He burns their villages.

Orestes *comes down to join* **Pylades**.

Aegisthus (*to* **The Speaker**)   In addition, who are these people the notes left by the vandals all say I am slaughtering?

The Speaker (*taking back the microphone*)   The Vietnamese.

Aegisthus   Oh, yes! Slaughter them!

Orestes (*standing, talking to* **Pylades**)   In what I have done to his statues and flags, does he not see his crimes? Does he not know that I, Orestes, am here? How can he not see his rotten soul crumbling in the dust of his shattered symbols?

Pylades   I have heard he intends to cut off Electra's hands.

Orestes   Cut off – but she is locked away, she –

Pylades   He feels that if she has no hands, no guard nor any man will want her.

Orestes   It is not possible.

Aegisthus   Cut off Electra's hands. I want her to have no hands, so that the desecration of my wonderful institutions will stop.

Electra *screams as another messenger comes running up to* **Pylades**.

Orestes   What has happened to my sister? I must go to her!

Pylades (*still reading*)   Aegisthus has ordered that her tongue be made so she will never speak. He is going to cut her tongue from her mouth.

Orestes   What?

Pylades (*handing him the note*)   With no hands or tongue, he says she will inspire no further destruction of his statues.

Electra *screams, collapsing to the floor*.

Orestes   No, no.

At the same time, **Jenny***,* **Sally***, and* **Becky** *enter and cower against the scaffolding before* **Aegisthus***.*

How is this possible?

Aegisthus   There are crowds of people each night below the windows of my jails. I have many, many jails.

Clytemnestra One *and* **Clytemnestra Two** *are strolling toward him.*

Orestes (*to* **Pylades**)   Who's that? Who's talking?

Pylades   Shhhhhhh. We must hide. Bow down. It is Aegisthus.

Trying to pull **Orestes** *to kneel amid the cowering people.*

Orestes   What?

Pylades (*forcing* **Orestes** *down as* **Aegisthus** *begins, grandly, to speak*)   Bow down. Be still.

Aegisthus   When you put one person in jail, another one appears in the street below. It's an equation. And they are all such odd ruined people below our jails – drunkards – foreigners, dwarfs – gathered in the streets. Now they are quiet, bowing down to me as you can see, but often they yell to one another of their lasting love – all accents and foreign words – they are indecent calling up and down. If that report that Orestes is yet alive should be true, I hope he has been sometimes among them, calling up to mute, despairing Electra. She would stare at me in fury and outrage and I would smile, going on about my business, cutting out her tongue. Call out to her, Orestes.

And then, whimsicality in his voice, he turns to **Clytemnestra One** *and* **Clytemnestra Two** *and gestures toward the sky.*

See that twinkling star – have you any wishes? I have many wishes. It is – isn't it – the first star. Oh, yes. Let us all wish quickly.

As both **Clytemnestra One** *and* **Clytemnestra Two** *cuddle with* **Aegisthus***.*

Orestes   Who's that with him?

Pylades   Clytemnestra.

Orestes   But she embraces him, she kisses him – the man who killed my father.

Pylades   It's your mother.

Orestes (*leaps out screaming as* **Pylades** *tries to restrain him*) You will not escape your crimes, Aegisthus!

Pylades   Run! Now you've done it!

Orestes   Whore! You whore!

Aegisthus   Who is that down there! Who is this criminal who speaks to me of crimes?

Orestes   You heard me!

Pylades   Run! With me. Please! RUN!

Aegisthus (*bellowing*)   Guards. Some vile revolting criminal accuses me of crimes!

Pylades (*fleeing*)   Now!

Aegisthus   Guards!

Orestes *and* **Pylades** *flee as a strobe light flashes on, the light shattering the images of moving people –* **Becky**, **Jenny**, **Sally**, **Pylades**, **Orestes**, *and* **The Girl** *– who all dash about while* **Aegisthus** *paces, receiving messages, reading them, gesturing in one direction and then another while* **The Speaker**'s *voice, amplified by her microphone, goes on.*

The Speaker   Strange indeed are objects at apparent rest upon the earth, for they are like beads of water upon a spinning wheel. So long as they spin slowly gravity holds them in place. It is, for example, a little-known fact that objects at the earth's equator are kept moving continually at rather more than one thousand miles per hour. Should we ever find ourselves spinning faster – say, sixteen times our present speed so that we had an eighty-five-minute day – how we would have to hurry, getting up, off to work, eating, playing, back to bed – we should, in addition, see the surprising spectacle of all objects at the earth's equator, winging off on tangents into outer space, the sea and air, of course, accompanying them on their new adventure.

Aegisthus   What do you mean you can not find him? He must be destroyed!

He stops pacing under the booth and hurls the message into the air, as the strobe cuts out and **Orestes** *bursts out from under the scaffolding with* **Pylades**.

Orestes   What are we running for? I'm sick of it. I don't care. I am Orestes. I want to know what happened. What am I to do?

As **Pylades** *tries to pull him on, he refuses.*

My sister is in jail. Some stranger is Aegisthus. Some stranger is my mother. You say! Who the hell are you? I must speak to my sister and she has no tongue. I was a child. I must learn who saved me. Did my mother in fact kill my father? What's going on? Why did he kill Iphigenia? I have nothing to work with but the names of the dead. Iphigenia! Agamemnon!

The Figure *steps out.*

The Figure   I am here, Orestes, if you wish to speak to me.

Pylades   Apollo.

Orestes   Who?

Pylades   It's Apollo. Called Delian, called Pythian. Called Delian because of Delos, the isle of his birth. Called Pythian for his battle with a serpent, called Phoebus meaning shining, called Lycian meaning wolf-God. Called Sminthian for mouse-God, the God of mice.

The Figure (*to* **Orestes**)   But whether because I protect mice or destroy them, no one knows.

As a number of other **Family Members** *enter.*

We are friendly people. We roam the hills, all strangers yet we live as a family.

Orestes (*to* **The Figure**)   Where have you been? I know you.

He looks at the others.

I know you all.

The Figure (*poking at* **Orestes'** *bags and books*)   What is all this? You have so many books, Orestes.

Orestes (*rooting through his books, documents*)   My notes. Papers. A journal of what I learned about my life, which I'm trying to understand. My mother, my father, and Aegisthus, who mutilates my poor sister.

The Figure   Tell Aegisthus of his crimes and he will call you 'criminal'!

Orestes   He has already done that.

The Figure (*as* **Becky**, **Sally**, *and* **Jenny** *gather around them*) How can words affect a man who thinks he is the source of all meaning? Once you say something to him, he simply takes it, makes it his own and says it back to you? Do you want these girls? They'll do whatever you want.

Girls *all laugh.*

The Figure   Are you hungry? We have food. You must be hungry.

Orestes   Yes.

The Figure (*to* **Jenny** *who rises and hurries off*)   Bread and wine.

And back to **Orestes**.

You should rest. We roam the hills.

Orestes   Have you cheese?

The Figure   Three kinds.

Becky *hands the cheese to* **Orestes**, *as* **The Figure** *is lighting up a hashish pipe.*

Would you care to smoke?

Pylades   I would.

They all laugh.

The Figure (*passing the pipe to* **Orestes**)   It is a pleasant weed.

Orestes *merely puffs.*

Becky   You must draw it deep.

Orestes *tries.*

The Figure   I have yearned to meet you for so long,
Orestes.

Orestes (*releasing the smoke*)   What do you mean?

The Figure   I have been awaiting you.

Orestes   You knew of my coming?

The Figure   There is in me a feeling of kinship for people of
the spirit. Are you not such a creature?

Orestes   I am looking to understand certain things that
have been so far very difficult to understand.

The Figure   Son of man, I am the issue of your dreams;
Apollyon, of the pit. Do with me as you will.

Orestes   What?

The Figure   It is all in your eyes.

He rises suddenly and moves to exit.

I shall sing for you and know your heart and you will be in my
army.

Orestes   What? What did you – Wait! I would like to talk to
you more.

He turns back to the group.

Where did he go?

Becky   He'll be back.

Pylades (*to* **Orestes**)   I used to be like you. Sometime. Way
back.

Orestes   That makes no sense to me. I am unique.

They all laugh. As **Becky** *snuggles up to him,* **Orestes** *smiles.*

I'm planning a lecture series soon – that's what I've decided.
It's our best hope – I must go about the land, trying to wake
the people up, delivering what I know that no one else knows.
'What is the basis on which people do brutal cruel things to
one another? And how can it be stopped?' I'm going to make
my thinking very clear.

Sally (*she settles onto the floor at* **Orestes**' *feet*)   It's a serious,
important question.

Orestes   In all my reading there was one unforgettable
thing more haunting than all the others. It is the riddle I must
come to know. Though I read scholarly tomes, I found this in
a diary. A father and daughter went into a desert seeking to
collect lovely flowers that grew only in that locale. And then in
the confusion of so much similarity they lost their way. He
returned alone. Quite calm. Perhaps a trifle confused. And he
said, and these are his exact words, 'The last I saw of her, she
was about two hundred yards behind me and she was calling,
but I couldn't understand her words. I waved and pointed out
the direction in which she should go. She'll be along in a
minute.' They found her dead the next morning, curled at the
base of a dune where, at a certain time each day, there must
have been shade.

Becky   Wow.

Orestes   How could such a thing have happened?

Pylades   And now you've let your sister suffer in jail, though
she begged your help. She's lost her hands and had her tongue
cut out, while you did nothing.

The Figure   I have mushrooms.

He steps in.

Orestes   What?

The Figure   Mushrooms – red and white. Known from all
time. We eat them, Orestes.

The Speaker   *Amanita muscaria* – clinically proven to bear a hallucinatory power.

The Figure (*to* **Orestes**)   They bear a visionary power. Ants seem huge as trees. Would you not like to see the light and color of sound streak off your fingers?

Sally   They enhance everything.

Pylades *and the other* **Girls** *laugh.*

The Figure   Releasing the ether of your soul.

Giving **Orestes** *a mushroom.*

Pylades   The purest taste of God's seed upon the earth.

Orestes   What is ether?

The Figure   You. Me, Orestes. Our great capacity is let loose.

Orestes *looks at the others smiling at him, and he pops the mushroom into his mouth.*

The Figure   We are the finest ether, Orestes, entangled through some accident in this catastrophic gore. The mushroom puts all bone and skin to sleep. We escape. We flee.

Music, airy and strange, begins.

Becky   It's true.

The Figure   She knows.

As **Becky** *kisses* **Orestes** *and they fall into an embrace on the ground,* **The Figure** *begins to sing.* **Pylades** *begins to kiss one of the other girls.*

> The trees beyond the sky
> Have a mushroom's glitter
> Each leaf an eye
> And each eye a star
> To see the sun and see the moon,
> To see the sun and see the moon
> To see the sun and kiss Apollo's gentle loving finger.

The lyric is repeated, and then the song quietly ends. They all lie there, quietly, looking at the sky. The mood is that of people around a campfire.

Orestes   I thought I would say the things I knew in my heart, and all men, possessed in some secret way of a heart not unlike my own, would hear me and nod as if they had merely forgotten goodness and I had reminded them. Do not the evil know what they are? I believe now they don't and their hearts are as strange to me as stones.

The Figure (*rising to stand over* **Orestes**)   On such a pleasant, dear sweet evening, would you not like to wipe your hand across the world and find the insect of Aegisthus taken from the air? (*He snatches at the air.*)

Orestes   It is obscene that a creature such as he and I are both called human.

The Figure   You are his opposite.

Orestes   Why is power always possessed by such ugly, arthritic hands?

The Figure   They envy you, Orestes.

Orestes   No.

The Figure   They have blunted your sister's hands and tongue.

Orestes   Out of envy?

Pylades   She had a beauty equaled only by your own.

The Figure   And on another evening, would you not like to wipe your hand again across our world and find your mother gone, a spot of empty air?

Orestes   I don't think my mother should be –

Pylades   It's what she deserves – her and your father and Aegisthus, too, sending us off to that goddamn war. After a couple a months, I was deranged, man. We were all deranged. So we went into this village, nobody knew if it was the right one or the wrong one, because there was this village on our maps called one name, but that wasn't what the people living there called it. They called it something I can't pronounce. But we went in shooting because it was an enemy stronghold on our maps and there was this one old lady, I remember, and everybody was shooting her, you could see the bone chips flying in the air. And there was this girl with this baby, so some of the guys fucked her and killed her. It was heavy, man, fillin' up these ditches with bodies; we had to stop to eat lunch.

Orestes   She has to suffer. My mother – that's what I'm saying. I have a plan to do a painting of her death that will terrorize her – it's going to be a drawing in cruel, hurting detail. I'll write a poem of all my hate of her.

The Figure   BUT SHE MUST KNOW NOTHING! Her slack, broken skin – she is the abomination – Clytemnestra – running back beyond Aegisthus to the hands of your father, corrupted into murdering infants.

Orestes (*kneeling, groping for his bag, his notes*)   No, no, I have letters – diaries – all here.

He waves them.

I've cross-checked and there's documented proof that it was not Arsinoe or Gellissa who saved me. It was my mother. Or Laodomaia. Laodomaia is a possibility. And regarding my father's murdering of infants – the accounts all show he fought difficult, dangerous campaigns – no doubt some child one time or the other –

The Figure *snatches the book from* **Orestes** *and snaps it shut.*

The Figure   Do you think both lies and bread are real?

Orestes   I'm trying to straighten you out, Apollo! Now right here in file 47 A, I have – (*As he digs out a file.*) – a letter in which Helen begs my father to help rescue her from Troy.

The Figure   Helen was a whore and they called her honor – and goodness, just like your mother. Those papers have put your sister into agony. Do you want to keep her there? They feed you lies, I feed you bread.

Pylades *puts the bread into* **The Figure***'s hand.*

The Figure   I have the bread! Do you want the bread?

Shoving bread into his mouth.

Or do you think the tribes your father conquered paid him tribute because he was a dear, kind man?

Orestes *has become preoccupied with his hand.*

Orestes   What?

The Figure   They were king and queen of theft and carnage!

Orestes   My hand . . . is odd . . .

Pylades   It is the mushroom.

He rises, takes the stool, and exits.

Orestes   No. It is my hand. It has no skin.

The Figure   Even she was a thing he pillaged and stole, and she welcomed it.

Orestes   I can't think anymore! But there's doubt, I know, about the way they got together in that courtyard. I've read it, and her handmaiden's diary contradicts his soldiers' letters, so that –

The Figure   I was there, Orestes, Apollo in that smoking courtyard, peering up from her I saw his cruelty, the murder in his look as he flung the child, and down from him I saw her wanton eyes begging for his body upon her, I saw his joy at conquest, her wonder at being taken, his simple soldier's heart. I saw the infant float with a startled look, a brief pleasure at his flight until the fabric of his skull crumbled. She drew him down; he took her like a dog. Or do you say that an infant hitting stone is a warrior? Or do you think the enormous wealth of this land all came since Aegisthus or from such goodness? Has it ever been that any land ever had such power because of goodness, because of virtue?

Orestes (*only interested in his hands now*)   I have no hands; is that good or bad?

The Figure   I am sickened that men go on and on believing motherhood most perfect. A seed is planted in a swamp – is that to the credit of the swamp and gore of a woman's belly that goes on wet and futile until a man enters seed to give it purpose? Are we never separate? The tree grown tall struggles toward the lightened sky from which it fell, in which its loving father lives. Only women love this dank cruel place! I have a madness on this point.

Orestes *goes for his notes, crawling away from* **The Figure**.

The Figure   You gesture to the air. She is a fungal place. Destroy her, Orestes, or I will make you outcast. I will make your flesh rot upon you like the ruin of age come in a single day. It is my curse. I am your friend, but it is my curse. Do you want my curse? I will take you to the sky.

Orestes *is flipping through his books, which he protects from* **The Figure**.

Orestes   I can't read my notes. Where is section II-A, page . . . ? I can't read them.

He hugs his notes and books to his chest.

I don't feel well, and I can't read . . . I dare not hurt my good mother.

The Figure   All that you are is your father's. Only your body is hers. What is Orestes? Nothing more than the simple swamp of his flesh? Or a man – a creature of air and ethics, aware beyond bone limits!

Orestes   I will be punished if I do injustice.

The Figure   No, no, you are too young, too beautiful. Take my hand.

Dropping his books, **Orestes** *swoons and* **The Figure** *catches him.*

Orestes   I dare not hurt my good mother.

The Figure (*cradling* **Orestes***, easing him to the ground*)   You go about fearful of corruption, and power. You think you are innocent, yelling at the air, believing that you are ordained and extraordinary. I will make you real, Orestes. I will make you real. The murderers of Agamemnon die at the hands of Orestes.

Orestes *sleeps.*

The Figure   Through the blood of the father to the hand of the son, falls the sword.

Fits the knife into **Orestes**' *hand, starts to leave.*

What goes around, comes around.

The Speaker   No longer is it thought that when a weary man collapses into bed, he goes into a firm and restful state. But rather, modern science has learned by attaching electrodes and an electroencephalograph to his scalp, forehead, chin, chest, and penis, that he tosses and moans.

Clytemnestra One *and* **Clytemnestra Two** *each holding a blanket wrapped as an infant in their arms enter, moving toward him.*

The Speaker   His eyes waggle behind closed lids, he whimpers and struggles, his penis becomes erect, and his heart pounds as rapidly as if running a race.

Orestes (*popping awake*)   I am a bubble. A button on the cloak of Aegisthus. A bubble in the sea. And there are . . . things nearby . . .

He is staring warily at **Clytemnestra One** *and* **Clytemnestra Two**.

Clytemnestra One   Orestes.

Clytemnestra Two   Orestes.

Orestes   I do not know if I am talking or thinking.

Clytemnestra One   Thinking.

Clytemnestra Two   Talking.

Clytemnestra One   We hold the infant of you in our arms.

She is kneeling beside **Orestes**.

See . . . !

Clytemnestra Two (*to the blanket in her arms, her back to*
Orestes *on the ground*)   Please don't come as you will and
must in times to see a guilt in us equal to the hate you feel.

Orestes (*to* **Clytemnestra Two**)   You must explain who
saved me.

Clytemnestra Two   We are your mother.

Clytemnestra One   But in no secret place within do we
feel unfit to live. Must you come?

Clytemnestra Two   Down the dimness toward us even as
the infant of you in our arms – stirs – in sleep. Do you see?

She bends toward **Orestes**, *kneels to his left side, as*
Clytemnestra One *is kneeling to his right. They are putting the
blankets like babies into his arms. As he takes up the babies, the knife is
left lying on the ground.*

See him looking toward us, nearly smiling?

Orestes   Ohhh . . . yes.

Clytemnestra One   Nothing in his eyes but need.

Clytemnestra One *and* **Clytemnestra Two** *are rising now,
retreating.*

Clytemnestra Two   Nothing in his eyes but need.

Orestes *is trying to hold the blankets to comfort them as*
Clytemnestra One *and* **Clytemnestra Two** *retreat.*
Agamemnon, *in a state of agitation, has entered behind* **Orestes**.

Clytemnestra One   Need.

Clytemnestra Two   Need.

Orestes   Why are you going? Don't go. We need to know,
the babies and me – who saved us?

Agamemnon (*loudly*)   Orestes!

Orestes (*huddling over to protect the babies*)   Shhhhhhh! We're
sleeping!

Agamemnon   Who is it that sits in my chair? I have told him, 'Get out.' All my robes, my rings, accept him. Do they not know that they are mine?

Orestes (*moving toward* **Agamemnon**)   Who are you?

Agamemnon   Avenge me! Give me rest!

Orestes   I don't know who you are!

Agamemnon   They stand about awaiting him. They do not seem to know that they are Agamemnon's chair and bed; Agamemnon's horse and courtyard, cart and house.

The Speaker   You don't have a car, Agamemnon!

Agamemnon   Cart! Cart! He has my cart!

Orestes (*realizing who he is*)   Agamemnon! Father, I have been looking for you! I'm Orestes!

Agamemnon   I have been looking for you. I wander with no sail. I spread my arms, I cup my hands to catch the changing air, but it eludes me. What will take me from this place? I must have wind.

Trying at **Orestes**' *blankets.*

Are those my sails?

Orestes (*protecting the babies*)   No, nooo! They are babies of me wrapped in blankets and sound asleep. We're all asleep.

Agamemnon   What is this place? I hate this place! What is it that you want that you brought me here? I don't know where I am. Once I picked up the drawing of my knee and thought it was the map of the ocean to Troy. I studied it for hours. Do I now sail it? Is this place my knee? Do I sail my knee? WAIT!

His hand probes the air.

Did you feel it? A call. A cry of air.

He starts to go, as if following a current of air.

Orestes (*running to him, stopping him*)   You must tell me what happened. I don't know what happened.

Agamemnon   Your mother stabbed my benevolence; she cut open my innocence. She murdered my virtue.

Orestes   Do you know what you're saying – what you're talking about?

Agamemnon   Avenge me!

Suddenly, he pummels the blankets, struggling to take them from **Orestes** *and hurl them to the ground.*

Avenge me!

Orestes   Stop it!

Agamemnon   Or you are no son of mine!

Orestes (*falling to his knees to comfort and re-form the babies, while* **Agamemnon** *stands there looking down at him*)   Oh, babies, poor babies. Has he hurt you? Where are you?

Agamemnon   Kill her! Kill her!

Orestes   Poor, poor babies, don't listen. Don't worry. I can not hurt my good mother for such a man. No more than could the weeds and nettles and daisies and dandelions rise up and slay the earth because he commands them too. Don't fear, Sweet Earth.

He holds the refolded blankets in one arm. With the other hand, he strokes the earth beneath him.

Sweet Earth, have I babies of me in my arms? Or are these blankets in which I sleep? Oh, Earth, do you know my mother? As you have cradled the seeds of trees and wheat, roses and clover my good mother cradled me in her center, as rich and grand and deep as you, I can not hurt her.

Looking up, sees his father glaring at him.

Father, I can not hurt her. From her I must rise to stand like you. Teach me a sport. We will play and have dinner.

He rises up to try and emulate his father. **Clytemnestra One** *and* **Clytemnestra Two** *are moving toward him.*

Clytemnestra One   Don't listen to him, Orestes.

Clytemnestra Two Don't look at him. Look at us.

Agamemnon You are a devious whore, a nagging bitch.

Orestes No, no; don't talk that way. We are together at last. If only Electra were here. If only Iphigenia were here.

And **Electra** *and* **Iphigenia** *come running on.*

Electra Hello.

Iphigenia Hello

Orestes Electra! Iphigenia.

Hugging **Iphigenia**.

Oh, happiness. You're alive, Iphigenia.

Iphigenia Yes, yes.

Orestes (*hugging* **Electra**) You have your tongue, Electra, you have your hands.

Electra Of course. I am as mother's womb delivered me into the world, a perfect baby. As she did all of us, Orestes. Each with all our arms and legs, our two ears and eyes, ten fingers, ten perfect toes. Mother's womb was so good to us.

Orestes (*to* **Clytemnestra One** *and* **Clytemnestra Two**) Thank you, Mother.

Electra *and* **Iphigenia** Thank you, Mother.

Electra And Father's perfect seed.

Orestes Thank you, Father.

Electra *and* **Iphigenia** Thank you, Father.

Orestes I love you, Father. What is a man? How am I to be a man?

Clytemnestra One You are a poem.

Clytemnestra Two A jewel.

Agamemnon It is not easy.

Orestes   You look angry, Father. No, no, don't be angry. I will make you happy.

As **Orestes** *moves toward his father,* **Clytemnestra One** *and* **Clytemnestra Two** *both groan.*

Clytemnestra One   No.

Clytemnestra Two   Come here.

Orestes   Don't worry, Mother. It's all right. Please. There is nothing to fear. It is only the mushroom.

He is hastening about, gathering them all, organizing them.

We are a family separated for too long, and now we have come together and we must stay together. Our blood runs back to Tantalus, but we are not like him. No, no, we move away from him, up from him. We progress. We advance so far away he is unknown, the other end of time. Not kind and good as we, his eyes are mean. But we are no longer like him. We must simply stay together and think one slow thought: 'We are not going mad. We are not going mad.'

He has brought them all together, his arms embracing their four heads in a row. He is trying to teach them, and they are trying to repeat the lesson, repeating by rote without inflection.

Agamemnon, **Clytemnestra One**, **Clytemnestra Two**, **Iphigenia** *and* **Electra**   We move away from him, up from him, we progress.

They are overlapping and repeating as is **Orestes** *as he moves backward from them, while facing them, preparing to take a photo of them. The camera flashes and* **Agamemnon** *breaks away to pick up the knife that* **The Figure** *put into* **Orestes'** *hand.*

Agamemnon   What's this? I don't know what this is.

Orestes   What? No, no.

Running to them.

To cut the bread. To cut the bread.

Agamemnon   To cut the bread?

Orestes   It is a picnic we are on, and that's to cut the bread and cheese. Here is the bread. I have the bread.

Holding up the bread.

Is this not the bread?

As **Iphigenia** *suddenly yelps with pain and leaps back from her father, who has thrust at her with the knife.*

Iphigenia   He cut me. Father cut me.

Orestes   No, Father.

Taking the knife and throwing it down onto the floor.

Stop it.

Agamemnon   I didn't.

Orestes   I won't stand for that, Father.

As **Clytemnestra Two** *leaps to pick up the knife.*

Agamemnon   Watch out for her!

Orestes   Mother, give that to me.

Moving to her, taking the knife.

Please. We must be careful with this thing. Look at what happened to Father. Look at what happened to Iphigenia. And they have said that I am to kill you, Mother, though I don't want to. Out of love for him, whom I have never actually seen. Yet they say I will. Because you abandoned me. Is that why? Did you send me yowling in my little cradle into endless exile away from you? If so, then duty to Father is an alibi. Or do I simply wish to wipe from the world what your body says about my own – we grow old. Do I yelp up at you even now from that cradle in which you put me down never to lift me? Is hatred then my motive, love my excuse? Apollo says you murder infants – you put them into the hands of men who break their little heads on swords and walls, and I must kill you, or his curse would ruin me with the plague of age in a single day. Is fear of him then my motive, hate of you my alibi, duty my excuse? You must tell me. I have a knife in my hand and I – they say – will pierce you with it, Mother!

During this tirade, the 'family portrait' has broken apart. Now **Pylades**, *carrying a telescope, is coming up behind* **Orestes**.

What is my motive, which my alibi – what is my excuse!?

Pylades   Look into this to find the answer, Orestes.

Orestes (*whirling*)   I'm fine. I'm doing fine!

Pylades   Have another mushroom.

As **Orestes** *takes the telescope.*

Orestes (*scolding* **Pylades**)   Forgive me.

Behind **Orestes**, *the neglected* **Family Members** *are going off in different directions.*

Orestes   Your words are bubbles, your bubbles float in the air. I hear in my ear.

Starting to look into the telescope, which is pointed directly at the ground.

It makes my foot big.

Pylades   Look in the other end. And have another mushroom.

Orestes *turns the telescope around as he lets* **Pylades** *put another mushroom into his mouth. He stares down at his foot again.*

Orestes   It makes my foot little. Where is my sister?

Pylades   In the heavens.

The phone starts to ring and **Orestes** *looks upward.*

Orestes   I see only the stars – I see only the Gods.

Pylades   Good-bye.

Orestes (*watching* **Pylades** *through the telescope*)   Good-bye. Oh, it makes you further and further away. You are so far away.

Turning the telescope away from **Pylades** *and looking around.*

Oh, it makes everything far away.

As he swings the telescope back, looking for **Pylades***, who has exited.*

It makes the world far, far away . . .

Swinging the telescope on and on. He lowers the telescope.

They're all gone. Mother, Father, sisters, friend.

The phone stops ringing and he looks up.

Iphigenia? I thought our father great, but he is a windy fool.
Oh, my sister in the heavens, you must tell me what
happened. Why our father killed you, and did your spirit
move the wind? Did our mother kill our father because of
you? Is that not a thing we can understand? I say there are
certain things that, if I am to remain a human man, I must not
ever cease to know them. What are they? Please tell me! Does
no one want to help me? Does no one care what happens to
poor Orestes fed so fucking long on bread and dreams he
thinks that both are real! How am I to ever begin my lectures?
I will never get it clear and I must – the thing that I know that
no one else knows, something sufficiently vile and disgusting,
so that I may begin my lectures all across this land. How is it
possible a father fails a daughter, a son fails a father, a wife a
husband. It is all paper.

He has begun tearing up his papers.

Notes. It is all notes.

*He throws the pieces high in the air. They fall back toward him and
beyond them he sees the hanging Godheads.*

That float in the air. Below . . . the Gods. My sister is not
there. Dear Gods, what in the air holds your head above me
that will not hold me? Is there only the air? This journey is too
long. God help me – I cannot find a friend. You must speak to
me. I can see in your form that you have all wisdom and
goodness, yet you tell me nothing, you break my little life. And
what is goodness and what is wisdom?

Now he is climbing amid the ropes of the cargo net, having reached up to pull himself so he can rise up near the Godheads, straining to get face to face with one of the Godheads.

I am here. Cold stony bubbles of eyes, you must think of me and make me other than I am. You must hear me. Rigid icy brain, hear me, see me. Rigid icy brain, you must think of me!

Orestes *is face-to-face with the Godhead, his nose almost touching, when suddenly there is a figure below him with a masked head that is white, skull-like, duplicating the hanging Godheads.*

Pylades   What do you want?

And the rest of the **Family Members** *are arriving, all masked in white skull-like Godheads. They carry wands that will light and flash.*

Orestes   What?

Pylades   What do you want to know?

Orestes *(still facing the Godhead)*   Do you speak? Do you speak to me, Gods?

Becky   Hello, I'm here.

Jenny   Here.

Sally   Hello, You called.

Startled, **Orestes** *looks down; he sees them.*

Jenny   You called.

Becky   Hello. Hello.

Orestes *(staring in amazement)*   What?

Becky   Don't you know us? Don't you know us?

And all yell, 'Hello, hello, don't you know us?' They wave.

The Speaker   It is not currently known whether consciousness is an electrochemical property of the brain or a product secreted by the lobes of the brain in the manner that bile is secreted by the liver.

Becky   Climbing to the Gods, you climbed into your brain.

Sally We are your thoughts, Orestes. We are your thoughts.

Pylades Apollo sent us, God of reason and the pit, called Apollyon.

Orestes I am in my brain? Hello!

Sally It is the mushroom. Hello!

Orestes No. It is my brain. I am in it, Iphigenia! Mother, Father, we are in my brain.

Pylades Have you ever been elsewhere?

Orestes *leaps in joy in the net above the happy figures of his brain, below the dangling skulls of his gods.* **The Speaker** *speaks and the figures of his brain begin to move the flashing wands. The ropes of the net and the ropes that entwine the set start to glow.*

The Speaker Because the activity in the brain is mainly electrical, an electrochemical change in a single neuron, and there are some thirteen trillion in the body, institutes a series of changes all along the nerves so that an electrical impulse flows along its fibers like a spark along a fuse toward an explosion.

Orestes *(laughing)* I am in my brain!

All You are in your brain.

Orestes I am in my skull; my thoughts have said so. I am seeing what I am thinking.

As high to his right a molecular structure of lights flashes on, and all the figures of his brain turn and point with their own flashing lights.

There! That's my question! How is it possible that a man claiming a father's love for a daughter could leave her alone in a desert to die?

All How is it possible?

And in answer, high to his left, another structure of lights flashing on. They all point and look.

Orestes There! He wishes to live and believes she will follow.

All   Logically.

Orestes   Logically. Reasonable conclusions based on a sound and logical premise based on other conclusions and a still more distant, unremembered premise.

More flashing.

All   It's the structures.

Orestes   The structures.

All   Of course.

Orestes   The myths and structures that are like floodlamps in the night, and they show you directly where to look while making it impossible for you to see anything should you look in another direction.

His face shimmers in light; the net and set glow and flicker as he points to a new structure.

There!

They all look to a molecular structure of lights flashing on high to his left.

That one. Again.

The lights go off and on.

That's it! Why Clytemnestra and Aegisthus ought to die – because they believe in the myths that make you blind to all they do not show – they believe in the structures and myths, and so they think that they are sane and civilized, king and queen, with more right to slaughter Electra than I have right to bring killing down on them. I mean, what would it be? What, brain? What, Gods? The measurable difference between motive –

And high in front of him another pattern of lights pops on, everyone pointing.

alibi –

All   – the same –

The lights flash and flash.

Orestes   – and excuse. Used, of course, as man applies them to himself and others apply them to him. Nothing! Science doesn't know. Not Pythagoras or Heraclides; they haven't the means.

He is leaning forward in the net, and slowly he flips forward, hovers briefly in the air, lands softly on the floor.

There is only the air in which we float and talk.

The Girl (*gently, wisely*)   What goes round comes round, O.

Orestes   What?

And the **Family Members** *are leaving as* **The Girl** *enters to stand behind him.*

The Speaker   Experimenters have sent out sounds wiggling through the fabric of the air two million miles beyond the moon where reflecting layers bounce them back.

Orestes (*facing* **The Girl**)   Hello.

The Girl   What goes around comes around. I mean, what's a moment?

Orestes   I don't know.

He settles beside her.

The Girl   People make squares where there's only circles in the entire height of God's universe. I mean, have you ever seen a square in the entire height of God's universe?

Orestes   No.

The Girl   It's not your choice. You just do it and you're the thing that does it, see. It won't happen if it isn't s'posed to. It won't happen if it isn't just. I did it, O.

Orestes   Did what?

The Girl   The thing you're worried about. Wearin' my sneakies, which are all black clothes to make it hard to see you in the night, and we wore 'em at first just to get the fear, sneakin' into people's houses, but we was kind when we killed 'em, not tellin' we was gonna kill 'em, so they could go in peace into all eternity.

Orestes   You killed people?

The Girl   We broke into this house and I looked into the rooms and there was this man and woman talkin' so I tole Tex, 'There's this man and woman talking.'

Orestes   You killed people? You already did it?

The Girl   There was knives, I know – big – I think, though I can't get any picture in my mind right now.

Orestes   You're so pretty and you already killed people.

The Girl   Long time ago, long time ago.

Orestes   Oh, wow.

The Girl   They were all fancy dressed. There was a guy sleepin' on the floor and Tex told me to tie him up and I very nearly couldn't find any rope the house was so big, I was so nervous, oh, wow. And Tex says – when they asked what we wanted – 'I'm Lucifer here to do Lucifer's business.'

Together they laugh a little at this, both smiling, whimsical.

And the one on the couch, he's the one who when I hesitated in my stabbing him, oh, wow, he reached up to get me by the hair and was pulling so I hadda fight for my life and six or seven times in self-defense I stabbed him in the leg until Tex shot him. And the pretty one, she kept talkin' how she wanted to live and have her baby, when I had her in the headlock – this was before we did the fancy writing on the walls – and it was so easy, kinda. The other woman running out the door and getting stopped – 'Okay,' she says, 'I give up,' and puts her hands up and Tex stabs her in the stomach. And meanwhile the pretty one's so still in my arms. Ohhh, I went home and I made love, I know I made love. Like I'd like to make love with you, O. I mean, we went in and we went out as natural as the wind that took us there. *Coyotes howl.*

She laughs.

Aren't we all just natural things in God's world? Is a person less a natural thing than a hurricane or an earthquake or pneumonia in the air of God's world? We went in there with knives as natural as the wind or rain or old age, O. They'da never survived Aulus, or My Lai, or you, O, or God's earthquakes or floods, anyway. If they weren't supposed to die, we wouldn'ta been there.

The Speaker (*indicating* **Orestes**, *pointing to various spots on his head*)   At each instant of our lives, some millions of neurons are firing. The task of the brain is to sort these many impulses, establish priorities, amid this popping, these explosions.

Orestes   Oh, I'm free of it – free at last to hate and hate this world in which I need and believe in honor, tenderness, and love, but find them nowhere.

Rushing to **The Girl**, *grabbing her.*

I will say: They are in me. All in me.

The Girl   They are, O. They are all in you.

Orestes   I will say my mother is a whore who knelt in sunlight in the courtyard of her first young murdered husband.

The Girl   That happens sometimes.

Orestes   As she surrendered her firstborn son into my father's killing hand, so she wished me to die at the hand of Aegisthus. It was Laodomaia who saved me. Good sweet Laodomaia.

The Girl   She was a good person. That's such a pretty name.

The music has begun.

Orestes   And I see dying only as a good and gracious friend grown as weary as I of my ordeal.

Together they sing to the building music, many other voices joining in and enriching them, though they are together and alone.

We will be a circle in the height of God's universe.
We will be a circle with no edges, no ledges
I am God and I am good Ooooo, Orestes
Circle is my name, circle is my name
We will be a bulb, a skull, a tear, a star, a sack of black air
To shut out the life of my mother
As a clot I will float in the blood of Aegisthus
As a clot I will float in the red and blue tubes of Aegisthus
I will crush his fat heart
I will choke his fat heart
Ooooo Aegisthus!
Ooooo Orestes!

In the final whirl and leap of the music, **The Girl** *and* **Orestes** *rush off, as* **Aegisthus**, *in a luxurious dressing gown, enters. He wears dress shoes and socks, but his legs are bare. He strides onto the stage.*

Aegisthus   It's been my goodness – I don't know how long since last I saw good, good Clytemnestra. It was either here or somewhere else. I get confused. It's morning at one time; night at another. It's morning, it's night. I get up, go to bed. 'Hello; good night.' I sleep, or I don't sleep. I get up. It occurs to me that I should worry, that I haven't eaten, that I am sitting when I'm standing and standing when I'm sitting.

Becky, *still wearing the white Godhead, but with a bowler hat upon it, rushes in to deliver a message.*

Aegisthus   Messengers come and go. They deliver and take messages. Sometimes in the deep of the night, I screw a maiden.

He laughs a little, nods; proud of this.

I screw her pretty good. And there are moments when I am having her I think of Clytemnestra. But sometimes when I was having Clytemnestra, I thought of maidens. I don't know what it all means. It seems I haven't seen Clytemnestra for so long. She could be in the corridor just beyond the wall and she might be gone forever. Who am I to say? It sometimes seems to matter if she's absent, but it rarely seems to matter if she's dead. She's always been absent at one time or another. Is there a difference if she's dead?

Another messenger, **Jenny**, *who wears the white Godhead mask and a straw hat and scarf, has come running in with another note for him. Handing the note, she flees.*

The messages say, 'No. Maybe.' The messengers come and go and tell me of this and that, and off they go. In the corridors of my castle, they scurry about, zipping here and there and back to me to tell me of my stocks and bonds, lungs and liver, the degree of lag between monetary and all other economic changes. It occurs to me that Clytemnestra is in danger. I have dreams of little people breaking her apart.

He sees the two **Clytemnestras** *strolling across the scaffolding.*

Oh, there she is, there she is.

They acknowledge him with a nod.

So good to see you. I've just been explaining our system. It's going well.

Sally *comes dashing in with a message. She wears the white Godhead mask, a top hat, sunglasses, and scarf.*

Aegisthus   And sometimes the word I receive pertains to Orestes. For instance, he just told me Orestes is in the castle. Now what am I to think of that? And even if it's true, how am I to know whether the Orestes of whom he is speaking is the one with whom I am concerned? There are a lot of Orestes.

He must correct himself.

Or-es-tee-ses. I mean, it's a common name.

He smiles, gestures grandly.

And the castle is enormous. What room is he in? Does he speak my language? The messenger didn't – didn't –

Pylades *is there, wearing a newsboy's cap and whispering into* **Aegisthus**'s *ear.*

Aegisthus   The most remote wing in the entire castle – way down beneath the basement even – in the tombs and ventricles. What's he doing there? I wonder. I'll have all the trapdoors barricaded. Soon there'll be wolves and antibodies lurking in all the ground-floor halls.

And **Becky** *is handing him another note.*

Well, well. Indeed. No, no, that's nothing to do with Orestes, but rather something to do with a certain portion of my business arrangements that seem to be collapsing. I'll have some of my men to do a little something to reorder it, buoy it up.

He gestures to **Pylades**, *standing off to the side, who turns to face* **Aegisthus**.

Go tell Michael and Edgar to sell all the fish and buy half back. Tell Russel and Harold to have all the farmers plant carrots.

As **Pylades** *goes running off,* **Jenny** *has hurried on from the opposite direction behind* **Aegisthus** *and is whispering another message.*

Well, now . . . she says Orestes has been reported in a closet on the ground floor. I have my doubts about that. I nevertheless suggested that they seal off that area. Little goes on there. There are, after all, whole sections, floors and chambers we scarcely ever use. Having it sealed off is merely a precaution, just as their word of his presence is merely a precaution, just as their word of his presence is merely a report. And what do reports and precautions deal with? Possibilities. So it is possible now that Orestes is in the castle. What's new in that? Hasn't it always been possible?

Becky *crosses to* **Aegisthus** *with a note.*

Aegisthus   That's not what I said. That's not what I said. 'Sell all and buy half. Sell all and buy half.'

He throws the note at her.

They sold half and bought all, which puts everything right back in the same mess I was trying to rearrange.

And already **Pylades** *is there whispering in his other ear.* **Aegisthus** *pushes him away.*

All right. So what? So he's on the third floor? Who cares. Fuck him. Fuck Orestes. Go fuck yourself, Orestes!

By the time he comes back center, **Jenny** *has another message for him. He reads it, then backs away from her.*

He is not. He couldn't be. No. No. There's an entire group of battle-notch-top-crack-big-troops; he couldn't be there. SEAL IT OFF! SEAL IT OFF! BLOCK THE WHOLE THING!

Turning, he finds **Sally** *with a note in her outstretched hand. He takes the note, looks at it. She shrugs and exits.*

What? He is not! He is not. Wouldn't I see him?

Warily, he looks about the empty room.

He says . . . Orestes . . . is in this room.

He looks about again.

Must . . . be . . . hiding. Your mother isn't home right now, if she's why you've come! I don't know where she is!

Pause; he thinks; he's not afraid.

I'm talking to the air. It's not that I'm not afraid because I don't think he'd hurt me if he was here. It's that I don't think he's here. I DON'T THINK YOU'RE HERE, ORESTES.

Slight pause.

But . . . if you are . . . you can have that side of the room over there . . .

Pointing front and backing up.

and I'll take this side over here.

Pylades *enters, whispers to* **Aegisthus**, *and exits.*

Aegisthus   He says he's not on that side of the room. He's on . . . this . . . on this . . .

Moving backward, groping backward for a safe place, his hand contacts a scaffold pole and **Jenny** *comes on with a rope and ties his hand to the pole. He looks at her.*

On . . . this . . . side of the . . . room . . . Well, I'll just go over
to that side –

*As he starts to move, he cannot, his hand bound to the pole. He stares at
the rope binding his wrist.*

I seem to – it seems – I'm all . . . entangled. Oh, well. I'll get
out of this in just a minute. Surely. It's nothing at all. I don't
feel so badly. I've been in worse spots, a lot worse spots.

Pause.

Is it because you're invisible that I don't see you? Do you . . .
see you . . . Orestes? I see me. Do you . . . see me?

The Speaker (*walking right up to* **Aegisthus**)   Maybe the
reason you can't see him, Aegisthus, is because something is
interfering with his light rays.

Aegisthus *stares at her.*

The Speaker   We don't really see one another anyway –
what we see is waves of different lengths of light bouncing off
us in the shape of us. Maybe his light was ricocheted or
something and off it bounced into outer space, and that's why
you don't see him. Maybe you'll see him later.

She turns, leaves.

Aegisthus   Will I see you later, Orestes?

Pause.

Oh, he's here. He is. I know it. We're both here. Oh, I don't –
Orestes – I don't – I've never dealt all that well with people –
you see, it's always been diagrams and – you understand –
maps – papers – letters – if you don't want to speak to me,
could you send me a letter? Could I send you a letter?

Sally *comes strolling by.*

Aegisthus   Would you . . . would you untie my hand? See
how it's all –

She ties his other hand to the scaffold.

No, no. This one over here. This one. Untie. Untie!

She exits.

No, no. UN! UN!

As from above him the letter falls and floats past him.

Oh, my goodness . . . the letter.

The Figure *leaps down from the scaffolding to the floor, as* **The Girl** *and* **Orestes** *push the tub, containing* **Clytemnestra One** *and* **Clytemnestra Two**, *racing in past* **Aegisthus***. Both of the* **Clytemnestras** *have their hands bound behind them and they are terrified. They are back-to-back in the tub, and they are blindfolded and gagged with masking tape.* **The Figure** *adds a mask or unlooses his hair and it falls long and black down to his shoulders as he advances close to* **Aegisthus***.*

The Speaker   That is Abaddon, who is . . .

Opening the Bible and reading from it.

'. . . the angel of the abyss, whose name in Hebrew is Abaddon, and in Greek, Apollyon, or the destroyer.' Revelations. Chapter Nine. Verse Eleven.

Aegisthus (*to* **The Figure**)   Hello.

And **The Figure** *leans to* **Aegisthus**' *ear and whispers something quickly.*

But . . . That's impossible. No, no I've got a perfect heart. Absolutely perfect. You didn't read my electrocardiogram or you wouldn't say that. My electrocardiogram is always perfect. Always absolutely perfect. Absolutely one hundred percent per – BULLSHIT!

As the **Clytemnestras** *begin crying out in terror behind their gags.*

The Figure (*to* **The Girl** *and* **Orestes**)   Let them speak!

Orestes *and* **The Girl** *tear the gags off the Clytemnestras.*

Aegisthus   BULLSHIT! BULLSHIT!

Clytemnestra One   What are you doing to my husband?

Aegisthus (**Orestes** *is whispering into his ear*)   BULLSHIT! BULLSHIT!

Clytemnestra Two   What are you doing to my husband?

Aegisthus   They are calling me pig.

Orestes (*bellowing at* **Aegisthus**)   Rich fucking pig!

Aegisthus   They are calling me rich fucking pig!

The Girl *puts a pillowcase over* **Aegisthus**' *head.*

Aegisthus   They are putting a hood over my head!

Clytemnestra Two   Don't hurt my husband

The Girl *has a large fork and an apple in her hands.*

Aegisthus   Open the letter! Open the – who did I hurt? I only hurt Agamemnon. Only Agamemnon!

Clytemnestra Two   I can't see my husband.

Clytemnestra One   Where is my husband?

Aegisthus   I killed you when you were an infant. 'Is that him?' I said. Spitting, smelly little thing! I hit you with my sword, Orestes!

Orestes (*moving near to* **Aegisthus**)   Think of yourself as a Vietnamese!

Aegisthus   A what? A who?

Orestes   Think of yourself as a duck, Aegisthus, a squirrel.

Aegisthus   No, no. Orestes says he loves everybody, but all his songs are all about himself. Only –

Orestes (*bellowing*)   WE WILL GET IT INTO YOU, ALL PARANOIA!

Aegisthus *shudders in terror, murmuring, 'No, no, no,' as* **The Figure** *moves from the end of the tub to stand behind* **Aegisthus** *under the scaffold.*

The Speaker   How is it now in the moment that we learn that we are insubstantial as a snowflake and of no more consequence? Is it with horror, consolation, tranquillity?

Aegisthus   Where is the letter? Read the –

As **The Figure**, *having snuck up behind* **Aegisthus** *and put his arms around him, squeezes savagely and lifts him upward and backward;* **Aegisthus**' *legs flail at the air.*

What, what? What are you doing? Why is this hood over my head? Why have you put this hood over my head? I have no life in this hood! I am a grocer! I run a grocery! I have no life in this hood!

The Girl *jams the apple against the pillowcase and drives it into* **Aegisthus**' *mouth. He hangs in the air, looking like a pig with an apple in his mouth as* **The Girl** *jams the fork into his heart. His feet kick helplessly at the air as she presses and he tries to breathe.*

The Speaker   The heart's fantastic powers as a pump add up to a lifetime of amazing statistics. Its job is to keep sixty thousand miles of veins and capillaries supplied. Not made of stone or steel or accessible for constant repair, it is a bundle of living cells, weighing less than a pound and small enough to hold in the palm of the hand.

Aegisthus *cries out in great pain, goes slack in the arms of* **The Figure**.

Clytemnestra One   What have you done to my husband?

Clytemnestra Two   What have you done to my husband?

The Figure   Is it Agamemnon you mean?

As he and **Orestes** *advance on her.*

Orestes   Or that other? The first?

The Figure   Do you mean Aegisthus?

Clytemnestra Two   What?

Clytemnestra One   What?

Orestes   Charlie says you are vain. He says you can not understand how you are not important anymore.

Clytemnestra One   You are children.

Orestes   He says you can not understand that you do not matter, you can not admit that you abandoned my good, brave father for this mediocre, cruel, stupid, little man.

Behind them **The Girl** *is smearing blood from a bowl all over the pillowcase. Plucking the apple from* **Aegisthus**' *mouth, she takes a bite.*

Clytemnestra One   Who are you?

Orestes   I am Orestes, here to do Agamemnon's business.

And he spins the tub and the blindfolded women scream.

Clytemnestra Two   I saved you!

The Figure   Clytemnestra, you are too rich to have ever been anything but a whore.

Clytemnestra One   You fix your eyes upon me and think that I agree with you. Orestes. No, Nooo!

Orestes *moves away, leaving her speaking to the air.*

Clytemnestra One   In no secret place within have I condemned myself. You don't know how good I feel, and how I still love you. Guilt is not a harsh unbearable thing. You do not know how it is easy. Eas –

Orestes   And now you seek to pretend innocence before me.

His voice behind her startles her. She does not know where he is.

Clytemnestra One   No, no, that is nothing. It is nothing that I want, nor did I ever want it or possess or lose it, no matter what I may have thought. He deserved to die. He deserved the death I gave him.

The Figure   Who?

Orestes   Who's that?

Clytemnestra One   Agamemnon.

Orestes   Who's talking about Agamemnon?

The Figure   We're talking about the infant.

Orestes The one you handed to my father for him to smash against a rock like an old bottle.

Clytemnestra Two I don't know what you're talking about.

Orestes (*kneeling left of the tub as* **The Figure** *kneels to the right*) In what part of town did it happen?

The Figure WHERE?

Clytemnestra Two Dirt.

Clytemnestra One Dirt. Courtyard.

Clytemnestra Two My husband is a grocer!

Clytemnestra One My husband is a grocer. My child. I love my child.

Clytemnestra Two No. Help. I love my child.

Orestes (*seizing* **Clytemnestra One** *by the hair*) You were in sunlight.

The Figure You were a pig beguiling him.

Orestes A whore beguiling him to do your murder. To make it seem you fought against the hands you guided as a lover, you conspired to kill my innocent father.

He puts a hood over her head.

Clytemnestra One Let me have my baby. Iphigenia!

Orestes *puts a hood over the head of* **Clytemnestra Two** *and the phone begins to ring and ring and ring.*

Clytemnestra Two (*as* **The Figure** *drifts away*) Answer, answer . . . !

Orestes *takes a knife from the tub. He slits* **Clytemnestra Two***'s throat.*

Clytemnestra One Hello.

Orestes *slits the throat of* **Clytemnestra One**, *as across the background the* **Family Members** *have drifted, led by* **The Girl**,

all wearing dark ski masks. **Orestes** *is writing 'Helter Skeelter' –
misspelled – on the wall in blood as the others have gathered, kneeling off
to the side to face* **The Girl***, who faces out. And the ringing stops and*
The Girl *smiles at the* **Family Members***.*

The Girl   So Abaddon says, 'Last time was sloppy,' and I
go, 'Okay, no talk about Lucifer tonight.'

To **Orestes***, still at the tub, looking in at the bodies.*

Did you see the pictures of their kids when we came in, oh,
wow!

Back to **The Family***.*

Maybe they'll come for Sunday dinner and find 'em.

They all laugh, and she looks to **Orestes***.*

Want some zu-zu's, O? Okay if I call you 'O'?

*He nods to her, smiles. She throws him a piece of candy that arcs across
the space between them. He catches it.*

When he was tying 'em up, the piggie kept saying how he was
a grocer or somethin' and the piggette keeps goin', 'What are
you doing to my husband?' We didn't say nothing to scare
'em. Just let 'em discorporate, see, 'cause when they scream
that's what they carry into infinity. But they were yelling all
the same – what could we do? – so we took off real fast after O
here writes 'Helter Skelter' in blood on the wall, only he
misspells it, oh, wow – and I had some chocolate milk in the
kitchen. And when we watched the newscast – I went like I
was an insane person, jumping and yelling – wow, it really
helped me to know all those people we got were so important
as they were.

Orestes (*leaving the knife in the tub, turns to face* **The Figure***, who
stands near the scaffolding, and the drooping body of* **Aegisthus***)*   I
thought it would take longer . . . be harder.

The Figure (*if he has worn a mask to be Manson, or added costume,
or changed his hair, it is all back now, so he is as he started*)   You
imagined furies would rush upon you. Did you think to hear

them screeching as you stood to look around? No, no, it will not happen.

Orestes   I feel so incredibly good.

The Figure (*moving to the end of the tub*)   You have killed your mother and it means nothing and you have seen the nothing that it means.

Orestes   I do.

The Figure   Of course.

Orestes   And yet I feel, there should be no more children.

The Figure (*moving farther down*)   Orphan! Orphan, what need of children, when you are all, the first and last. I have a golden rope.

Orestes   A what?

The Figure (*bounding suddenly away and up into the scaffolding*) Come here. Come with Apollo. A golden rope – to take you higher. You would be higher, would you not?

Orestes   I would, I would.

Follows, eagerly, and then he stops.

And yet sometimes, Apollo, I look at you and you seem many shells of skin behind which you receded from me to a center I have never seen . . . a hideous lunatic eye.

The Figure   Sometimes you seem exactly that same way to me, Orestes.

Orestes   I do?

The Figure   Let me raise you up. I want to raise you to the heights.

Orestes *moves, onto the net where* **The Figure** *is pointing.*

Orestes (*suddenly erect, facing out,* **The Figure** *behind him*)
And it is my verdict that vile, cunning Agamemnon, noble and cruel, butchered his most sweet and foul Iphigenia, and good Clytemnestra, out of heat and hate, passion and reason, pity

and self-deceiving self-revelation, murdered good
Agamemnon, and I am innocent.

The Figure   Orestes!

Orestes (*leaning backward to* **The Figure** *for support; in a way
giving himself over to* **The Figure**)   Apollo.

The Figure   Apollo and Orestes.

Orestes (*rising slowly up into the air*)   I thought I would be
destroyed. I thought I could not kill. I let fear run me all over
the world, but I have caressed my demon, picked up my
monster, and I know now I can kill and survive. What a joke.
My whole life. I had no sense of humor till now. Don't you
agree? I could just throw my head back and my hands up and
roar with laughter at the colossal joke of my life up till now.
All those years of taking myself so seriously. All that struggle.
That worry.

The Figure   You're the best, Orestes. Do you not feel like
the best?

Orestes   I do. I am.

The Figure   You're the brightest, finest, most aware and
sincere.

Orestes   I am tall. I am handsome.

The Figure (*looking up in worship*)   And I am with you. I am
here.

Orestes   I have killed my mother and there is no
punishment.

He hangs suspended, **The Figure** *looking up in love and awe, as
music begins.*

The Figure   For I am nothing without you. What am I
without you?! For you are all. All. You are all, Orphan! Ohhh,
Orphan, beautiful, beautiful Orphan.

Orestes (*hanging amid the planets, the Godheads, the fragments of
white debris, he starts to sing*)

I wake up in the morning,
The morning's aflame
Lines of power mark my brain.
In the morning sun awakening
I wear a lion's mane
In some magic corner of my brain.

In this moment now reborn,
I am tall and free,
With nothing left to mourn,
Orestes, Orestes, Great, Great Orestes.

The Speaker (*in the dimness, she stands, looking upward,* **The Figure** *beside her, but retreating, as she has her microphone and flashlight; beginning to speak, she uses her flashlight to pick out the Godheads hanging in the dark above her as if they are the planets of which she speaks*)   There are nine planets moving around the sun – one, two, three, four, five, six, seven – (*On seven she hits* **Orestes**, *who now hangs among the other planets.*) – eight, nine – and the Earth . . . (*The light, having hit* **Orestes** *and moved on, now jumps back to him, as he hangs there humming the tune of his song.*) . . . is but one. Of the other eight, five have been known from prehistoric times. It would be difficult to imagine any planet less inviting than Jupiter – (*Her light flickers on planet three.*) but Uranus, Neptune and Pluto – (*Hitting heads four, five, and six.*) fill the bill. Only the Earth so far, has proven hospitable to man.

Her light holds on **Orestes** *for a beat.*

And Mercury (*Planet one.*) completes its journey around the sun in far less time than Pluto. (*Planet six*).

Then her light turns out. **Orestes** *hangs there, humming in a feeble light.*

Orestes (*singing*)   Orestes, Orestes, Great, Great Orestes.

As his light goes to black.